Compulsive Buying

Compulsive Buying

Clinical Foundations and Treatment

Edited by Astrid Müller
and James E. Mitchell

Routledge
Taylor & Francis Group
New York   London

Routledge
Taylor & Francis Group
270 Madison Avenue
New York, NY 10016

Routledge
Taylor & Francis Group
27 Church Road
Hove, East Sussex BN3 2FA

Printed in the United States of America on acid-free paper
10 9 8 7 6 5 4 3 2 1

International Standard Book Number: 978-0-415-88463-1 (Hardback) 978-0-415-87642-1 (Paperback)

Library of Congress Cataloging-in-Publication Data

Compulsive buying : clinical foundations and treatment / edited by Astrid Müller,
James E. Mitchell.
   p. ; cm. -- (Practical clinical guidebooks)
Includes bibliographical references and index.
Summary: "Rooted in research and clinical practice, Compulsive Buying
examines the drive that compels people to compulsively purchase and hoard their
acquisitions. The authors and contributors cover the entire scope of this behavior
and discuss what clinicians need to know in order to better understand and treat
their clients. Among the key subjects examined are case reports, correct diagnosis,
assessment and instruments, comorbidity, treatment, research, and directions for
future research. The book ends with a useful guide for therapists, which includes
data and research, and a treatment manual, which includes questionnaires and
exercises for clinician and client alike"--Provided by publisher.
   ISBN 978-0-415-88463-1 (hardback : alk. paper) -- ISBN 978-0-415-87642-1 (pbk. :
alk. paper)
   1. Compulsive shopping. 2. Compulsive shopping--Treatment. I. Müller, Astrid,
1963 Feb. 14- II. Mitchell, James E. (James Edward), 1947- III. Series: Practical clinical
guidebooks series.
   [DNLM: 1. Impulse Control Disorders. 2. Compulsive Behavior. WM 190 C738
2010]
   RC569.5.S56C68 2010
   616.85'84--dc22
                       2010021218

Visit the Taylor & Francis Web site at
http://www.taylorandfrancis.com

and the Routledge Web site at
http://www.routledgementalhealth.com

Dedication

To Steffen and Karen

Who are always there for us

Contents

Preface   ix
Acknowledgments   xiii
Contributors   xv

Part 1   Clinical Foundations

1 Diagnosis and Epidemiology of Compulsive Buying   3
   RONALD J. FABER, PHD

2 Etiology of Compulsive Buying   19
   TROY W. ERTELT, MA, JOANNA M. MARINO, MA, AND
   ASTRID MÜLLER, MD, PHD

3 Assessment of Compulsive Buying   27
   DONALD W. BLACK, MD

4 The Measurement of Compulsive Buying and Its Application
   to Internet Buyers   51
   NANCY M. RIDGWAY, PHD, MONIKA KUKAR-KINNEY, PHD, AND
   KENT B. MONROE, PHD

5 The Neural Basis of Compulsive Buying   63
   GERHARD RAAB, PHD, CHRISTIAN E. ELGER, MD,
   MICHAEL NEUNER, PHD, AND BERND WEBER, MD

6 Psychiatric Comorbidity and Compulsive Buying   87
   MARTINA DE ZWAAN, MD

7 Personality and Compulsive Buying Disorder   105
   LAURENCE CLAES, PHD AND ASTRID MÜLLER, MD, PHD

8 Hoarding and Compulsive Buying   115
   ASTRID MÜLLER, MD, PHD AND RANDY O. FROST, PHD

Part 2 Treatment

9 Overview of Treatment for Compulsive Buying   129
   KRISTINE J. STEFFEN, PHARMD, PHD AND JAMES E. MITCHELL, MD

10 Case Examples   149
   APRIL BENSON, PHD, LISA A. PETERSON, MA, TROY W. ERTELT,
   MA, AND AIMEE ARIKIAN, MA

11 Therapist's Guide to the Treatment Manual   161
   JAMES E. MITCHELL, MD

12 Compulsive Buying Disorder Group Treatment Manual   169
   JAMES E. MITCHELL, MD

   Index   279

Preface

We have had an interest in the problem of compulsive buying for several years. James originally became interested in it about 18 years ago when he was on the faculty of University of Minnesota. He had seen several patients with this problem and developed a cognitive behavioral intervention that he piloted on a few groups, modifying the manual in the process. He then moved to the Neuropsychiatric Research Institute (NRI) 14 years ago and put the project on hold.

Several years ago Martina de Zwaan from the University of Erlangen in Germany came to NRI as a visiting scientist to work with James and the rest of the staff on eating disorders and obesity research. She was there for a little more than a year. At that time James had again activated research in this area and was conducting groups. Martina ran some of these groups as well. This work resulted in the first published trial comparing the outcomes of those treated in the group to a waiting list control group. When Martina returned to Erlangen she carried this new interest in compulsive buying with her, and Astrid, her colleague in Erlangen, became interested in the problem as well. They then translated the manual into German and did a replication study in the form of a randomized controlled trial. Astrid then came to NRI for a year and worked with James and others on several projects, one of which was a new compulsive buying treatment study that is still in progress. She also did several other studies in the area including a large population-based prevalence study in Germany. All of this work will be reviewed in this text.

Astrid, Martina, and James published the manual as well as a litera-ture review in German under the title "Pathologisches Kaufen" (Deutscher Ärzte-Verlag) in 2008. Astrid and James subsequently decided it would be important to publish an extended version that included a review of all that was known about compulsive buying as well as an updated manual in English. James had previously edited a book for Routledge titled *Bariatric Surgery: A Guide for Mental Health Professionals*. At that time he had worked with an editor there, George Zimmar, and had found working with George was a great experience. George is a very thoughtful, very well-read and enthusiastic man. James had lunch with him at the American Psychiatric Association meeting in San Francisco in May of 2009 and proposed this book. Following an exchange of e-mails over the next few months it was decided to move forward with the project and that Astrid and James would serve as editors.

It was our pleasure to include as chapter authors a number of people who have done some of the most important work in this area. James had known Ron Faber when he was at the University of Minnesota. Ron had developed the screening instrument most widely used in diagnosing compulsive buying and had published some of the important early work in this area. Don Black, from the University of Iowa, also agreed to be involved. Don had been publishing important work in this area for many years and was kind enough to join the project. Gerhard Raab, who is an expert in neuroeconomics, agreed to contribute, as did our colleague Martina de Zwaan. Kristine Steffen, who works with James, contributed an overview on pharmacological treatment. Laurence Claes from Belgium had spent some time in North Dakota while Astrid was there and also became interested in this problem and began doing research on this issue with Astrid and Martina. Randy Frost, who is clearly the world's expert on hoarding behavior, also agreed to be involved, given the significant overlap of hoarding and compulsive buying. Several graduate students who worked with James, Joanna Marino, Troy Ertelt, Lisa Peterson, and Aimee Arikian, were also doing some research in this area and agreed to contribute. April Benson, who had written two books on the topic and practices in Manhattan, also contributed case material. Lastly, Nancy Ridgway and her colleagues, who recently developed an important new scale to measure compulsive buying, also agreed to contribute. In short, we were very pleased that we were able to put together a team of contributors who have been responsible for much of the important published research in this area.

The book is broken down into two sections. The first, "Clinical Foundations," reviews the available data from the literature and attempts to translate this into useful clinical information on topics ranging from diagnosis and epidemiology to the relationship with hoarding. The second section, "Treatment," begins with an overview of treatment principles and a series of case examples. Next is a therapist guide to the treatment manual as well as the compulsive buying group treatment manual itself. Individuals who purchase this manual are granted permission to reproduce the manual as often as they wish for their clinical use. The manual is designed to be used as a group or individual manual, where both the patient(s) and the therapist have a copy. The patient's copy is his or hers to keep, as he or she is instructed to do the homework assignments in the manual itself.

Our main goal in publishing this work is to alert clinicians to this problem and to provide them with skills in the assessment and treatment of these patients. Our overarching concern is the dissemination of what we think is a useful treatment for patients with compulsive buying.

Astrid Müller
James E. Mitchell

Acknowledgments

We would like to thank George Zimmar at Routledge for his kindness and enthusiastic support for this project.

Contributors

Aimee Arikian, MA
Clinical Psychology Doctoral
 Candidate
University of Minnesota
 Department of Psychiatry
Minneapolis, Minnesota

April Benson, PhD
Psychologist
New York

Donald W. Black, MD
Professor of Psychiatry
Roy J. and Lucille A. Carver
 College of Medicine
University of Iowa
Iowa City, Iowa

Laurence Claes, PhD
Professor in Clinical Assessment
 and Psychopathology
Department of Psychology
Catholic University of Leuven
Leuven, Belgium

Christian E. Elger, MD
Professor of Neurology and
 Epileptology
Clinic for Epileptology
University Hospital
Bonn, Germany

Troy W. Ertelt, MA
Clinical Psychology Doctoral
 Candidate
Department of Psychology
University of North Dakota
Grand Forks, North Dakota

Ronald J. Faber, PhD
Professor of Advertising and Mass
 Communication
University of Minnesota
Minneapolis, Minnesota

Randy O. Frost, PhD
Professor of Psychology
Smith College
Northampton, Massachusetts

Monika Kukar-Kinney, PhD
Assistant Professor of Marketing
University of Richmond
Richmond, Virginia

Joanna M. Marino, MA
Clinical Psychology Doctoral
  Candidate
Department of Psychology
University of North Dakota
Grand Forks, North Dakota

James E. Mitchell, MD
Professor and Chair of Clinical
  Neuroscience
President of the Neuropsychiatric
  Research Institute
University of North Dakota
Fargo, North Dakota

Kent B. Monroe, PhD
Professor of Marketing Emeritus
University of Richmond
Richmond, Virginia

Astrid Müller, MD, PhD
Assistant Professor
University of Erlangen-Nuremberg
Department of Psychosomatic
  Medicine and Psychotherapy
University Hospital
Erlangen, Germany

Michael Neuner, PhD
Senior Researcher
Ludwigshafen University of
  Applied Sciences
Transatlantic Institute
Ludwigshafen, Germany

Lisa A. Peterson, MA
Clinical Psychology Doctoral
  Candidate
Department of Psychology
University of North Dakota
Grand Forks, North Dakota

Gerhard Raab, PhD
Professor of Marketing and
  Psychology
Ludwigshafen University of
  Applied Sciences
Transatlantic Institute
Ludwigshafen, Germany

Nancy M. Ridgway, PhD
Professor of Marketing
University of Richmond
Richmond, Virginia

Kristine J. Steffen, PharmD, PhD
Research Scientist
Neuropsychiatric Research
  Institute
Fargo, North Dakota

Bernd Weber, MD
Head of Neuroimaging
University Hospital of Bonn
Clinic for Epileptology
Bonn, Germany

Martina de Zwaan, MD
Professor and Chair of
  Psychosomatic Medicine and
  Psychotherapy
University of Erlangen-Nuremberg
University Hospital
Erlangen, Germany

PART 1

Clinical Foundations

CHAPTER 1

Diagnosis and Epidemiology of Compulsive Buying

RONALD J. FABER, PHD

Contents

Introduction 3
Diagnosis 5
Excessive versus Compulsive Buying 7
Classification of Compulsive Buying as a Disorder 7
Epidemiology 9
Onset 11
Who is at Risk? 12
Conclusion 14
References 15

Introduction

Compulsive buying (CB) is an often misunderstood disorder. Many people confuse it with impulse buying, excessive buying, and other more normal behaviors. While CB may share a number of behavioral characteristics with these other forms of purchasing, its causes, triggers, and outcomes differ in important ways.

Impulse buying is a common situation that almost everyone experiences at one time or another. It has been defined as occurring when our desire for a specific item outweighs our willpower to resist it (Hoch & Loewenstein, 1991). This may involve grabbing a candy bar or magazine while standing on the checkout line of the supermarket or seeing a beautiful coat and just "having to have it." Generally, impulse buying is triggered by external stimuli such as the item or the store environment.

CB, however, is typically more about the desire or need to buy than wanting a particular item (O'Guinn & Faber, 1989). Those with CB often report experiencing an urge or tension to buy. This frequently occurs well before the individual is even in a buying environment. In overly simplified terms, CB is about the act of buying, while impulse buying is about the item being bought.

Studies that have interviewed those with CB have reported that they do not seem to have a great desire for products. Several studies that looked at materialism among those with CB (Edwards, 1992; O'Guinn & Faber, 1989; Scherhorn, Reisch, & Raab, 1990) found that while some relationship exists, it is not due to possessiveness or a desire for objects, but rather due more to the envy dimension of materialism (particularly in regard to envy of relationships rather than goods). O'Guinn and Faber (1989) further found that those with CB were actually lower on a measure of object attachment than were other consumers. This lack of interest in the item purchased helps to explain why many researchers have reported that those with CB frequently never use the items they buy and that these items often remain unopened in the bags they were bought in or hang in closets with tags still on them (Black, 1996; Faber & O'Guinn, 2008; Lejoyeux, Haberman, Solomon, & Ades, 1999).

The consequences of impulse buying tend to be far less severe than those of CB. Many people only engage in impulse purchasing occasionally and such purchases generally have little consequence in their lives. Some people may habitually engage in impulse buying, and this may create some financial or interpersonal difficulties, but these are generally mild. Those with CB, however, tend to consistently engage in buying either daily or whenever they experience negative affect. As a result, they eventually reach a point where their buying creates major conflicts in their lives.

Finally, both impulsive buying and CB can be linked to failures in self-regulation (Faber & Vohs, 2004). However, they involve different types of failure. Impulse buying typically represents individual instances of self-regulatory failure. A specific failure is frequently due to a depletion of regulatory resources that leads to underregulation of the behavior. Following this temporary lapse, however, the person is able to re-establish control over his purchasing behavior (at least for a while).

On the other hand, CB is seen as a chronic and more profound breakdown of the self-regulatory process. This generally occurs because one experiences conflicting self-regulatory goals. Typically this involves a need for emotional or affective relief versus the need to maintain spending goals. Research in self-regulation has shown that affective needs are given priority over behavioral ones when a trade-off must be made (Tice, Bratslavsky, & Baumeister,

2001). In this situation, CB can be said to be due more to misregulation rather than underregulation (Baumeister, Heatherton, & Tice, 1994).

Diagnosis

As early as 1915, CB was identified in psychiatric textbooks under the term oniomania (Kraepelin, 1915). It was listed as being one of a number of monomanias or impulse disorders along with kleptomania and pyromania. Oniomania was initially defined as impulsively driven buying that resulted in a senseless amount of debt (Kraepelin, 1915). Patients with oniomania were said to be unable to control their behavior or even to recognize the senseless consequences of their actions (Bleuler, 1924).

Very little discussion of CB or oniomania appeared again until the mid-1980s when media attention was given to self-help groups that were trying to treat this problem (Holmstrom, 1985; Mundis, 1986), and a few academic articles in the fields of addiction (Glatt & Cook, 1987), psychotherapy (Krueger, 1988; Winestine, 1985), and consumer behavior (Faber, O'Guinn, & Krych, 1987; O'Guinn & Faber, 1989) began to be published. Research in consumer behavior tried to describe the phenomenon of CB and distinguished it from more normal types of excessive buying. O'Guinn and Faber (1989), for example, stated that CB is "chronic, repetitive purchasing that occurs in response to negative events and feelings" (O'Guinn & Faber, 1989, p. 149). They went on to state that the alleviation of these negative feelings is the primary motivation for CB and that ultimately the behavior leads to detrimental effects.

The chronic nature of this behavior is an important element in distinguishing CB from isolated buying sprees. Some people may engage in what might be viewed as excessive purchasing if they suddenly came into a lot of money, around certain events such as Christmas, as a reward for some achievement, or just to cheer themselves up. However, for those with CB the behavior is highly repetitive. Some with CB report shopping almost every day and feeling anxious on days they don't go shopping (O'Guinn & Faber, 1989). Many report experiencing uncontrollable urges and a mounting tension that can only be relieved by buying (Christenson, Faber, de Zwaan, Raymond, Specker, Eckert, et al., 1994; DeSarbo & Edwards, 1996; McElroy, Keck, Pope, Smith, & Strakowski, 1994). The behavior of others with CB appears to be more episodic. For these individuals, buying becomes a repetitive, almost automatic, response to a specific set of negative feelings or circumstances. On average, it appears that those with CB report experiencing this behavior two to three times per week, although reports of the frequency of binge buying range from once a month to multiple times per day (Christenson et al., 1994; Schlosser, Black, Repertinger, & Freet, 1994).

Edwards (1992) provides a somewhat similar definition to that of O'Guinn and Faber. She defined CB as:

> ... an abnormal form of shopping and spending in which the afflicted consumer has an overpowering, uncontrollable, chronic and repetitive urge to shop and spend, compulsive spending characteristically functions as a means of alleviating negative feelings of stress and anxiety. (p. 67)

As with the prior definition, there is a focus on the problem being repetitive and alleviating negative feelings (at least in the short term). However, Edwards' definition expands this disorder to including shopping as well as purchasing and emphasizes that the sense of an uncontrollable urge to buy that is experienced as intrusive.

Probably the most widely accepted definition in the clinical literature is that proposed by McElroy and her colleagues (Goldsmith & McElroy, 2000; McElroy, Keck, Pope, Smith, & Strakowski, 1994). They have proposed three criteria:

1. Maladaptive preoccupation with buying or shopping, or maladaptive buying or shopping impulses or behavior, as indicated by at least one of the following:
   a. Frequent preoccupation with buying or impulses to buy that are experienced as irresistible, intrusive, or senseless.
   b. Frequent buying of more than can be afforded, frequent buying of items that are not needed, or shopping for longer periods of time than intended.
2. The buying preoccupations, impulses, or behaviors cause marked distress, are time-consuming, significantly interfere with social or occupational functioning, or result in serious financial problems (e.g., indebtedness or bankruptcy).
3. The excessive buying or shopping behavior does not only occur exclusively during periods of hypomania or mania. (Goldsmith & McElroy, 2000, p. 218)

This definition combines elements of both of the previous definitions and articulates them in terms that can be easily used in determining indicators for a diagnosis in a clinical setting. Evidence of excessive behavior can be seen in the number of shopping trips, the time spent shopping or buying, the total amount spent on purchases, purchasing multiples of the same item, and the amount of debt amassed. Studies have reported that, on average, those with CB devote almost 50 percent of their take-home pay toward payment of nonmortgage-related debt compared to a little more than 20 percent for other consumers (Christenson et al., 1994; O'Guinn & Faber, 1989).

Negative consequences from shopping and buying can range from distress caused by taking time away from more important events and the amount of debt incurred, as well as more serious consequences such as major family disputes and divorce, stealing, embezzling, and writing bad checks to pay for more purchases, and even suicide attempts (Christenson et al., 1994; Faber, O'Guinn, & Krych, 1987; O'Guinn & Faber, 1989). Typically it is not until these serious consequences emerge that compulsive buyers actually admit that they have a problem.

Excessive versus Compulsive Buying

Another area of potential confusion exists between CB and other people who may buy excessively. While those with CB buy excessively, not all excessive buyers have CB. Excessive buying can occur on the basis of amount of things purchased or the amount of money spent. For some people, their purchasing may appear to be excessively high simply because they can afford to spend almost limitless amounts. Others may spend far beyond their means because of a high level of materialism or desire for things, poor financial skills, or for other reasons. Therefore to identify people who truly have CB, it is important to examine the motivations for buying, the situations in which excessive buying occurs, and the use or enjoyment from the items purchased, in addition to the frequency and amount of buying and the consequences of this behavior.

The potential to confuse those with excessive buying for those with CB and the importance of distinguishing these two groups can be seen in a study done by DeSarbo and Edwards (1996). They examined a sample of those with CB in order to determine the degree of homogeneity in their behavior and the underlying motivations for this behavior. They found those with CB formed two separate clusters. The first cluster seemed to be more motivated by internal feelings such as low self-esteem, greater anxiety, and having a short-term sense of power or control. This group appeared most similar to those with pathological CB. People in the second cluster seemed to be driven more by materialism and a desire for objects. They also tended to be more impulsive and have poor coping skills. The buying behavior of this second cluster appears to be motivated more by environmental factors and a high level of avoidance as a coping strategy for dealing with stress. This cluster seems to represent excessive rather than truly CB.

Classification of Compulsive Buying as a Disorder

Differences exist in how to best classify CB as a psychiatric disorder. Some authors have labeled it as an addiction (Goldman, 2000; Glatt & Cook, 1987).

However, most tend to classify it as either a form of obsessive-compulsive disorder (OCD) (Frost, Kim, Bloss, Murrey-Close, & Steketee, 1998; Ridgway, Kukar-Kinney, & Monroe, 2008), or as an impulse control disorder (ICD) (Black, 2001; Christenson et al., 1994; Hollander & Allen, 2006; Koran, Bullock, & Hartston, et al. 2002). It may be that CB has some characteristics of both types of disorders (Goldsmith & McElroy, 2000; Schlosser et al., 1994).

Frost, Kim, Morris, Bloss, Murray-Close, and Steketee (1998) pointed out that CB is experienced as uncontrollable, distressing to the individual, time consuming, and results in negative consequences. They suggested that these characteristics resemble OCD in that the behavior occurs in response to intrusive urges, these urges lead to a mounting anxiety, and this behavior is done to reduce the anxiety. They also noted that CB often occurs in conjunction with hoarding, and hoarding is characterized as an OCD. To test this belief, they correlated scores on the Compulsive Buying Scale (CBS) with those on the Padua Inventory (Sanavio, 1988) that assesses symptoms of OCD. They found that scores on the CBS were significantly correlated with three of the four subscales on the Padua Inventory. However, it should be pointed out that the subjects in this study were normal college students and the relationship reported is based on continuous scores on each measure. Thus the relationship found here does not demonstrate a relationship at pathological levels.

Christenson et al. (1994) overcame this problem by comparing a group with CB with a matched control group. They found that two-thirds of those with CB described buying in a compulsive manner (intrusive thoughts, attempts to resist these thoughts, and repetitive behavior). Furthermore those with CB scored significantly higher than the normal control subjects on the Maudsley Obsessive Compulsive Inventory. However, they note that the scores of those with CB were only minimally elevated. Only 12.5 percent described any other OCD behaviors that met DSM criteria. This is somewhat surprising if CB actually is a form of OCD since multiple obsessions and compulsions are commonly found among people with OCD (Rasmussen & Tsang, 1987).

CB also resembles Impulse Control Disorders (ICD) in several ways. ICD involves an inability to resist urges or impulses to perform an act that is harmful to the person or others. A feeling of pleasure, gratification, or relief is experienced after engaging in the behavior (American Psychiatric Association, 2000). Feelings of regret or guilt may soon follow the behavior. Christenson et al. (1994) reported that almost all of those with CB in their study (95.8 percent) reported experiencing irresistible urges or a mounting tension that could only be relieved by buying. One major distinction between OCD and ICD is whether the action is associated with pleasure, gratification, or a relief from tension or anxiety (Frosch & Wortis, 1954).

ICD is associated with such gratification as well as linked to more exciting or arousing behaviors, while OCD is typically more related to avoiding harm and is not seen as pleasurable (Goldsmith & McElroy, 2000). Those with CB tend to report that their buying leads to an immediate sense of tension reduction and pleasure, but that this is very quickly replaced by guilt and depression (Christenson et al., 1994; Faber & Christenson, 1996). They describe episodes of CB in highly arousing or exciting terms such as recounting the experience as a "high" or a "rush" (Faber, 2000). Several researchers have found that those with CB have a lifetime history of having other ICDs such as pathological gambling, trichotillomania, or kleptomania, further suggesting this disorder may be a form of ICD (Christenson et al., 1994; McElroy et al., 1994; Schlosser et al., 1994).

It appears that CB has some characteristics of ICD such as experiencing irresistible urges, mounting tension, and relief from this tension through purchasing, as well as feelings of excitement. It also seems to have some commonalities with OCD such as intrusive thoughts. This has led several authors to suggest that both OCD and ICD might be part of a broader classification of disorders termed affective spectrum disorders or impulsive-compulsive disorders (Goldsmith & McElroy, 2000; Hollander & Dell'Osso, 2005; McElroy, Keck, & Phillips, 1995). Such a determination may be forthcoming in the DSM-V in which compulsive buying is being considered for inclusion (Hollander & Allen, 2006). At this point, however, most clinicians have chosen to label it as an Impulse Control Disorder—Not Otherwise Specified (Black, 2001; Goldsmith & McElroy, 2000).

Epidemiology

Most research and treatment of those with CB is based on people who initially self-identify themselves. As a result, it was difficult to obtain an accurate estimate of the prevalence of this disorder. Only recently have a few attempts been made to determine how many people may have this disorder and who is most at risk.

The first published attempt to determine the prevalence of CB was conducted by Faber and O'Guinn (1992) as part of their initial effort to develop the CBS. This scale was created by empirically determining the items that best served to differentiate between self-identified compulsive buyers and a general population sample drawn from the state of Illinois. The authors developed an algorithm for scoring, and based on the distributions for the general consumers and those with CB, they established a cut point to identify those with CB. By applying their algorithm and cut point to the general population sample in their study they developed an initial estimate of what percent of the general population might be classified as having CB. While the authors noted several limitations to using this approach (e.g., using same sample for creation of the scale and estimation, very small sample size, population from only one state), it provided the first indication of how widespread the disorder might be. Using their recommended cut point, their results suggested the prevalence might be as high as 8.1 percent of the U.S. adult population. Using a much more conservative cut point dropped the estimate to 1.8 percent.

A more recent study used the CBS with a larger and more appropriate national population sample to achieve a better estimate of prevalence (Koran et al., 2006). A survey organization with interviewers experienced in conducting health-related studies was employed to do a national household telephone survey. A random-digit dialing sample, stratified by states, was utilized, and up to 15 calls to each selected number were made in an attempt to approximate a random sample of the U.S. population. A total of 4461 phone numbers were selected, and calls to these numbers yielded 2513 completed interviews with adults ages 18 and older (a 56.3 percent response rate). Respondents were asked to answer the items on the CBS as well as several additional questions for validation purposes. The scoring algorithm for the CBS was then applied to the scale responses, and anyone whose score reached the criterion of ≤ 1.34 was classified as having CB. This yielded an estimated point prevalence of 5.8 percent. Thus it seems that a little less than 6 percent of the adult U.S. population may have CB. Using the more conservative cut point (three standard deviations above the mean) produced an estimated prevalence rate of 1.4 percent.

To date, the Koran et al. (2006) study is the best estimate of the prevalence of CB in the United States. However, prevalence studies have also been conducted in Germany (Neuner, Raab, & Reisch, 2005; Mueller, Mitchell, Crosby, Gefeller, Faber, Martin et al., in press). One article reported on two separate prevalence estimates of CB conducted 10 years apart (Neuner et al., 2005). Thus it is able to provide some information on the changing level of prevalence over time.

Their first study was conducted in 1991 and sampled more than 1500 German consumers age 14 or over. Approximately two-thirds of their respondents came from West Germany, while the other one-third lived in East Germany. Since East Germany was transitioning from a planned socialist economy to a Western capitalist economy, this also provides some indication of the importance of culture, economic development, and socialization in the prevalence of CB.

The authors used the German Addictive Buying Scale (Scherhorn et al., 1990) to estimate prevalence. This scale was not originally designed to identify those with CB, but rather to assess attitudes and behaviors that might relate to CB along a continuum in the general population. The authors made the decision to treat any score greater than two standard deviations above the mean for the West German sample as indicative of having CB. Using this criterion, they estimated that in 1991, 5.1 percent of the West German population (age 14 or over), could be classified as having CB. Additionally, 1 percent of the East German population met this criterion.

A survey using the same methodology was again conducted in 2001. In the intervening 10 years, the percentage of those with CB in West Germany had increased to 8.1 percent and reached 6.5 percent in East Germany. This rapid growth in the prevalence rate among East Germans suggests that changes in economic conditions, product availability, and buying norms may facilitate the development of this disorder.

Since different scales were used in the German and U.S. prevalence estimates, one should not draw any conclusions about similarities or differences in prevalence across the two countries based just on these data. However, a recent study in Germany used a translated version of the CBS used by Koran et al. (2006) to develop a prevalence estimate and compared the results using this scale with the findings from Neuner et al. (2005), which used the German Addictive Buying Scale. This study found that the CBS produces a slightly more conservative estimate than does the German Addictive Buying Scale (Mueller et al., in press). While Neuner et al. reported a prevalence of 8.1 percent of West German adults in 2001, the German translation of the CBS estimated the prevalence of this population to be about 7 percent. Additionally, using the CBS produced a much lower estimate for the East German population (3 percent compared to the 6.5 percent reported by Neuner et al.). Thus while prevalence estimates appear to be somewhat affected by the instrument used, it seems reasonable to conclude that the prevalence in both the United States and Germany is somewhere between 5.5 percent and 8 percent.

CB has been reported to exist in a wide range of different countries around the world. For example, along with the United States and Germany, reports of CB have come from Brazil (Bernik, Akerman, Amaral, & Braun, 1996), Canada, and South Korea (Kwak, Zinkhan, & Crask, 2003), to name just a few countries. The only prerequisite seems to be that there are enough resources and goods available for people to be able to buy things. This may minimize the overall prevalence in many countries, but it is still likely to affect some members of the elites in these nations who have the resources and opportunities to buy.

Onset

The onset of CB behavior generally does not occur until the late teens or 20s (Black, 1996; Christenson et al., 1994; Schlosser et al., 1994). For example, one study reported a mean age at onset of 17.5 (with a range of 6–30) (Christenson et al., 1994). Another study (Schlosser et al., 1994) found a similar age of onset (mean = 18.7), but a third study (McElroy et al., 1994) indicated a much later mean age of onset (mean = 30; range from 12 to 52). Typically it seems that CB doesn't start until people are able to financially support themselves.

The actual onset of this disorder may be difficult to assess and subject to some error since those with CB don't recognize or admit that they have a problem until well after onset. For example, while Christenson et al. (1994) report an average age of onset of 17.5, these same individuals with CB indicated that, on average, they did not realize they had a buying problem until they were 29.5. The realization that they have a buying problem generally doesn't occur until people have either incurred large amounts of debt, experienced repeated conflicts with family members over their spending, encountered legal or criminal problems related to their buying, or began to see their behavior being repeated by their children (Christenson et al., 1994; Faber, 2000).

Assessing CB in young people can also be particularly problematic because many other factors common in this age group can cause people to get into financial difficulty. These can include poor financial skills, the easy availability of credit, lack of experience managing money, unrealistic expectations about financial risk or future gains, and low incomes. Thus it is important to distinguish between people who actually have CB from those who encounter financial or spending problems for other reasons.

Who is at Risk?

Several studies have examined demographic characteristics of those with CB to identify specific groups who might be particularly at risk for this disorder. Unfortunately, however, data from these studies are often conflicting.

One variable that might be thought to be related to CB is income. However, a few studies have reported that people at widely varying income levels are equally susceptible to developing CB (Christenson et al., 1994; O'Guinn & Faber, 1989; Scherhorn, Reisch, & Raab, 1990). Instead, what seems to be affected by income is where and what those with CB purchase. People with limited income may manifest this behavior by buying at thrift shops and garage sales, while those with very large incomes may be more likely to buy in exclusive boutiques or excessively spend on expensive items such as cars and real estate. It is also conceivable that among the very rich disruption of normal life functioning might be significantly delayed. However, while financial resources may not run out for these people, other problems such as family conflicts are likely to occur.

While studies relying on self-identification have tended to find no significant income differences, one study identifying those with CB in the broader population did report differences by income (Koran et al., 2006). They reported that a greater percentage of those with CB had incomes under $50,000 relative to those who did not have CB. However, in the one prevalence study in Germany that reported on household income, there was no significant difference on this variable between people classified as having CB and those who were not (Mueller et al., in press).

The studies involving population samples have also tended to find that those with CB are somewhat younger than other consumers (Koran et al., 2006; Mueller et al., in press; Neuner et al., 2005). This seems to be primarily due to a higher percentage of people with CB under 35 years of age. Other demographics such as marital status, education, and ethnicity have not differed between those with CB and other consumers.

The one demographic consideration that has yielded the greatest controversy is whether CB is more likely to be a problem for women rather than men. Some gender difference would be consistent with what has been found for most other impulse control disorders. For example, women have historically been more likely to engage in kleptomania and, during adulthood, trichotillomania, while men are more likely to develop problems with pathological gambling, pyromania, and intermittent explosive disorder (Goldsmith & McElroy, 2000). These differences may be due, at least in part, to cultural and socialization differences between genders in the likelihood and frequency of engaging in the specific behavior. Since in Western culture women typically do more of the shopping and spend significantly more time in this activity, it would seem possible that CB may be a more common problem among women.

Most of the initial research on CB supported this expectation. In Kraepelin's (1915) initial discussion of oniomania, he stated that this was primarily a problem for women. Research in more recent times also supported this belief. In studies that relied on psychiatric patients as well as those that advertised for subjects or used self-identified as having CB seeking help, virtually all noted that the vast majority of their participants were women (Christenson et al., 1994; McElroy et al., 1994; O'Guinn & Faber, 1989; Schlosser et al., 1994). Typically these studies reported that at least 80 percent of those with CB were women. For this reason, it was generally believed that women were more prone to CB than men.

However, relying on data that comes just from volunteers and those seeking treatment is likely to overestimate the percentage of women who have a disorder. Both volunteering in general and seeking treatment for all ailments are more common among women than men (Kessler, Brown, & Broman, 1981; Wilson, 2000). Data that identify those with CB in the general population are needed to provide a more meaningful indication of any gender imbalance in this disorder.

Somewhat surprisingly, the one prevalence study conducted in the United States (Koran et al., 2006) reported only a small, nonsignificant difference in prevalence estimates for women (6 percent) and men

(5.5 percent). A similar finding of no significant difference by gender is also reported in the most recent German prevalence study (Mueller et al., in press). However, in the earlier German prevalence studies a significant gender effect was found with a greater percentage of women having this disorder than men (Neuner et al., 2005). Thus more research is needed before a definitive conclusion can be reached.

Conclusion

Research suggests that CB is qualitatively different from normal buying. It is less about the item purchased and much more about the need to obtain some short-term relief from mounting tension or negative feelings. It generally starts in the late teens or early 20s, although people often don't recognize that they have a problem until much later. Acceptance that this is a problem generally only occurs when problem buying creates some financial, interpersonal, or legal problem for the individual.

CB seems to have some elements of an ICD as well as some characteristics of OCD. Many, but not all, of those with CB report experiencing unwanted urges and a mounting tension to buy. Buying relieves this tension and seems to provide short-term feelings of relief and excitement. However, these are generally quickly followed by feelings of guilt and remorse.

The best estimate of the prevalence of CB in Western nations appears to be between 5.5 percent and 8 percent of the adult population. Even using the most extreme criteria would indicate at least 1.4 percent of the population has this problem. This certainly indicates a need for both more research and more extensive and better treatment for this disorder.

More research is needed to determine who may be particularly at risk for this disorder. Research is especially needed to determine if gender plays a role in this and other related disorders. It seems reasonable to imagine that there are a number of common underlying risk factors for several different types of ICDs or forms of OCD. The particular behavioral manifestation of the disorder may, in some part, be due to socialization and trial-and-error learning that a particular behavior can provide some short-term relief to the individual. Escape theory, for example, states that a behavior needs to be fully absorbing for the individual to allow him to experience cognitive narrowing where undesirable thoughts are blocked out. Some evidence has shown that this occurs in those with CB and those with eating disorders (Faber & Vohs, in press). A greater understanding of the underlying similarities in related disorders and what makes them manifest in particular behaviors would be helpful in understanding the etiology of these disorders and potential approaches to treatment.

References

American Psychiatric Association (2000) *Diagnostic and Statistical Manual of Mental Disorders*, rev. 4th ed., Washington, DC: American Psychiatric Association.

Baumeister, R.F., Heatherton, T.F., & Tice, D.M. (1994) *Losing Control: How and Why People Fail at Self-Regulation*, San Diego: Academic Press.

Bernik, M.A., Akerman, D., Amaral, J.A., & Braun, R.C. (1996) Cue exposure in compulsive buying (letter), *Journal of Clinical Psychiatry*, 57:90.

Black, D.W. (2001) Compulsive buying disorder: definition, assessment, epidemiology and clinical management, *CNS Drugs*, 15:17–27.

Black, D.W. (1996) Compulsive buying: a review, *Journal of Clinical Psychiatry*, 57:50–4.

Bleuler, E. (1924) *Textbook of Psychiatry*, New York: McMillan.

Christenson, G.A., Faber, R.J., de Zwaan, M., Raymond, N., Specker, S., Eckert, M.D., Mackenzie, T.B., Crosby, R.D., Crow, S.J., Eckert, E.D., Mussell, M.P., & Mitchell, J. (1994) Compulsive buying: descriptive characteristics and psychiatric comorbidity, *Journal of Clinical Psychiatry*, 55:5–11.

d'Astous, A. (1990) An inquiry into the compulsive side of "normal" consumers, *Journal of Consumer Policy*, 13:15–31.

DeSarbo, W.S. & Edwards, E.A. (1996) Typologies of compulsive buying behavior: a constrained clusterwise regression approach, *Journal of Consumer Psychology*, 5:231–62.

Edwards, E.A. (1992) The measurement and modeling of compulsive buying behavior, *Dissertation Abstracts International*, 53:11–A.

Elliott, R. (1994) Addictive consumption: function and fragmentation in postmodernity, *Journal of Consumer Policy*, 17:159–79.

Faber, R.J. (2000) The urge to buy: a uses and gratifications perspective, in S. Ratneshwar, D.G. Mick, & C. Huffman (eds.), *The Why of Consumption: Contemporary Perspectives on Consumer Motives, Goals, and Desires*, London: Routledge, 177–196.

Faber, R.J. & Christenson, G.A. (1996) In the mood to buy: differences in the mood states experienced by compulsive buyers and other consumers, *Psychology and Marketing*, 13:803–20.

Faber, R.J. & O'Guinn, T.C. (2008) Compulsive buying: review and reflection, in C.P. Haugtvedt, P.M. Herr, & F.R. Kardes (eds.), *Handbook of Consumer Psychology*, New York: Taylor & Francis, 1039–56.

Faber, R.J. & O'Guinn, T.C. (1992) A clinical screener for compulsive buying, *Journal of Consumer Research*, 19:459–69.

Faber, R.J., O'Guinn, T.C., & Krych, R. (1987) Compulsive consumption, in Wallendorf, M. & Anderson, P. (eds.), *Advances in Consumer Research*, Provo, UT: Association for Consumer Research, 132–5.

Faber, R.J. & Vohs, K.D. (in press) New insights on self-control and the implications for mitigating compulsive and impulsive consumer behaviors, in D. Mick, S. Pettigrew, C. Pechmann, C., & J. Ozanne (eds.), *Transformative Consumer Research for Personal and Collective Well Being*, New York: Taylor & Francis.

Faber, R.J. & Vohs, K.D. (2004) To buy or not to buy? Self-control and self-regulatory failure in purchase behavior, in Baumeister, R. & Vohs, K. (eds.), *The Handbook of Self-Regulation*, New York: Guilford, 509–24.

Frosch, J. & Wortis, S.B. (1954) A contribution to the nosology of the impulse disorders, *American Journal of Psychiatry*, 111:132–8.

Frost, R.O., Kim, H., Morris, C., Bloss, C., Murray-Close, M., & Steketee, G. (1998) Hoarding, compulsive buying and reasons for savings, *Behaviour Research and Therapy*, 36:657–64.

Glatt, M.M. & Cook, C.C. (1987) Pathological spending as a form of psychological dependence, *British Journal of Addiction*, 82:1257–8.

Goldman, R. (2000) Compulsive buying as an addiction, in A.L. Benson (ed.) *I Shop, Therefore I Am: Compulsive Buying and the Search for Self*, Northvale, N.J.: Aronson Press.

Goldsmith, T. & McElroy, S. (2000) Compulsive buying: associated disorders and drug treatment, in A.L. Benson (ed.) *I Shop, Therefore I Am: Compulsive Buying and the Search for Self*, Northvale, N.J.: Aronson Press.

Hoch, S.J. & Loewenstein, G.F. (1991) Time inconsistent preferences and consumer self-control, *Journal of Consumer Research*, 18:492–507.

Hollander, E. & Allen, A. (2006) Is compulsive buying a real disorder, and is it really compulsive? *American Journal of Psychiatry*, 163:1670–2.

Hollander, E. & Dell'Osso, B. (2005) New developments in an evolving field, *Psychiatric Times*, 22:17.

Holmstrom, D. (1985). Controlling compulsive spending, *American Way*, 18:67–9.

Kessler, R.C., Brown, R.L., & Broman, C.L. (1981) Sex differences in psychiatric help-seeking: evidence from four large-scale surveys, *Journal of Health and Social Behavior*, 22:49–64.

Koran, L.M., Bullock, K.D., Hartston H.J., Elliott, M.A., & D'Andrea, V. (2002) Citalopram treatment of compulsive shopping: an open-label study, *Journal of Clinical Psychiatry*, 63:704–8.

Koran, L.M., Faber, R.J., Aboujaoude, E., Large, M.D., & Serpe, R.T. (2006) Estimated prevalence of compulsive buying in the United States, *American Journal of Psychiatry*, 163:1806–12.

Kraepelin, E. (1915) *Psychiatrie* (8th edition), Leipzig: Verlag Von Johann Ambrosius Barth.

Krueger, D. (1988) On compulsive shopping and spending: a psychodynamic inquiry, *American Journal of Psychotherapy*, 42:574–85.

Kwak, H., Zinkhan, G.M., & Crask, M.R. (2003) Diagnostic screener for compulsive buying: applications to the USA and South Korea, *Journal of Consumer Affairs*, 37:161–9.

Lejoyeux, M., Haberman, N., Solomon, J., & Ades, J. (1999) Comparison of buying behavior in depressed patients presenting with or without compulsive buying, *Comprehensive Psychiatry*, 4:51–6.

McElroy, S.L., Keck Jr., P.E., Pope Jr., H.J., Smith, J.M., & Strakowski, S.M. (1994) Compulsive buying: a report of 20 cases, *Journal of Clinical Psychiatry*, 55:242–8.

McElroy, S.L., Keck Jr., P.E., & Phillips, K.A. (1995) Kleptomania, compulsive buying and binge-eating disorder, *Journal of Clinical Psychiatry*, 56:14–26.

Mueller, A., Mitchell, J.E., Crosby, R.D., Gefeller, O., Faber, R.J., Martin, A., Bleich, S., Glaesmer, H., Exner, C., & de Zwaan, M. (in press) Estimated prevalence of compulsive buying in Germany and its association with sociodemographic characteristics and depressive symptoms, *Psychiatry Research*.

Mundis, J. (1986) A way back from deep debt, *New York Times Magazine*, Jan. 5:22–6.

Neuner, M., Raab, G., & Reisch, L. (2005) Compulsive buying in maturing consumer societies: an empirical re-inquiry, *Journal of Economic Psychology*, 26:509–22.

O'Guinn, T.C. & Faber, R.J. (1989) Compulsive buying: a phenomenological exploration, *Journal of Consumer Research*, 16:147–57.

Rasmussen, S.A. & Tsang, M.T. (1987) Epidemiology and clinical features of obsessive-compulsive disorder, in Jenike, M.A., Baet, L., and Minichiello, W.E. (eds.), *Obsessive Compulsive Disorders: Theory and Management*, Littleton, MA: PSG Publication Co.

Ridgway, N.M., Kukar-Kinney, M., & Monroe, K.B. (2008) An expanded conceptualization and a new measure of compulsive buying, *Journal of Consumer Research*, 35:622–39.

Sanavio, E. (1988) Obsessions and compulsions: the Padua Inventory, *Behaviour Research and Therapy*, 26:169–77.

Scherhorn, G., Reisch, L.A., & Raab, G. (1990) Addictive buying in West Germany: an empirical study, *Journal of Consumer Policy*, 13:355–87.

Schlosser, S., Black, D.W., Repertinger, S., & Freet, D. (1994) Compulsive buying: demography, phenomenology, and comorbidity in 46 subjects, *General Hospital Psychiatry*, 16:205–12.

Shoham, A. and M.M. Brencic (2003) Compulsive buying behavior, *Journal of Consumer Marketing*, 20:127–38.

Tice, D.M., Bratslavsky, E., & Baumeister, R.F. (2001) Emotional distress regulation takes precedence over impulse control: if you feel bad, do it! *Journal of Personality and Social Psychology*, 80:53–67.

Wilson, J. (2000) Volunteering, *Annual Review of Sociology*, 26:215–40.

Winestine, M.C. (1985) Compulsive shopping as a derivative of childhood seduction, *Psychoanalytic Quarterly*, 54:70–2.

CHAPTER 2

Etiology of Compulsive Buying

TROY W. ERTELT, MA, JOANNA M. MARINO,
MA, AND ASTRID MÜLLER, MD, PHD

Contents

Introduction   19
Social Factors   20
Cognitive and Emotional Factors   21
Behavioral Factors   22
Psychodynamic Factors   23
Biological Factors   23
Toward a Biopsychosocial Model   23
References   25

Introduction

The etiological factors that may be causal for the development of compulsive buying (CB) have been examined by a number of theoretical perspectives. However, there has been a generally limited amount of research dedicated to the etiological pathways to CB behavior (Kyrios, Frost, & Steketee, 2004). Some have argued that manifestations of CB behavior are consistent with a biopsychosocial model of psychopathology (Faber & Christenson, 1996). As with many behavioral pathologies, etiological factors can differ among individuals and contexts. This chapter aims to provide a review of our understanding of the relationship between CB and possible social (including consumerist and materialistic values and ideals), cognitive, emotional, behavioral, and psychodynamic factors related to etiological theories of CB.

Social Factors

By and large, the act of shopping can be conceptualized as a social behavior. At the same time, the ways in which we shop and make purchases are socially constructed and influenced both by our individual microsystems of family and friends, as well as by macrosystemic cultural and societal attitudes toward consumption and the value placed on it. For decades, consumer research has examined the ways in which consumers make purchases and how best to market items to consumers. In CB, the sequence of acquisition is often preceded by social pressures from the microsystem—family, friends, coworkers, and others peers—and the macrosystem—advertisers, merchandisers, and individual cultures.

In most industrialized nations, shopping serves various functions—social activity, leisure activity, and necessity. Beyond this, the social pressures to acquire a large number of items (e.g., collections of baseball cards or dolls) or the desire to have the best quality items (e.g., large screen televisions or designer shoes) are apparent. Consumers may experience a feeling of achievement through purchasing these items or being able to provide these items as gifts to others. These buying behaviors occur across socioeconomic strata, genders, and age groups (d'Astous, 1990; Christenson, Faber, de Zwaan, Raymond, Specker, Ekern et al., 1994). From the consumer research perspective, CB can be conceptualized as an extreme variant of normal buying behavior.

In a descriptive examination of those with CB, it was observed that CB was often well established by the early 30s, but often began in late adolescence, and often ran a chronic course (Christenson et al., 1994). One study observed a significant correlation between CB in adolescents and their perceptions of CB among their parents (d'Astous, Maltais, & Roberge, 1990). This suggests that social modeling and social transmission of attitudes about materialism and consumerism are associated with the onset of CB. Also regarding adolescents and CB, a positive correlation between the number of hours spent watching television and CB behavior has been observed (d'Astous, Maltais, & Roberge, 1990). This finding provides support for the notion that attitudes leading to the development of CB behavior are transmitted from the macrosystem as well. Predictive modeling of CB among adolescents has found that gender (typically female), youth, peer influence, parental CB behavior, family resources, family stressors, and poor family communication may predict the development of CB behavior (d'Astous, Maltais, & Roberge, 1990; Gwin, Roberts, & Martinez, 2005).

In clinical samples, CB is more frequently identified in women than in men, and this may be due to the somewhat gender-specific role of shopping (Dittmar & Drury, 2000). Black (2001) has suggested that CB and compulsive gambling might be gender-typed variations on a theme (i.e., shopping and buying behavior are viewed as more socially appropriate impulsive-compulsive behaviors in women, while gambling behavior is viewed as a more socially appropriate impulsive-compulsive behavior in men).

Materialism, defined as a belief "that the acquisition of material goods is a key to self-definition and happiness, a central life goal, and a prime indicator of success" (Dittmar, 2005, p. 837), has been associated with compulsive buying. One study observed that those with CB focus on image over functionality of goods in advertisements, and this finding supports the idea that those with CB endorse materialistic beliefs and derive self-fulfillment from the acquisition of socially desirable items (Dittmar, 2005).

Credit cards and their influence on CB behavior are important to discuss in an examination of social factors associated with the onset of CB. Those with CB have been observed to have more credit cards than their non-CB counterparts, and the balance on credit cards held by those with CB are closer to their spending limits than are credit cards held by typical consumers (O'Guinn & Faber, 1989). Having large lines of credit available has been associated with overconsumption (Dittmar, 2005). In the United States, access to credit cards and attitudes and beliefs about the use of credit can often lead to overspending, even among typical consumers. Those with CB frequently have irrational attitudes toward money and carry substantial personal financial debt (Miltenberger, Redlin, Crosby, Stickney, Mitchell, Wonderlich et al., 2003).

Cognitive and Emotional Factors

Kyrios, Frost, and Steketee (2004) have developed a cognitive model of CB and acquisition. They posit that CB's etiological roots are derived from negative mood states, low self-esteem, perfectionism, problematic beliefs about the uniqueness and opportunity to purchase items (i.e., an exclusive opportunity to attain a product), decision-making difficulties, and incorrect beliefs about the emotional outcome of buying. Beyond these cognitive factors, there appears to be an emotional component that perpetuates a negative reinforcement cycle that is involved in CB behavior.

Negative emotions are often reported prior to a compulsive shopping episode (e.g., boredom, depressed mood, anxiety), although in some cases excitement for the shopping can manifest in feelings of power and happiness (Miltenberger, Redlin, Crosby, Stickney, Mitchell, Wonderlich et al., 2003; Faber & Christenson, 1996; Christenson, Faber, de Zwaan, Raymond, Specker, Ekern et al., 1994). In a self-monitoring study, Miltenberger and colleagues (2003) observed that those with CB reported that their negative mood states improved somewhat during shopping episodes but deteriorated after shopping episodes subsided. This pattern suggests that those with CB engage in CB in order to alleviate negative mood states, and that this is achieved during CB episodes. However, negative mood states return as negative consequences of CB episodes are realized after episodes are over.

Rose (2007) has suggested that narcissism correlates with CB, as previous research has supported the correlation between materialism and narcissism. He argues that, given that those with narcissistic tendencies have a need for admiration, the value of materialistic goods is apparent in narcissistic individuals. This need for admiration is likely diminished if the narcissistic individual perceives that others are aware of his or her problem or inability to afford his or her spending habits (Rose, 2007). This relationship is mediated by materialism and impulse control insufficiencies. Conversely, CB has been related to negative self-esteem (Faber & O'Guinn, 2008; Hanley & Wilhelm, 1992), in which acquisition is an attempt to improve self-esteem or wherein self-esteem is reduced due to the cyclical pattern of spending and indebtedness. Additionally a relationship between CB and risk-taking behaviors (e.g., smoking, alcohol and drug use, and unsafe sexual practices) has also been reported (Roberts & Tanner, 2000). In considering these findings, it is important to note that the results are typically based on nonclinical samples and thus have inherent limitations.

Behavioral Factors

The preceding discussion of social, cognitive, and emotional factors implicated in the development of CB are all relevant to the behavioral development and maintenance of CB behavior. In the context of social, cognitive, and emotional aspects of CB, reinforcing and punishing contingencies can be identified that are associated with CB. For example, literature on the social aspects of CB has identified that making expensive purchases might enhance feelings of power and prestige in those with CB and make them feel more acceptable to those in their environments. Feelings of power, prestige, and acceptance are positively reinforcing, and this creates a situation wherein CB behavior is more likely to occur in the future.

In data presented by Miltenberger and colleagues (2003), negative mood states were observed to precede CB episodes, and negative mood states decreased during buying episodes. Negative mood states, however, returned after buying episodes after consequences of buying episodes became apparent. This creates a situation in which buying episodes are negatively reinforcing (i.e., the buying episodes remove the negative mood state and make the buying episodes more likely to occur in the future), but also punishing (i.e., the buying episodes introduce negative consequences that should make buying episodes less likely to occur in the future). However, that resultant negative mood state can also act as a trigger for another

CB episode, thus creating a chain of behavior in which CB episodes are both reinforcing and punishing. Recently, Kellett and Bolton (2009) suggested a similar theoretical model of CB that has not yet been validated.

Psychodynamic Factors

Psychodynamic theory has been used to explain the etiology of CB within its own context. For example, Lawrence (1990) has suggested that CB serves the function of providing nurturing to the self that is not provided by the outside world. Krueger (1988) reported a small case series of those with CB who were treated with psychodynamic psychotherapy. In discussing the psychodynamic roots of the CB behavior in his patients, Krueger stated that CB behavior was an attempt "to regulate the affect and fragmented sense of self and to restore self object equilibrium" (Krueger, 1988, p. 581) on the part of those with CB.

Biological Factors

Evidence of possible biological pathways related to the development of CB has been put forth in the research literature. For example, a number of small medication studies have been conducted with subjects who have CB, and the results of these studies might provide some clues as to neurotransmitters involved in CB behavior. Medication studies provide some weight to the notion of possible disruptions of the opioid, dopaminergic, and serotonergic systems (Black, Gabel, Hansen, & Schlosser, 2000; Grant, 2003; Koran, Aboujaoude, Solvason, Gamel, & Smith, 2007; Koran, Bullock, Hartston, Elliott, & D'Andrea, 2002; Koran, Chuong, Bullock, & Smith, 2003; Ninan et al., 2000). Medication management of CB is also examined in detail in another chapter in this volume. Additionally, neuroeconomics, an examination of the neurological correlates of weighing options in decisions making, is discussed as one approach to differentiate generally normal consumers from those with CB behavior (e.g., Schaefer, 2009).

Toward a Biopsychosocial Model

The preceding review has identified a number of possible etiological factors that have been associated with CB in the research literature. The goal of the following section is to synthesize this information into a proposed biopsychosocial model of CB. To this end, the following case example is presented to provide a meaningful context in which to examine this biopsychosocial model. A graphical depiction of the biopsychosocial model for the case example is presented in Figure 2.1.

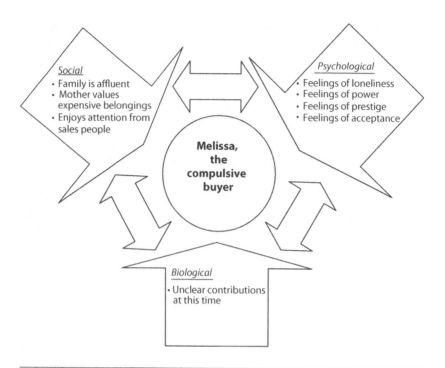

Figure 2.1 Biopsychosocial model of compulsive buying.

Melissa is a 20-year-old college student who works part time at a cosmetics counter in a mall department store. As a child, Melissa lived in an intact family in an affluent suburb of a major city. Melissa and her mother spent much of their leisure time together shopping when Melissa was a child and adolescent. Melissa's mother placed a high premium on buying expensive dishes, stemware, and decorations that she would use to impress her friends during social gatherings at the family's home. As Melissa grew into adolescence, Melissa's mother would often bring her to the mall for "retail therapy" after she had a fight with Melissa's father. As an adolescent, Melissa was impressed by the attention that she received from the salespeople as her mother was trying on new clothes or deciding on new items for their home.

Melissa obtained her first credit card when she was a senior in high school and turned 18. Melissa would frequently take her friends out for dinner and she enjoyed the feelings of prestige that this gave her. When Melissa moved away from her family of origin to begin college, she experienced depressed mood due to loneliness. Melissa began engaging in "retail therapy" on her own and would often spend hours at the local mall trying on clothes and jewelry. Her feelings of loneliness would briefly subside as she interacted with the salespeople, and she eventually befriended some of them. Melissa enjoyed the compliments that she received about her new clothes, and she also experienced feelings of power when she purchased items that others her age could not afford, even though all of her purchases were being charged to credit cards. This led to her taking a job at a department store in the mall, and she was happy that her position granted her a discount on many of the items that she most liked to buy.

References

Black, D.W. (2001) Compulsive buying disorder: Definition, assessment, epidemiology, and clinical management, *CNS Drugs*, 15:17–27.

Black, D.W., Gabel, J., Hansen, J., & Schlosser, S. (2000) A double-blind comparison of fluvoxamine versus placebo in the treatment of compulsive buying disorder, *Annals of Clinical Psychiatry*, 12:205–11.

Christenson, G.A., Faber, R.J., de Zwaan, M., Raymond, N.C., Specker, S.M., Ekern, M.D., Mackenzie, T.B., Crosby, R.D., Crow, S.J., Eckert, E.D., et al. (1994) Compulsive buying: Descriptive characteristics and psychiatric comorbidity, *Journal of Clinical Psychiatry*, 55:5–11.

d'Astous, A. (1990) An inquiry into the compulsive side of "normal" consumers, *Journal of Consumer Research*, 13:15–31.

d'Astous, A., Maltais, J., & Roberge, C. (1990) Compulsive buying tendencies of adolescent consumers, *Advances in Consumer Research*, 17:306–12.

Dittmar, H. (2005) Compulsive buying—a growing concern? An examination of gender, age, and endorsement of materialistic values as predictors, *British Journal of Psychology*, 96:467–91.

Dittmar, H. & Drury, J. (2000) Self-image—is it in the bag? A qualitative comparison between "ordinary" and "excessive" consumers, *Journal of Economic Psychology*, 21:109–42.

Faber, R.J. & Christenson, G.A. (1996) In the mood to buy: Differences in the mood states experienced by compulsive buyers and other consumers, *Psychology & Marketing*, 13:803–19.

Faber, R.J. & O'Guinn, T.C. (2008) Compulsive buying: review and reflection, in C.P. Haugtvedt, P.M. Herr, & F.R. Kardes (eds.), *Handbook of Consumer Psychology*, New York: Taylor & Francis, 1039–56.

Grant, J. (2003) Three cases of compulsive buying treated with naltrexone, *International Journal of Psychiatry in Clinical Practice*, 7:223–5.

Gwin, C.F., Roberts, J.A., & Martinez, C.R. (2005) Nature vs. nurture: The role of family in compulsive buying, *Marketing Management Journal*, 15:95–107.

Hanley, A. & Wilhelm, M.S. (1992) Compulsive buying: An exploration into self esteem and money attitudes, *Journal of Economic Psychology*, 13:5–18.

Kellett, S. & Bolton, J.V. (2009) Compulsive buying: A cognitive-behavioral model, *Clinical Psychology and Psychotherapy*, 16:83–99.

Koran, L.M., Aboujaoude, E.N., Solvason, B., Gamel, N.N., & Smith, E.H. (2007) Escitalopram for compulsive buying disorder: A double-blind discontinuation study, *Journal of Clinical Pharmacology*, 27:225–7.

Koran, L.M., Bullock, K.D., Hartston, H.J., Elliott, M.A., & D'Andrea, V. (2002) Citalopram treatment of compulsive shopping: An open-label study, *Journal of Clinical Psychiatry*, 63:704–8.

Koran, L.M., Chuong, H.W., Bullock, K.D., & Smith, S.C. (2003) Citalopram for compulsive shopping disorder: An open-label study followed by double blind discontinuation, *Journal of Clinical Psychiatry*, 64:793–8.

Krueger, D.W. (1988) On compulsive shopping and spending: A psychodynamic inquiry, *American Journal of Psychotherapy*, 42:574–84.

Kyrios, M., Frost, R.O., & Steketee, G. (2004) Cognitions in compulsive buying and acquisition, *Cognitive Therapy and Research*, 28:241–58.

Lawrence, L. (1990) The psychodynamics of the compulsive female shopper, *American Journal of Psychoanalysis*, 50:67–70.

Miltenberger, R.G., Redlin, J., Crosby, R.D., Stickney, M., Mitchell, J., Wonderlich, S., Faber, R., & Smyth, J. (2003) Direct and retrospective assessment of factors contributing to compulsive buying, *Journal of Behavior Therapy Experimental Psychiatry*, 34:1–9.

Ninan, P.T., McElroy, S.L., Kane, C.P., Knight, B.T., Casuto, L.S., Rose, S.E., Marsteller, F.A., & Nemerott, C.B. (2000) Placebo-controlled study of fluvoxamine in the treatment of patients with compulsive buying, *Journal of Clinical Psychopharmacology*, 20:362–6.

O'Guinn, T.C. & Faber, R.J. (1989) Compulsive buying: A phenomenological exploration, *Journal of Consumer Research*, 16:147–57.

Roberts, J.A. & Tanner, J.F. (2000) Compulsive buying and risky behavior among adolescents, *Psychological Reports*, 86:763–70.

Rose, P. (2007) Mediators of the association between narcissism and compulsive buying: The role of materialism and impulse control, *Psychology of Addictive Behaviors*, 21:576–81.

Schaefer, M. (2009) Neuroeconomics: in search of the neural representation of brands, *Progress in Brain Research*, 178:241–52.

CHAPTER 3

Assessment of Compulsive Buying

DONALD W. BLACK, MD

Contents

Introduction   27
Identification and Assessment   28
Screening   29
Psychiatric History   30
Other Assessments   32
Shopping Diaries   36
A Patient Example   37
Conclusion   38
References   38
Appendix A: Compulsive Buying Scale   41
Appendix B: Edwards Compulsive Buying Scale   43
Appendix C: Questionnaire about Buying Behavior   45
Appendix D: Yale-Brown Obsessive-Compulsive Scale-Shopping
Version (YBOCS-SV)   47

Introduction

Compulsive buying (CB) has been a focus of increasing attention in both the lay and the professional literature (Black, 2007). Yet for many clinicians, CB has been off the "radar screen," and they may be unaware their patients have problematic shopping and spending behaviors. Possibly the patient will consider the symptoms as part of a larger financial problem of no interest to the clinician. Alert clinicians will know that CB is common and widespread, particularly among a psychiatric patient population, and is associated with subjective distress and impaired functioning in important life domains.

While many individuals will be hesitant to discuss these problems, occasional patients will seek help from mental health professionals for CB, especially those who have read about it or seen media portrayals. Others may present at the behest of a concerned spouse, on the recommendation of a friend, or sometimes at the suggestion of an attorney or law enforcement officer if there have been legal entanglements.

This chapter reviews the clinical assessment of those with CB, and includes discussion of instruments used by clinicians and researchers to diagnose and assess CB.

Identification and Assessment

When CB is a presenting problem, the patient will likely have been referred by a financial counselor, lawyer, law enforcement officer, family member, or spouse (Black, 2000). More frequently CB reveals itself in the course of ongoing treatment. Some patients will begin to talk openly about the problem. With others, CB emerges in the context of inquiries relating to financial independence and responsibility, relationship problems, difficulties at work, or parenting problems. CB may also present itself indirectly; for example, a patient might wear something new or different to each appointment, or arrive with shopping bags week after week, or repeatedly bring gifts to the therapist or staff, or fall behind in paying the bill (Benson, 2000).

People with CB tend to be secretive about their disorder because it is a source of shame and embarrassment, perhaps even more so than alcoholism or drug abuse. The latter are commonly thought of as diseases requiring treatment, while CB may be trivialized by some who see it as an excuse to "medicalize" behavioral problems (Lee & Mysyk, 2004). But those with CB, who are largely unaware of these controversies, worry that they will be considered materialistic and vacuous by clinicians—judgments that likely reflect their poor self-image (Benson, 2000).

Regardless of how CB comes to clinical attention, the following steps can be taken to evaluate the disorder. This is particularly important when CB becomes a focus of clinical attention and is necessary when treatment is being considered.

The first step in assessing patients with possible CB is to assure them of the confidential nature of the physician–patient (or therapist–patient) relationship. The clinician should explain that to provide appropriate diagnostic assessment and comprehensive treatment recommendations the disorder must be thoroughly assessed. The clinician should then proceed

Table 3.1 Diagnostic Criteria for Compulsive Buying

A. Maladaptive preoccupation with buying or shopping, or maladaptive buying or shopping impulses or behavior, as indicated by at least one of the following:

    1. Frequent preoccupation with buying or impulses to buy that is/are experienced as irresistible, intrusive, and/or senseless.

    2. Frequent buying of more than can be afforded, frequent buying of items that are not needed, or shopping for longer periods of time than intended.

B. The buying preoccupations, impulses, or behaviors cause marked distress, are time-consuming, significantly interfere with social or occupational functioning, or result in financial problems (e.g., indebtedness or bankruptcy).

C. The excessive buying or shopping behavior does not occur exclusively during periods of hypomania or mania.

Source: McElroy, S.L., Keck, P.E., Pope, H.G., Smith, J.M.R., & Strakowski, S.M. (1994). Compulsive buying: a report of 20 cases. *Journal of Clinical Psychiatry,* 55:242–8. Reprinted with permission.

to construct an accurate history of the disorder, which will form the most important basis for diagnosing CB.

Because the assessment of CB begins with its recognition, clinicians need to become familiar with the syndrome. To help clinicians and researchers, McElroy, Keck, Pope, Smith, and Strakowski (1994) developed a set of operational criteria (see Table 3.1). Their definition recognizes that CB involves cognitions (or preoccupations) and behaviors, each component potentially leading to impairment. Impairment can be manifested through personal distress; social, marital, or occupational dysfunction; or financial or legal problems. Mania and hypomania will have been ruled out as a cause of the disturbance. Designed primarily for use in research settings, the criteria can easily be used for clinical purposes.

As with any psychiatric assessment, the interview should begin with a sincere attempt to develop rapport with the patient, perhaps beginning by asking the patient about himself or herself. For example, the clinician might ask what kind of work the patient does, where he or she goes to school, or whether he or she is married or has a significant other. The questions should be asked in a manner that conveys genuine interest. Once rapport is established, the questions can gradually become more detailed and specific, circling in on the patient's problems.

Screening

The initial goal of evaluation is to define the buying problem through relatively nonintrusive inquiries about the person's attitudes about shopping and spending, and then to focus on specific shopping behaviors and patterns. Once the buying problem has been acknowledged, the patient can be questioned in greater detail about the extent of the preoccupation and behavior. For most persons with CB, preoccupation with shopping and spending is a hallmark of the disorder (Black, in press).

For general screening purposes a clinician might ask:

- Do you feel overly preoccupied with shopping and spending?
- Do you ever feel that your shopping behavior is excessive, inappropriate, or uncontrolled?
- Have your shopping desires, urges, fantasies, or behaviors ever been overly time-consuming, caused you to feel upset or guilty, or led to serious problems in your life (e.g., financial or legal problems, relationship loss)?

Any positive response should be followed up with more detailed questions about shopping and spending. For example, the clinician will want to ask when the behavior began, how frequently it occurs, what the individual likes to buy, and how much money is spent. Patients with CB are often anxious or embarrassed about their symptoms, and may need considerable reassurance before disclosing their thoughts and behaviors.

Family members and friends can become important informants in the assessment of those with CB, able to fill in the gaps in the patient's history or to describe the patient's behavior they may have witnessed. Patients may not always be accurate in describing the extent of their problem, but close relatives affected by the consequences of the behavior are usually able to quantify the problems. Of course, the clinician will need to seek the patient's consent in order to interview other informants.

Psychiatric History

The patient's psychiatric history should be carefully explored because research has shown that most persons with CB have substantial current and lifetime psychiatric comorbidity (Black, Repertinger, Gaffney, & Gabel, 1998; Christenson, Faber, de Zwaan, Raymond, Specker, Ekern et al. 1994; McElroy, Keck, Pope, Smith, & Strakowski, 1994; Mueller, Mitchell, Black, Crosby, Berg, & de Zwaan, 2010). Evaluation of psychiatric comorbidity may help the clinician to develop a treatment plan, but may also provide helpful explanations for the excessive spending and shopping that may be used in counseling patients. For instance, an individual's excessive shopping and spending might be triggered by anxiety, which could suggest treatment with a serotonin reuptake inhibitor antidepressant. Clinicians should take note of past psychiatric treatment, including medications, hospitalizations, and psychotherapy. The patient's history of physical illness, surgical procedures, drug allergies, and medical treatment is important, as it may help rule out unusual medical illnesses as explanations for CB (e.g., neurological disorders, brain tumors), or reveal conditions that may contraindicate the use of certain medications the clinician might prescribe to treat the disorder. Since many patients with CB often have histories of depression, anxiety disorders, eating disorders, and substance use disorders, particular attention should be focused on these conditions (Mueller et al., 2010).

Family history should be obtained. Though the causes of CB are unknown, it is clear that the disorder runs in some families—families that are often troubled by depression, alcoholism, and drug addiction (Black, Repertinger, Gaffney, & Gabel, 1998). Information about the emotional and psychiatric health of the parents, grandparents, aunts, uncles, and offspring can help identify risk factors linked to the patient's heredity or home environment, and suggest possible diagnoses. Possibly having grown up in a dysfunctional home in which one or both parents had an emotional disorder or substance abuse may have indirectly contributed to the patient's CB. On the other hand, the patient may have learned inappropriate buying and spending behavior from her mother or other relatives. For these reasons family information may be helpful both in understanding the patient's disorder and in designing a therapeutic strategy for the patient. For example, in some patients, understanding the family constellation will help with the process of individual psychotherapy, or may help inform family therapy recommendations.

The patient's personal and social history should be explored, including early family life. Details about the home and the community, and any history of physical, emotional, or sexual abuse, should be obtained. Educational background, relationships, occupational history, and questions about marriage will also be helpful in evaluating the patient. Details about the patient's living arrangements, finances, and children are additional aspects of the personal history that can help fill in the overall picture of the patient's life. This information will help in planning a comprehensive approach to the patient's problems.

The CB itself must be fully evaluated. This should begin with inquiries about when the behavior began, how it began, and what prompted its origin. Typically patients will report the onset of the disorder in their late teens or early 20s, often at times when they began their first job, obtained their first credit card, or opened their first checking account, or achieved personal independence (Schlosser, Black, Repertinger, & Freet, 1994). The course of the disorder needs to be explored. Has it been chronic? Episodic? Has its severity fluctuated over time? Have there been periods of remission? Patients often indicate that their disorder is chronic but fluctuates depending on life circumstances and finances (Christenson et al., 1994).

The clinician should ask the patient what she buys. Clothing? Jewelry? Collectibles? Electronic goods? Does the buying occur in upscale department stores? Discount stores? Consignment or thrift shops? Does the patient make a habit of attending garage sales? Does the patient spend time looking through newspaper ads or catalogues? Or spending hours searching the Internet? Is the shopping year round, or does it occur in sprees associated with birthdays and major holidays? Does the shopping occur when the patient is alone, or is she accompanied by a friend or family member? Is the shopping impulsive, or is it preceded by careful planning? Does the patient use cash, personal checks, debit cards, or credit cards? If the patient uses credit cards, how many cards does the patient have and what is the current level of debt (excluding the home mortgage and car payment)?

Does the patient associate any particular emotions or affects with buying? How does the patient feel after a purchase? Does the patient have to buy, or can she be satisfied by window shopping? Has the shopping affected the patient's spousal relationship or family life? Does the patient ignore her spouse or children in order to shop? Does the patient take her children along with her on shopping sprees? Has she ever sought treatment for her shopping disorder? If so, what treatment did the patient receive, and how long did it last? Was the treatment effective? Lastly the examiners should ask patients what they believe caused the disorder. Most patients offer an explanation for their behavior, which may yield clues to what prompted the shopping initially and what they view as important historically in their lives.

Other Assessments

A thorough assessment of any patient generally involves conducting a physical examination or arranging for one to be done and obtaining routine screening laboratories. For most persons with CB, it is unlikely that the physical examination or laboratory test will be helpful, although test results may be consistent with medical problems the patient reports. For example, alcoholic patients may show evidence of liver enlargement or display palmar erythema, while laboratory testing may show evidence of liver enzyme elevations. There is no reason to administer other tests, such as brain imaging studies or electroencephalography, unless they are used to rule out brain disorders (e.g., mass lesion, seizure disorder) suggested by the differential diagnosis or physical examination findings.

In collecting the patient's history, the clinician should train his or her attention on the patient's appearance, habits, and demeanor, noting any peculiarities in dress, attitude, or speaking style. Orientation to time, place, and person, ability to reason, and memory can be assessed informally as part of a mental status examination (MSE). The MSE can help to identify patients with psychotic symptoms, severe depression or suicidal ideations, or cognitive impairment. Most of those with CB display a normal sensorium, are well groomed and dressed, show good eye contact, and exhibit relevant and coherent speech. Some show evidence of current psychiatric comorbidity, such as major depression, panic disorder, or social phobia. Others will have evidence of alcohol or drug addiction. As a group, those with CB tend to be highly interested in their disorder, often show good insight, and are able to describe the driven, compulsive quality of their disorder. They may describe a feeling of anxiety that builds until it is relieved by shopping and spending. Afterwards, they may convey a sense of shame and guilt, while admitting to the pleasure they experienced while shopping and spending.

In any evaluation normal shopping and spending behavior must be distinguished from CB, though it may sometimes be difficult to draw a clear distinction. The clinician should also be aware of the inherent differences in shopping behavior of typical men and women, and understand that shopping and spending generally occur within a cultural context. In contemporary American society, shopping is typically viewed from a female perspective, a fact not lost on advertisers, who aim their advertisements mainly at women. Additionally persons may go through periods when their shopping and spending behavior may take on a compulsive quality—for example, around special holidays and birthdays. The clinician needs to be mindful of the fact that those with CB typically do not confine their overspending to certain times of the year, but have a chronic pattern of excessive shopping and spending (Black, 1996; Christenson et al., 1994). The clinician should exercise judgment in applying the criteria of McElroy et al. (1994), and be aware of the need for evidence of distress or impairment.

Several researchers have developed useful instruments to help identify and diagnose CB. Canadian researchers Valence, d'Astous, and Fortier (1988) developed the Compulsive Buying Measurement Scale. They selected 16 items thought to represent four basic dimensions of CB (a tendency to spend, feeling an urge to buy or shop, postpurchase guilt, and family environment). A reliability analysis based on results from a sample of 38 individuals with CB and 38 individuals characterized as normal shoppers led the investigators to delete three items representing family environment; the remaining 13 items had high internal consistency (Cronbach's alpha = 0.88). Construct validity was established by demonstrating that those with CB achieved significantly higher scores than the control group, and the higher scores correlated with higher levels of anxiety and more commonly with a family history of psychiatric illness. A modified version of the scale containing 16 items, each rated on a four-point scale, was tested by German researchers (Scherhorn, Reisch, & Raab, 1990). Their Addictive Buying Indicator was found to have high reliability (Cronbach's alpha = 0.87). Construct validity was demonstrated by significant correlations between scale scores and scores assessing psychasthenia, depression, and self-esteem. Like the Canadian instrument, the

Addictive Buying Indicator was able to discriminate between those considered to be normal and those with CB.

These early efforts led Faber and O'Guinn (1992) to develop the Compulsive Buying Scale (CBS), an instrument designed to identify those with CB. They began with 29 items based on preliminary work, and each was rated on a five-point scale chosen to reflect important characteristics of CB. Their scale was administered to 388 individuals self-identified as having CB and 292 persons drawn randomly from the general population. Using logistic regression, seven items representing specific behaviors, motivations, and feelings associated with buying significantly were found to correctly classify approximately 88 percent of the subjects. This instrument is reproduced in Appendix A.

The CBS also showed excellent reliability and validity. One measure of reliability, internal consistency, was verified using principal components factor analysis as well as by calculating Cronbach's alpha (0.95). Criterion and construct validity were assessed by comparing those with CB from the general population sample (classified by the screener) to those self-identified as having CB and to the other members of the general population on variables previously found to relate to CB (Faber & O'Guinn, 1989). The comparison provides good support for the validity of the screener.

Another use of this instrument is in prevalence estimation. Based on a probability distribution, Faber and O'Guinn (1992) recommend a cut point of 0.70 (i.e., the probability of having CB), which corresponds with a scale score of –1.34, a figure approximately two standard deviations above the normal population mean. Using this criterion, they classified 8.1 percent of their general population sample as being (or at risk of developing) CB. Using a more conservative probability level of 0.95 produced a prevalence estimate of 1.8 percent of the general population.

Christenson et al. (1994) have developed the Minnesota Impulsive Disorder Interview (MIDI), which is used to assess the presence of CB, kleptomania, trichotillomania, intermittent explosive disorder, pathological gambling, compulsive sexual behavior, and compulsive exercise. This diagnostic instrument is fully structured and designed for use in research settings. The MIDI begins by gathering demographic data, and then progresses through various screening modules. It is followed by a section on family history and personality characteristics. The section on compulsive buying consists of four core questions and five follow-up questions. The developers recommend administering their 82-question expanded module to persons screening positive for compulsive buying. Expanded modules are also available for trichotillomania and compulsive sexual behavior. While the MIDI and its expanded modules have not been tested for reliability or validity, its developers report excellent inter-rater reliability among themselves and believe that the instrument has good face validity (G. Christenson, personal communication). Grant, Levine, Kim, and Potenza (2005) reported that the instrument had a sensitivity of 100 percent and a specificity of 96.2 percent for CB when comparing the instrument to the diagnostic criteria of McElroy et al. (1994).

Edwards (1993) and DeSarbo and Edwards (1996) have developed a 13-item self-report scale designed to identify those with CB and to rate its severity. Each item is rated along a five-point Likert-like scale. In a study comparing the responses of 104 individuals with CB recruited through support groups and 101 persons from the general population, the authors identified five factors concerning compulsive spending: compulsion/drive to spend, feelings about shopping and spending, tendency to spend, dysfunctional spending, and postpurchase guilt. Based on their results, the authors pared the scale from 29 to 13 items. The scale and its subscales showed good to excellent internal consistency as estimated by Cronbach's alpha (range, 0.76 to 0.91). The developers of the scale observe that it can be used by counselors and therapists to help identify a person's compulsive spending tendencies, as well as the severity of those tendencies, which they hypothesize to fall along a continuum from non-CB to "addicted" buying behavior. The instrument is reproduced in Appendix B.

Other research groups have also developed scales. Lejoyeux, Tassian, Solomon, and Adès (1997) developed a questionnaire consisting of 19 items that tap the basic features of CB. These dimensions include: impulsivity; urges to shop and buy; emotions felt before, during, and after purchasing; postpurchase guilt and regret; degree of engagement of short-term gratification; tangible consequences of buying; and avoidance strategies. Its psychometric properties have not been examined. This instrument is reproduced in Appendix C.

Weun, Jones, and Beatty (1998) developed the Impulse Buying Tendency Scale to assess the proclivity for impulse buying, which they distinguish from CB. Ridgway, Kukar-Kinney, and Monroe (2008) developed the Compulsive-Impulsive Buying Scale that measures CB as a construct incorporating elements of both an obsessive-compulsive and an impulse-control disorder. The scale appears to be reliable and valid, and performs well in correlating with other theoretically related constructs. These instruments will be of interest mainly to researchers.

Monahan, Black, and Gabel (1996) modified the Yale-Brown Obsessive-Compulsive Scale (YBOCS) (Goodman, Price, Rasmussen, Mazure, Delgado, Heninger et al., 1989) to create the YBOCS-Shopping Version (YBOCS-SV) to assess cognitions and behaviors associated with CB. The authors concluded that their scale was reliable and valid in measuring severity and change during clinical trials. For example, those with CB were reported to describe repetitive problematic buying, intrusive thoughts about buying, and resistance to such thoughts. This instrument is reproduced in Appendix D.

These investigators compared a group of individuals clinically identified as having CB and control subjects and showed that the scale separated the two groups. Inter-rater reliability was demonstrated for those with CB (r = 0.81), control subjects (r = 0.96), and for both groups combined (r = 0.99). The instrument showed a fairly high degree of internal consistency using Cronbach's alpha coefficients. Evidence for construct validity was good as well, showing that YBOCS-SV scores were the best indicators of severity of illness, not other scales that were administered, including the Clinical Global Impression Scales (Guy, 1976) and the National Institute of Mental Health Obsessive-Compulsive Scale (NIMHOCS) (Murphy, Picker, & Alterman, 1982). The YBOCS-SV was sensitive to clinical change and was able to detect improvement during clinical trials (Black et al., 1997, 2000).

Like its sister instrument, the YBOCS-SV consists of 10 items, five of which rate preoccupations and five of which rate behaviors. For assessing both preoccupations and behaviors subjects are asked about time involved, interference due to the preoccupations or behaviors, distress associated with shopping, the resistance to the thoughts or behavior, and degree of control over the symptoms. Items are rated from zero (none) to four (extreme), and scores can range from zero to 40. In the sample described by Monahan et al. (1996), the mean YBOCS-SV score for untreated compulsive shoppers was 21 (range 18–25) and four (range one to seven) for those considered to be normal shoppers.

Shopping Diaries

Any effort to understand and treat those with CB will benefit by having patients keep a daily log of their shopping and spending behavior. For both assessment and therapeutic purposes, it may be helpful to have patients regularly record their shopping experiences: where they shop, how much they spend, and what they buy. It also may be helpful to have patients record their mood at the time and to note whether the buying episode was prompted by anything in particular. The data collected can be used to gain a sense of the patient's typical buying behavior, as well as to provide data that can be directly monitored during a treatment trial. The data can be used to supplement (and externally validate) the rating scale scores. Benson (2008) describes how this can be embedded within a self-help program.

The use of a daily log may be therapeutic as well. In our experience patients almost uniformly report that keeping a log is the most valuable part of their treatment. The log enables them to become fully aware of the extent and severity of their disorder; acknowledging the disorder to a therapist is probably the first step toward any improvement. Any formal effort at behavior therapy will benefit from the use of a log, as the therapist can design an individualized program for the patient to interrupt unwanted behaviors, to help the patient learn typical cues that prompt the behavior, and to assist the patient in learning new ways to spend her time (Bernik, Akerman, Amaral, & Braun, 1996). The data can provide a description of the patient's buying behavior that may be helpful during treatment, for example, in a medication or behavior therapy trial (Benson, 2006; Black et al., 1997; Bernik et al., 1996). The use of a daily log may be therapeutic as well, by fostering the patient's awareness of the extent of the problem.

A Patient Example

Mary, a 47-year-old divorced woman, had compulsively shopped since she first obtained credit cards at 19 (Black, 2001). She knew her shopping behavior was excessive, and reported that it had been continuous for nearly its entire duration. She had only controlled her shopping briefly for two short periods, both coinciding with bankruptcy proceedings.

Mary's history strongly suggested CB. Her CBS was −4.19, which indicated that her shopping and spending habits were extreme. The criteria of McElroy et al. (1994) were applied, and she acknowledged meeting each criterion. There were no other current or past Axis I disorders.

Mary's disorder was assessed with the MIDI, using the expanded module for CB. Among the information learned was that Mary was currently in debt on four credit cards. Her life revolved around shopping and spending, even though she worked full time. Spending gave her a "rush," despite the guilt she experienced afterwards. She would either return items or give them away. She enjoyed shopping—mostly alone—at expensive department stores and would spend her money mainly on clothing and shoes. She was unhappy with her inability to control her spending, and was ashamed that her behavior had contributed to her divorce, as well as to her serious financial problems. She described the shopping behavior as relatively spontaneous and impulsive, and generally not planned.

Mary entered the 9-week experimental drug trial. At intake her YBOCS-SV score was 15, her Clinical Global Impression (CGI) severity score was 4 ("moderately ill").

She was randomized to receive fluvoxamine and was begun on 50 mg/day, a dose that was gradually increased to 150 mg/day. She met weekly with the researchers to discuss her shopping compulsions and other concerns. Mary was asked to bring her shopping diary to these sessions, where it was reviewed. She was asked about each shopping experience listed, including date and time, duration of shopping, what was purchased, and how much was spent. The researchers also inquired about her feelings and attitudes toward the shopping and spending, and whether she felt any regret or remorse. As she improved, Mary was also asked about how she was spending the time she had previously used for shopping. She was also asked about drug side effects, use of other medications, new illnesses, and about her general mood and level of anxiety. She was not given any specific instructions on how to reduce her shopping or spending behaviors.

By the end of week three, Mary's YBOCS-SV score had dropped to 6 and she was given a CGI improvement rating of 1, indicating "very much" improvement. By week nine, the end of the trial, her YBOCS-SV had dropped to 2 and her CGI improvement rating remained at 1. Mary responded well to the treatment, and reported that she thought less frequently about shopping, felt less compelled to shop, and spent less money shopping. She reported that her self-esteem was better as she was able to exercise greater control of her shopping and spending behaviors.

Conclusion

CB is common in the general population, and even more common in mental health settings. For this reason, clinicians should familiarize themselves with its characteristic symptoms and, as with other disorders, gather historical data, obtain confirmatory evidence when possible, and proceed with a differential diagnosis. Because psychiatric comorbidity is the rule, clinicians should pay particular attention to the patient's mental health history. Several instruments and rating scales are available to assist in the recognition, diagnosis, and assessment of CB including the Compulsive Buying Scale, the Minnesota Impulsive Disorders Interview, and the Yale-Brown Obsessive Scale modified for CB (YBOCS-SV). Patients may also be evaluated through daily shopping logs, which can help with assessment as well as with behavioral therapies aimed at interrupting the cycle of CB.

References

Benson, A.L. (ed.) (2000) *I Shop, Therefore I Am: Compulsive Buying and the Search for Self*, Northvale, New Jersey: Jason Aronson.

Benson, A.L. (2008) *To Buy or Not to Buy: Why We Overshop and How to Stop*, Boston: Trumpeter.

Bernik, M.A., Akerman, D., Amaral, J.A.M.S., & Braun, R.C.D.N. (1996) Cue exposure in compulsive buying (letter), *Journal of Clinical Psychiatry*, 57:90.

Black, D.W. (1996) Compulsive buying: a review, *Journal of Clinical Psychiatry*, 57:50–5.

Black, D.W. (2000) Assessment of compulsive buying, in A. Benson (ed.), *I Shop, Therefore I Am: Compulsive Buying and the Search for Self*, Northvale, New Jersey: Jason Aronson, 191–216.

Black, D.W. (2001) Compulsive buying disorder: definition, assessment, epidemiology and clinical management, *CNS Drugs*, 15:17–27.

Black, D.W. (2007) Compulsive buying disorder: a review of the evidence, *CNS Spectrums*, 12:124–32.

Black, D.W. (in press) Epidemiology and phenomenology of compulsive buying disorder, in J. Grant & M. Potenza (eds), *Oxford Handbook of Impulse Control Disorders*, New York: Oxford University Press.

Black, D.W., Monahan. P., & Gabel, J. (1997) Fluvoxamine in the treatment of compulsive buying, *Journal of Clinical Psychiatry*, 58:159–63.

Black, D.W., Repertinger, S., Gaffney, G.R., & Gabel, J. (1998) Family history and psychiatric comorbidity in persons with compulsive buying: preliminary findings, *American Journal of Psychiatry*, 155:960–3.

Black, D.W., Gabel, J., Hansen, J., & Schlosser, S. (2000) A double-blind comparison of fluvoxamine versus placebo in the treatment of compulsive buying disorder, *Annals of Clinical Psychiatry*, 12:205–11.

Christenson, G.A., Faber, R.J., de Zwaan, M., Raymond, N.C., Specker, S.M., Ekern, M.D., Mackenzie, T.B., Crosby, R.D., Crow, S.J., Eckert, E.D., et al. (1994) Compulsive buying: descriptive characteristics and psychiatric comorbidity, *Journal of Clinical Psychiatry*, 55:5–11.

DeSarbo, W.S. & Edwards, E.A. (1996) Typologies of compulsive buying behavior: a constrained clusterwise regression approach, *Journal of Consumer Psychology*, 5:231–52.

Edwards, E.A. (1993) Development of a new scale for measuring compulsive buying behavior, *Financial Counseling and Planning*, 4:67–84.

Faber, R.J. & O'Guinn, T.C. (1989) Classifying compulsive consumers: advances in the development of a diagnostic tool, *Advances in Consumer Research*, 16:738–44.

Faber, R.J. & O'Guinn, T.C. (1992) A clinical screener for compulsive buying, *Journal of Consumer Research*, 19:459–69.

Goodman, W.K., Price, L.H., Rasmussen. S.A., Mazure, C., Delgado, P., Heninger, G.R., & Charney, D.S. (1989) The Yale-Brown Obsessive-Compulsive Scale: II: Validity, *Archives of General Psychiatry*, 46:1012–6.

Grant, J.E., Levine, L., Kim, D., & Potenza, M.N. (2005) Impulse control disorders in adult psychiatric inpatients, *American Journal of Psychiatry*, 162:2184–88.

Guy, W. (1976) ECDEU Assessment Manual for Psychopharmacology, Washington, D.C.: U.S. Department of HEW Publication, 217–222.

Lejoyeux, M., Adés, J., Tassian, V., & Solomon, J. (1996) Phenomenology and psychopathology of uncontrolled buying, *American Journal of Psychiatry*, 153:1524–9.

Lee, S. & Mysyk, A. (2004) The medicalization of compulsive buying, *Social Science and Medicine*, 58:1709–18.

Lejoyeux, M., Tassian, V., Solomon, J., & Adés, J. (1997) Study of compulsive buying in depressed patients, *Journal of Clinical Psychiatry*, 58:169–73.

McElroy, S.L., Keck, P.E., Pope, H.G., Smith, J.M.R., & Strakowski, S.M. (1994) Compulsive buying: a report of 20 cases, *Journal of Clinical Psychiatry*, 55:242–8.

Monahan, P., Black, D.W., & Gabel, J. (1996) Reliability and validity of a scale to measure change in persons with compulsive buying, *Psychiatry Research*, 64:59–67.

Mueller, A., Mitchell, J., Black, D.W., Crosby, R.D., Berg, K., & de Zwaan, M. (2010) Latent profile analysis and comorbidity in a sample of individuals with compulsive buying disorder. *Psychiatry Research*, 178:348–53.

Murphy, D.L., Pickar, D.L., & Alterman, I.S. (1982) Methods or the quantitative assessment of depressive and manic behavior, in E.I. Burdock, A. Sudilovski, & S. Gershon (eds.) *The Behavior of Psychiatric Patients*, New York: Marcel Dekker, 355–391.

Ridgway, N.M., Kukar-Kinney, M., & Monroe, K.B. (2008) An expanded conceptualization and a new measure of compulsive buying, *Journal of Consumer Research*, 35:350–406.

Scherhorn, G., Reisch, L.A., & Raab, G. (1990) Addictive buying in West Germany: an empirical study, *Journal of Consumer Policy*, 13:355–87.

Schlosser, S., Black, D.W., Repertinger, S., & Freet, D. (1994) The demography, phenomenology, and comorbidity of compulsive buying, *General Hospital Psychiatry*, 16:205–12.

Valence, G., d'Astous, A., & Fortier, L. (1988) Compulsive buying: concept and measurement, *Journal of Clinical Policy*, 11:419–33.

Weun, S., Jones, M.A., & Beatty, S.E. (1998) Development and validation of the Impulse Buying Tendency Scale, *Psychological Reports*, 82:1123–33.

Appendix A: Compulsive Buying Scale

1. Please indicate how much you agree or disagree with each of the statements below. Place an X on the line that best indicates how you feel about each statement.

	Strongly Agree (1)	Somewhat Agree (2)	Neither Agree nor Disagree (3)	Somewhat Disagree (4)	Strongly Disagree (5)
If I have any money left at the end of the pay period, I just have to spend it.	____	____	____	____	____

2. Please indicate how often you have done each of the following things by placing an X on the appropriate line.

	Very Often (1)	Often (2)	Sometimes (3)	Rarely (4)	Never (5)
a. Felt others would be horrified if they knew of my spending habits.	____	____	____	____	____

	Very Often (1)	Often (2)	Sometimes (3)	Rarely (4)	Never (5)
b. Bought things even though I couldn't afford them.	____	____	____	____	____
c. Wrote a check when I knew I didn't have enough money in the bank to cover it.	____	____	____	____	____
d. Bought myself something in order to make myself feel better.	____	____	____	____	____
e. Felt anxious or nervous on days I didn't go shopping.	____	____	____	____	____
f. Made only the minimum payments on my credit card.	____	____	____	____	____

Scoring equation = $-9.69 + (Q1 \times .33) + (Q2a \times .34) + (Q2b \times .50) + (Q2c \times .47) + (Q2d \times .33) + (Q2e \times .38) + (Q2f \times .31)$.

Substitute your score 1 to 5 on each question for its place in the equation. For example, if you marked Question 1 as 2 (somewhat agree), use 2 in place of Q1 and multiply it by .33. When you have answered each question, add your individual scores together and subtract 9.69 to determine your overall score. If your overall score is a higher negative score than −1.34 (for example, −2.04), you would be classified as a compulsive buyer.

Source: Faber, R. & O'Guinn, T. (1992) A clinical screener for compulsive buying, *Journal of Consumer Research*, 19:459–69. Reprinted with permission.

Appendix B: Edwards Compulsive Buying Scale*

1. I feel driven to shop and spend, even when I don't have the time or money.
2. I get little or no pleasure from shopping.
3. I hate to go shopping.[†]
4. I go on buying binges.
5. I feel "high" when I go on a buying spree.[†]
6. I buy things when I don't need anything.[†]
7. I go on a buying binge when I'm upset, disappointed, depressed, or angry.
8. I worry about my spending habits, but still go out and shop and spend money.
9. I feel anxious after I go on a buying binge.
10. I buy things even though I cannot afford them.
11. I feel guilty or ashamed after I go on a buying binge.
12. I buy things I don't need or won't use.

---

* Edwards, E.A. (1993) Development of a new scale for measuring compulsive buying behavior, *Financial Counseling and Planning*, 4:67–81. Reprinted with permission.
† Indicated that the item should be reverse-coded.

Appendix C: Questionnaire about Buying Behavior*

Directions: Each of the questions below contains two choices, yes and no. Please indicate on you answer sheet which choice most describes the way you act and feel. Do not leave any blanks and please respond to all questions with only one answer (yes or no).

1. Have you ever had the irresistible urge to spend money on anything at all?
2. Have you ever bought something that you later found useless?
3. Have you ever felt on edge, agitated, or irritable when you haven't been able to buy something?
4. Have you ever avoided certain stores because you were afraid you would buy too much?
5. Have you ever asked someone to go shopping with you so you wouldn't buy too much?
6. Have you ever hidden your purchases from your family or friends?
7. Has the craving to buy something ever caused you to miss a date with friends?
8. Have you ever left work in order to buy something?
9. Has one or several of your purchases ever provoked the reproach of your family or friends?
10. Has one or several of your purchases ever provoked a prolonged misunderstanding or separation?
11. Has any of your purchases ever resulted in problems with your bank?
12. Has any of your purchases ever resulted in legal problems?
13. Have you ever continued to buy things in spite of the financial and family problems your purchases caused?
14. Do you regularly regret your purchases?
15. Do you regularly feel tense or nervous before you buy something?
16. Do you regularly feel relieved after you've bought something?
17. Do you have excessive buying periods accompanied by overwhelming feelings of generosity?
18. Do you buy something "on the spur of the moment" at least once a month?
19. Do your "spur-of-the-moment" or excessive purchases represent at least 25 percent of your wages?

---

* Lejoyeux, M., Tassain, V., Solomon, J., & Adés, J. (1997) Study of compulsive buying in depressed patients, *Journal of Clinical Psychiatry* 58:169–73. Reprinted with permission.

Appendix D: Yale-Brown Obsessive-Compulsive Scale-Shopping Version (YBOCS-SV)*

1. TIME OCCUPIED BY THOUGHTS ABOUT SHOPPING. How much of your time is occupied by thoughts about shopping?

   0   None.
   1   Mild, less than 1 hr/day or occasional intrusion.
   2   Moderate, 1 to 3 hrs/day, or frequent intrusion.
   3   Severe, greater than 3 and up to 8 hrs/day or very frequent intrusion.
   4   Extreme, greater than 8 hrs/day or near constant intrusion.

2. INTERFERENCE DUE TO THOUGHTS ABOUT SHOPPING. How much do your thoughts about shopping interfere with your social, work, or role functioning? Is there anything you don't do because of them?

   0   None.
   1   Mild, slight interference with social or occupational activities but overall performance not impaired.
   2   Moderate, definite interference with social or occupational performance, but still manageable.
   3   Severe, causes substantial impairment in social or occupational performance.
   4   Extreme, incapacitating.

3. DISTRESS ASSOCIATED WITH THOUGHTS ABOUT SHOPPING. How much distress do your thoughts about shopping cause you?

   0   None.
   1   Mild, not too disturbing.
   2   Moderate, disturbing but still manageable.
   3   Severe, very disturbing.
   4   Extreme, near constant and disabling distress.

4. RESISTANCE AGAINST THOUGHTS ABOUT SHOPPING. How much of an effort do you make to resist the thoughts about shopping? How often do you try to disregard or turn your attention away from these thoughts as they enter your mind?

---

* Monahan, P., Black, D.W., & Gabel, J. (1996) Reliability and validity of a scale to measure change in persons with compulsive buying, *Psychiatry Research*, 64:59–67. Reprinted with permission.

0   Makes an effort to always resist, or symptoms so minimal doesn't need to actively resist.
1   Tries to resist most of the time.
2   Makes some effort to resist.
3   Yields all thoughts without attempting to control them, but does so with some resistance.
4   Completely and willingly yields to all thoughts about shopping.

5. DEGREE OF CONTROL OVER THOUGHTS ABOUT SHOP-PING. How much control do you have over your thoughts about shopping? How successful are you in stopping or diverting your thoughts about shopping? Can you dismiss them?

0   Complete control.
1   Much control, usually able to stop or divert thoughts with some effort and concentration.
2   Moderate control, sometimes able to stop or divert thinking.
3   Little control, rarely successful in stopping or dismissing thinking, can only divert attention with difficulty.
4   No control, experience is completely involuntary, rarely able to even momentarily alter thoughts about shopping.

6. TIME SPENT SHOPPING. How much time do you spend shopping? How much time do you spend compulsively shopping?

0   None.
1   Mild, spends less than 1 hr/day shopping.
2   Moderate, spends 1 to 3 hrs/day shopping.
3   Severe, spends more than 3 and up to 8 hrs/day shopping.
4   Extreme, spends more than 8 hrs/day shopping or near con-stant shopping episodes.

7. INTERFERENCE DUE TO SHOPPING BEHAVIOR. How much does your shopping behavior interfere with your social, work, or role functioning? Is there anything you don't do because of the shopping?

0   None.
1   Mild, slight interference with social or occupational activities, but overall performance not impaired.
2   Moderate, definite interference with social or occupational performance, but still manageable.
3   Severe, causes substantial impairment in social or occupa-tional performance.
4   Extreme, incapacitating.

8. DISTRESS ASSOCIATED WITH COMPULSIVE SHOPPING BEHAVIOR. How would you feel if prevented from shopping? How anxious would you become?

0   None.

1   Mild, only slightly anxious if shopping prevented, or only slightly anxious while shopping.

2   Moderate, reports that anxiety would mount but remains manageable.

3   Severe, prominent and very disturbing increase in anxiety if shopping interrupted.

4   Extreme, incapacitating anxiety from any intervention aimed at modifying activity, or incapacitating anxiety develops during performance of shopping.

9. RESISTANCE AGAINST COMPULSIVE SHOPPING. How much of an effort do you make to resist the compulsion?

0   Makes an effort to always resist, or symptoms so minimal doesn't need to actively resist.

1   Tries to resist most of the time.

2   Makes some effort to resist.

3   Yields to almost all compulsions without attempting to control them, but does so with some reluctance.

4   Completely and unwillingly yields to almost all compulsions.

10. DEGREE OF CONTROL OVER COMPULSIVE SHOPPING. How strong is the drive to compulsively shop? How much control do you have over the compulsion?

0   Complete control.

1   Much control, experiences pressure to perform the behavior but usually able to exercise voluntary control over it.

2   Moderate control, strong pressure to perform behavior, can control it only with difficulty.

3   Little control, very strong drive to perform behavior, must be carried to completion, can only delay with difficulty.

4   No control, drive to perform behavior experienced as completely involuntary and overpowering, rarely able to even momentarily delay activity.

CHAPTER 4

The Measurement of Compulsive Buying and Its Application to Internet Buyers

NANCY M. RIDGWAY, PHD, MONIKA KUKAR-KINNEY, PHD,
AND KENT B. MONROE, PHD

Contents

Introduction	51
Definition and Positioning of Compulsive Buying Disorder	52
Compulsive Buying and the Internet	55
Motivations to Shop and Buy on the Internet versus from Bricks-and-Mortar Stores	55
Ability to Buy Unobserved on the Internet	56
Product and Information Variety	56
Immediate Positive Feelings	57
Survey	57
Findings	58
Implications of Internet Buying	59
General Conclusions and Public Policy Implications	60
References	61

Introduction

It has been more than 20 years since the issue of compulsive buying behavior was introduced to the consumer research literature (Faber, O'Guinn, & Krych, 1987). This pioneering research has helped to awaken researchers' interest in a troubling issue in consumer behavior. The incidence of compulsive buying (CB) was estimated to range between 2 percent and 8 percent of consumers in the United States 15 years ago (Faber & O'Guinn, 1992).

More recently, 5.8 percent of U.S. consumers were estimated to have CB (Koran et al., 2006). However, other researchers believe that these estimates are too low and that there is an increasing tendency by consumers to buy compulsively in both the United States and other developed countries (Müller & de Zwaan, 2004; Neuner, Raab, & Reisch, 2005). The continuous stream of research articles, books, television documentaries, and Web sites addressing CB and the problems it creates shows that the issue remains a concern (Benson, 2008; Chaker, 2003; McElroy, Phillips, & Keck, 1994; Mellan & Christie, 1997; www.stoppingovershopping.com). Therefore it is imperative that consumer researchers better understand and accurately measure the tendency of consumers to compulsively buy.

Definition and Positioning of Compulsive Buying Disorder

In this chapter, CB is defined as a consumer's tendency to be preoccupied with buying that is revealed through repetitive buying and a lack of impulse control over buying. Many researchers believe that CB should be considered as exhibiting elements of both obsessive-compulsive and impulse-control disorders, calling this theory obsessive-compulsive spectrum disorder (Hollander & Allen, 2006; Hollander & Dell'Osso, 2005; McElroy, Phillips, & Keck, 1994). Other conditions within this spectrum include anorexia nervosa, binge eating, impulsive Internet addiction, pathological gambling, trichotillomania, and kleptomania (Hollander, 1999).

The definition and measurement of CB used in this chapter are based on this emerging theoretical foundation and incorporate both impulse-control disorder (ICD) and obsessive-compulsive disorder (OCD) characteristics. An ICD is characterized by irresistible impulses to repeatedly perform harmful behaviors. On the other hand, OCD is an anxiety disorder, with obsessions (thoughts, preoccupations) and compulsions (behavior) that cause distress and anxiety, consume large amounts of time, and interfere with an individual's everyday functioning (McElroy et al., 1994). The rationale for classifying CB as an obsessive-compulsive spectrum disorder is that, like OCD, the consumers' thoughts are preoccupied with buying, and repetitive buying behavior is performed to reduce anxiety. Moreover, like ICD, these consumers lack control over the urge to buy. Both disorders involve an urge to perform an act followed by a loss of control over the urge (Hollander & Dell'Osso, 2005). Recognizing this overlap, CB should be classified as a disorder with elements of both OCD and ICD (Ridgway, Kukar-Kinney, & Monroe, 2008).

There is strong evidence for considering CB as an obsessive-compulsive spectrum disorder. McElroy and colleagues (1994) found that 80 percent of those identified with CB had lifetime diagnoses of anxiety disorders (OCD is classified as an anxiety disorder in DSM-IV-TR 2000), and 40 percent had an ICD. Also, Christenson, Faber, de Zwaan, Raymond, Specker, Eckern et al. (1994) found that 67 percent of those with CB were diagnosed with OCD and 96 percent were diagnosed with ICD. Clearly, there is overlap between the two disorders, and characteristics of both disorders should be included in a conceptualization and measurement of CB. Thus these definitions and measurement of CB include the extent to which consumers' buying behaviors are repetitive and consuming (characteristics of OCD) and the extent to which consumers are unable to control repeating harmful behavior (characteristic of ICD). Both of these dimensions are reflective of the underlying consumer tendency of being preoccupied with buying.

Although there are currently six separate scales to measure CB, a new measure of CB that includes both aspects of the obsessive-compulsive spectrum disorder construct—ICD and OCD—is needed. In addition, the existing CB scales possess several other limitations (Christenson et al., 1994; d'Astous, 1990; Valence, d'Astous, & Fortier, 1988—developed together; Edwards, 1993; Faber & O'Guinn, 1982; Lejoyeux, Tassain, Solomon, & Ades, 1997; Monahan, Black, & Gabel, 1996). The shortcomings include a sole focus on either ICD or OCD but not both, difficulty administering the scale (personal interview format only tested only on psychiatric patients), wording problems (such as referring only to shopping not buying, items that ask two questions in one, making it impossible to tell which question the respondent is answering), inadequate reliability and validity (with some scales not testing these at all), arbitrary cutoffs for classifying those with CB, and the inclusion of consequences (especially financial) of CB in the scale itself. The major problem with this last shortcoming is that by including outcomes within the scale (or trait) measure itself, one is not able to separate compulsive buying tendency from financial consequences. According to Benson (2005), there are many individuals with CB who can "afford" their buying and who suffer no financial consequences. She refers to these individuals with CB as being psychologically or emotionally bankrupt. Thus financial harm should not be included in the scale measure itself but should be considered a possible outcome of CB.

The scale used in the compulsive Internet research was rigorously tested using three very different samples, multiple analytical approaches, and nomological correlates to show its psychometric properties (see Ridgway, Kukar-Kinney, & Monroe, 2008). One of the samples contained actual buying data to add confidence to the usual self-report measures on which all other studies have depended. The current scale proved to be both reliable and valid. The final formatted scale as presented to the respondents is comprised of four seven-point agree–disagree scales and two 7-point frequency (never–very often) scales (see Table 4.1). In the three studies that were conducted, 15.5 percent, 8.9 percent, and 16 percent of the respondents were

Table 4.1 Compulsive Buying Scale

	Strongly Disagree						Strongly Agree
	1	2	3	4	5	6	7
1. My closet has unopened shopping bags in it.	___	___	___	___	___	___	___
2. Others might consider me a shopaholic.	___	___	___	___	___	___	___
3. Much of my life centers around buying things.	___	___	___	___	___	___	___
4. I consider myself an impulse purchaser.	___	___	___	___	___	___	___

	Never						Very Often
	1	2	3	4	5	6	7
5. I buy things I don't need.	___	___	___	___	___	___	___
6. I buy things I did not plan to buy.	___	___	___	___	___	___	___

Note: Scoring 25 or higher is considered compulsive buying.

classified as having CB. These percentages are much higher than what has been reported in the past.

Next, the applicability of the newly developed measure of CB is demonstrated by examining a widely used form of buying for many consumers—the Internet. As the Internet grows in importance in consumer behavior, it is critical to study its relationship to CB. One study in particular links CB to the Internet (Lejoyeux, Mathieu, Embouazza, Huet, & Lequen, 2007). In this study, French women were questioned as they entered a famous Parisian department store. Interestingly based on a different measure of CB, the incidence was 32.5 percent. Of most importance, however, was the fact that those with CB had a connection to online shopping sites that was longer and more frequent than those without CB. Similar connection was also shown in another study (Wang & Yang, 2007), where it was found that consumers with an obsessive passion went online more days per week, spent more hours per day shopping online, enjoyed their online shopping experience more, and felt dependent on their online shopping. The purpose of the following application linking CB to the Internet is to determine what attracts those with CB to buying on the Internet in comparison with those without CB (Kukar-Kinney, Ridgway, & Monroe, 2009).

Compulsive Buying and the Internet

In addition to the current interest in and importance of CB, use of the Internet for retailing purposes also has been growing steadily. Reports indicate that approximately 86 percent of Internet users are using the Internet to buy products. Total retail Internet sales (excluding travel) were estimated to reach $146 billion in 2008, with an annual growth rate at 14.3 percent (eMarketer.com, 2009). Moreover, relative to bricks-and-mortar sales, the percentage of Internet sales is increasing.

In this research, the purpose is to further investigate how consumers' motivations to shop and buy on the Internet differ depending on their CB tendencies (as measured with the new CB scale). Investigating the relationship between Internet buying and CB is important because the Internet retail environment possesses characteristics that seem to encourage CB. For example, the Internet offers the opportunity to buy frequently, at any time, and unobserved. Also, the Internet allows consumers to satisfy an urge to buy more quickly. Indeed, many Internet retailers encourage "Express Checkout," which means that once a customer enters their e-mail and password, just one click completes the order. In addition, Internet retailers send e-mails to their customers (especially their heavy users) frequently, as often as once a day. Many e-tailers offer a "what's new" category so that those customers who frequent the site often and know the product offerings can check only the newest merchandise. Finally, many Internet retailers provide persistent shopping carts, which save items that have been placed in the cart but not purchased. Some of these e-tailers send reminders to consumers with items in their cart asking if they would like to purchase the items now (e.g., www.urbanoutfitters.com).

Motivations to Shop and Buy on the Internet versus from Bricks-and-Mortar Stores

Retail shopping motivations include product-oriented motives, experiential and hedonic motives, shopping convenience, information search, recreational shopping, and variety seeking (e.g., Arnold & Reynolds, 2003; Dawson, Bloch, & Ridgway, 1990). One typology focusing specifically on Internet shoppers includes the convenience shopper, the variety seeker, the store-oriented shopper, and the balanced buyer (Rohm & Swaminathan, 2004). Further researchers found significant differences between Internet shoppers with utilitarian and hedonic motives (To, Liao, & Lin, 2007). Noble, Griffith, and Adjie (2006) compared information search, price comparison, uniqueness seeking, product assortment, convenience seeking, social interaction, and browsing as Internet shopping motives. The present research focuses on the shopping motivations that would most likely differ across those with and without CB. Rationale for the likely relationships between the chosen shopping motivations and CB is discussed next.

Ability to Buy Unobserved on the Internet

Those with CB experience shame, guilt, and regret because of their frequent buying episodes (O'Guinn & Faber, 1989). Because of these feelings, they may not want others (including family members) to see what, how frequently, and how much they buy. Consequently these consumers may feel the need to hide their buying activities. They may also fear that instant recognition by sales clerks labels them as having CB (Lee, Lennon, & Rudd, 2000). Compared to the bricks-and-mortar stores, the Internet enables consumers to be alone while shopping and buying, and offers a low to nonexistent level of social interaction. Because of these features, the motivations to shop and buy unobserved and to avoid social interactions were expected to be more strongly associated with preferences for Internet buying by those with CB versus those without CB.

Product and Information Variety

Those with CB desire to experience positive, stimulating feelings while buying (Faber & O'Guinn, 1992). When feeling down, buying can help them relieve the negative feelings by producing a temporary "high" (Ridgway, Kukar-Kinney, & Monroe, 2008). Greater product variety provides those with CB with a way to achieve more positive feelings, as it offers a more stimulating and exciting buying experience (McAlister & Pessemier, 1982). In addition, given a positive relationship between CB and fashion interest (Park & Burns, 2005), the desire to be aware of the most current fashion trends is relatively more important to those with CB. The ability to find the newest fashions as well as information about and reviews of the newest fashions on the Internet and being able to receive continuous electronic updates about new product offerings should thus be an important online shopping motivator for those with CB. Relative to bricks-and-mortar stores, the Internet enables consumers to access information and shop for and buy products across a much larger number and variety of stores, products, and brands that may otherwise be inaccessible.

Immediate Positive Feelings

Experiential or hedonic motives are a well-known driver of shopping and buying behavior. Those with CB experience an emotional lift from buying (Faber & O'Guinn, 1992). As such the positive feelings obtained during the buying process motivate these consumers to buy more. Thus those with CB strongly focus on the buying process and the immediate relief of prior negative feelings along with the stimulation of the positive feelings that it brings. When feeling blue, Internet (as compared to bricks-and-mortar) buying may elicit these positive feelings more quickly, given the speed and ease of making a purchase (e.g., most fashion e-tailers offer express checkout by "remembering" your personal and payment information). Hence it was expected that the online buying of those with CB should be more strongly motivated by the immediate positive feelings associated with the Internet shopping and buying experience than would be for those without CB.

Survey

To examine the relationship between shopping and buying motivations and CB, a survey of customers of an Internet women's clothing retailer was conducted. An invitation to participate with the link to the survey was successfully sent to 1294 customers, from which 314 people from 42 states responded, resulting in a response rate of 24.3 percent. The sample consisted of 98.5 percent women, 63 percent of the respondents were married, average age was 53 years (range 28 to 75 years), and average household income was $82,000. The survey contained questions about general shopping and buying behavior (including CB) at Internet and bricks-and-mortar stores, shopping motivations, individual consumer characteristics, and demographics.

Consumers' tendency to buy compulsively was measured using the six-item CB scale shown in Table 4.1. In the present research, reliability (Cronbach's alpha) for the scale was .85, and all items displayed item-to-total correlations above .50. An index of CB was composed by summing the responses to the six items.

Shopping and buying motivations were measured with 16 seven-point disagree–agree statements (Kukar-Kinney, Ridgway, & Monroe, 2009). The respondents provided answers to the following general statement: "In comparison to retail stores, I shop on the Internet when buying clothing and accessories for myself because ..." Sample responses to this statement were: "No one can see me buy" (a sample item for ability to buy unobserved); "I can avoid other shoppers in retail stores" (a sample item for avoiding social interaction); "There are more product choices" (a sample item for product and information variety); and "I can get more immediate pleasure from buying" (a sample item for immediate positive feelings). Construct reliabilities for individual motivational factors were .94 for ability to buy unobserved, .75 for avoiding social interaction, .82 for product and information variety, and .88 for immediate positive feelings.

Findings

To analyze the relationship between CB and motivations to shop and buy on the Internet, linear regression analysis was conducted. Social desirability bias was significantly correlated with CB, and was used as a covariate in all analyses. The findings indicate that the greater the CB tendency, the stronger the consumers' motivation to shop and buy on the Internet in comparison to bricks-and-mortar stores due to the ability to hide buying behavior (i.e., buy unobserved) ($\beta = .34$, $p < .01$). In addition the results confirm that motivation to avoid social interaction is positively associated with respondents' CB tendencies ($\beta = .13$, $p < .05$). Data also provide evidence that motivation to quickly obtain positive feelings has a positive association with respondents' CB tendencies ($\beta = .42$, $p < .01$). However, even though the correlation between product and information variety motive and CB index is significant, regression results indicate that this relationship does not significantly contribute to explaining CB behavior above and beyond other investigated motives ($\beta = .06$, $p > .10$).

To offer additional insights into the differences between shopping and buying behavior of consumers with different levels of CB tendencies, variables such as average monthly amount spent on clothing and accessories at Internet and bricks-and-mortar stores, average amount spent at the top five retail and top five brick-and-mortar stores per month, and frequency of buying from the top five retail and top five Internet stores per month were examined. A positive relationship existed between all of these behavioral variables and the CB scores. Specifically those respondents who scored highest on the CB index reported spending more on clothing as well as buying more frequently at both traditional retail and Internet stores than the respondents with lower levels on the CB index.

To determine whether a CB segment can be identified based solely on their motives to shop and buy online, the next step was to conduct cluster analysis. The goal was to uncover existing consumer segments relative to online shopping motivations and to see whether any segments match the shopping motivations of those identified with CB. Four clusters (segments) resulted from the analysis. Using data from two sources, self-report and actual (provided by the e-tailer), the four segments on four dimensions were examined: CB index, total dollar amount spent at the Internet retailer in question over the period 2001–2004, total number of purchases from this e-tailer during the same period, and the highest amount of any single purchase from this retailer. There was a segment identified only by their shopping motivations as having CB that indeed scored the highest on all variables. In contrast, the "bricks-and-mortar buyers" scored the lowest on the CB index, total Internet dollars spent, and total number of Internet purchases from the retailer, as anticipated. These findings use actual consumer purchase data to support the existence of the identified segments and show that shopping and buying motives can serve as an Internet shopper segmentation technique. The motives can also predict whether a consumer exhibits CB tendencies.

Implications of Internet Buying

The research findings indicate that consumers' preferences for shopping and buying on the Internet as opposed to bricks-and-mortar stores indeed differ depending on their tendency to buy compulsively. All motives and additional behavioral variables but the product and information variety showed a significant positive relationship with CB. Therefore, people who exhibit strong tendencies to buy compulsively experience stronger feelings with respect to shopping and buying, stronger buying and shopping motivations, and exhibit more extreme shopping and buying behaviors.

Overall, the findings show that as their CB tendency increases, consumers are more strongly motivated to buy on the Internet than at retail stores. This motivation appears to be due to the consumers' ability to buy unobserved and avoid social interaction while shopping and buying online, as well as the immediate positive feelings associated with their Internet buying experience. To buy unobserved and to quickly experience strong positive feelings during buying are two motivations most common to those with CB. While prior research indicated that the lack of social interaction on the Internet was a limitation of the online shopping environment (Grewal, Iyer, & Levy, 2004), it was found here that it may, in fact, not be a limitation for those with CB. The Internet allows these consumers to buy secretly and without contact with others. Moreover, although an Internet shopping experience may be considered as less stimulating than shopping in the bricks-and-mortar retail stores, it may still produce positive feelings in some consumers. In fact, those with CB may find it more stimulating due to a greater variety of products they can access online. Further, because they are preoccupied with buying and lack impulse control, individuals with CB desire an immediate release of negative feelings and an accompanying surge of positive feelings that the Internet buying brings them. Also, they are willing to exchange this immediacy of positive feelings for postponing the actual receipt and consumption of purchased products to a later time.

The present research also has implications for public policy officials. Since the Internet retail environment allows for ease of shopping, enables consumers to buy unobserved, and provides a stimulating experience, it may encourage CB. This claim is supported by our finding that consumers in the CB cluster segment reported spending 50 percent more of their fashion dollars on the Internet than at traditional retail stores (i.e., 60/40 percent), compared to consumers in the noncompulsive cluster segments, who reported spending about equally across the two retail channels (50 percent of fashion budget spent on the Internet versus 49 percent in retail stores). The Internet appears to be the preferred buying medium for individuals with CB and may in fact further contribute to conversion of more vulnerable consumers into developing CB. In addition, the Internet has been found to stimulate an addiction to online buying (e.g., Black, Belsare, & Schlosser, 1999). This finding could be due to the ease of accumulating a large number of items in a shopping cart and the ease of paying (e.g., express checkout). This relative ease may, in turn, lead to a greater accumulation of consumer debt.

General Conclusions and Public Policy Implications

In contrast to previous research, we argue that CB should not be defined or measured in terms of its consequences (e.g., the extent of financial harm incurred by CB). Thus separating the consequences of CB from the measure itself allows us to demonstrate that this buying disorder may affect a larger percentage of consumers than has been identified previously. As mentioned at the beginning of this chapter, using the new scale, in study one, 15.5 percent of student respondents were classified as compulsive buyers. In study two, 8.9 percent of university staff respondents were classified as having CB, while in study three, the Internet sample, the CB estimate was 16 percent.

The current research also has important public policy implications. As our findings suggest, the CB tendency may affect a larger percentage of consumers than has been previously documented. Moreover, CB appears to be increasing in the United States, in Europe, and elsewhere. Thus many people worldwide are either currently affected or are at risk of becoming so and may consequently experience negative emotional, social, economic, or even legal consequences because of their CB tendencies. Public policy officials should work on determining what can be done to stem this increasing trend as well as to establish help programs for affected consumers. Concerted efforts could be made to publicly inform consumers of the characteristics of CB and problems it may cause (e.g., using public service announcements that lead consumers to helpful Web sites). These

Web sites could provide links to CB chat rooms, to symptoms lists and outcomes, self-help books, and free online content.

References

Arnold, M.J. & Reynolds, K.E. (2003) Hedonic shopping motivations, *Journal of Retailing*, 79:77–95.

Benson, A.L. (2000) *I Shop, Therefore I Am: Compulsive Buying and the Search for Self*, New York: Aronson.

Benson, A.L. (2008) *To Buy or Not to Buy*, Boston: Trumpeter.

Benson, A.L. (2005) Personal communication, Sept. 30, San Antonio, Texas.

Black, D. (2007) A review of compulsive buying disorder, *World Psychiatry*, 6:14–18.

Black, D., Belsare, G., & Schlosser, S. (1999) Clinical features, psychiatric comorbidity, and health-related quality of life in persons reporting compulsive computer use behavior, *Journal of Clinical Psychiatry*, 60:839–44.

Chaker, A.M. (2003) Hello, I'm a Shopoholic! There's a move afoot to make compulsive shopping a diagnosable mental disorder. But should it be? *Wall Street Journal*, Jan. 14, F-1.

Christenson, G., Faber R., de Zwann, M., Raymond N., Specker, S., Ekern M., MacKenzie, T., Crosby, R., Crow, S., Echert, E., Mussell, M., & Mitchell, J. (1994) Compulsive buying: descriptive characteristics and psychiatric comorbidity, *Journal of Clinical Psychiatry*, 5:5–11.

d'Astous, A. (1990) An inquiry into the compulsive side of normal consumers, *Journal of Consumer Policy*, 13:15–31.

Dawson, S.C., Bloch, P.H., & Ridgway, N.M. (1990) Shopping motives, emotional states and retail outcomes, *Journal of Retailing*, 66:408–27.

Edwards, E.A. (1993) Development of a new scale for measuring compulsive buying behavior, *Financial Counseling and Planning*, 4:67–84.

eMarketer.com, http://www.emarketer.com/Reports/All/Emarketer_2000492.aspx, accessed on Dec. 16, 2009.

Faber, R.J. & O'Guinn, T.C. (1992) A clinical screener for compulsive buying, *Journal of Consumer Research*, 19:459–69.

Faber, R.J., O'Guinn, T.C., & Krych, R. (1987) Compulsive consumption, in *Advances in Consumer Research*, Vol. 14, M. Wallendorf & P. Anderson (eds.), Provo, UT: Association for Consumer Research, 132–35.

Grewal, D., Iyer, G.R., & Levy, M. (2004) Internet retailing: enablers, limiters and market consequences, *Journal of Business Research*, 57:703–13.

Hollander, E. (1999) Managing aggressive behavior in patients with obsessive-compulsive disorder and borderline personality disorder, *Journal of Clinical Psychiatry*, 60:38–44.

Hollander, E. & Allen, A. (2006) Is compulsive buying a real disorder, and is it really compulsive? *American Journal of Psychiatry*, 163:1670–2.

Hollander, E. & Dell'Osso, B. (2005) New developments in an evolving field, *Psychiatric Times*, 22:17.

Koran, L., Faber, R.J., Aboujaoude, E., Large, D.J., & Serpe, R.J. (2006) Estimated prevalence of compulsive buying behavior in the United States, *American Journal of Psychiatry*, 163:1806–12.

Kukar-Kinney, M., Ridgway, N.M., & Monroe, K.B. (2009) The relationship between consumers' tendencies to buy compulsively and their motivations to shop and buy on the Internet, *Journal of Retailing*, 85:298–307.

Lee, S., Lennon, S.J., & Rudd, N.A. (2000) Compulsive consumption tendencies among television shoppers, *Family and Consumer Sciences Research Journal*, 28:463–89.

Lejoyeux, M., Tassain, V., Solomon, J. &, Ades, J. (1997) Study of compulsive buying in depressed patients, *Journal of Clinical Psychiatry*, 58:169–73.

Lejoyeux, M., Mathieu, K., Embouazza, H., Huet, F., & Lequen, V. (2007) Prevalence of compulsive buying among customers of a Parisian general store, *Comprehensive Psychiatry*, 48:42–6.

McAlister, L. & Pessemier, E. (1982) Variety-seeking behavior: an interdisciplinary review, *Journal of Consumer Research*, 9:311–22.

McElroy, S., Phillips, K., & Keck, P. (1994) Obsessive compulsive spectrum disorder, *Journal of Clinical Psychiatry*, 5:33–53.

Mellan, O. & Christie, S. (1997) *Overcoming Overspending: A Winning Plan for Spenders and Their Partners*, New York: Walker & Co.

Monahan, P., Black, D.W., & Gabel, J. (1996) Reliability and validity of a scale to measure change in persons with compulsive buying, *Psychiatry Research*, 64:59–67.

Müller, A. & de Zwaan, M. (2004) Current status of psychotherapy research on pathological buying, *Verhaltenstherapie*, 14:112–9.

Neuner, M., Raab, G., & Reisch, L. (2005) Compulsive buying in maturing consumer societies: an empirical re-inquiry, *Journal of Economic Psychology*, 26:509–22.

Noble, S.M., Griffith, D.A., & Adjei, M.T. (2006) Drivers of local merchant loyalty: understanding the influence of gender and shopping motives, *Journal of Retailing*, 82:177–88.

O'Guinn, T.C. & Faber, R.J. (1989) Compulsive buying: a phenomenological exploration, *Journal of Consumer Research*, 16:147–57.

Park, H. & Burns, L.D. (2005) Fashion orientation, credit card use, and compulsive buying, *Journal of Consumer Marketing*, 22:135–41.

Ridgway, N.M., Kukar-Kinney, M., & Monroe, K.B. (2008) An expanded conceptualization and a new measure of compulsive buying, *Journal of Consumer Research*, 35:622–39.

Rohm, A.J. & Swaminathan, V. (2004) A typology of online shoppers based on shopping motivations, *Journal of Business Research*, 57:748–57.

To, P., Liao, C., & Lin, T. (2007) Shopping motivations on Internet: a study based on utilitarian and hedonic value, *Technovation*, 27:774–87.

Valence, G., d'Astous, A., & Fortier, L. (1988) Compulsive buying: concept and measurement, *Journal of Consumer Policy*, 11:419–33.

Wang, C-C. & Yang H-W (2007) Passion and dependency in online shopping activities, *CyberPsychology & Behavior*, 10:296–8.

www.urbanoutfitters.com.

CHAPTER 5

The Neural Basis of Compulsive Buying

GERHARD RAAB, PHD, CHRISTIAN E. ELGER, MD,
MICHAEL NEUNER, PHD, AND BERND WEBER, MD

Contents

Introduction   63
Compulsive Buying   64
Neural Basis of Compulsive Buying   66
    Striatum (Nucleus Accumbens)   67
    Ventromedial and Ventrolateral Prefrontal Cortex (vmPFC)   69
    Insular Cortex   70
Method   71
    Participants (Phase One)   71
    fMRI Analysis (Phase Two)   72
    fMRI Acquisition and Analysis   74
    Postscan Analysis (Phase Three)   74
Results   75
    fMRI Product Phase Results (Hypothesis One)   75
    fMRI Price Phase Results (Hypothesis Two)   75
    fMRI Decision Phase Results (Hypothesis Three) 75
    Postscan Results   76
Discussion   77
Acknowledgment   80
References   80

Introduction

In the last two decades compulsive buying (CB) behavior has increasingly become a focus with consumer (e.g., d'Astous, 1990; Dittmar, 2005a,b;

Faber & O'Guinn, 1988; Hirschman, 1992; Manolis & Roberts, 2008; Raab, Neuner, Reisch, & Scherhorn, 2005; Ridgway, Kukar-Kinney, & Monroe, 2008; Scherhorn, Reisch, & Raab, 1990) and clinical researchers (e.g., Black, 1996; Koran, Faber, Aboujaoude, Large, & Serpe, 2006; Krueger, 1988; Lawrence, 1990; McElroy, Keck, Pope, Smith, & Strakowski, 1994; Mueller, de Zwaan, & Mitchell, 2008; Mueller & de Zwaan, 2008). Furthermore, CB has been generating growing interest among the general public. Along with popular science publications (Benson, 2009; O'Connor, 2005), and reports in various types of media (daily newspapers, magazines, radio, television, Internet), the movie "Confessions of a Shopaholic" (Bruckheimer, 2009) is illustrative of that interest. The first comprehensive studies of CB were conducted by an American (Faber, O'Guinn, & Krych, 1987; Faber & O'Guinn, 1989), a German (Scherhorn et al., 1990), and a Canadian research group (d'Astous, 1990; Valence, d'Astous, & Fortier, 1988). Contemporaneously in the clinical-therapeutic literature there appeared individual case studies regarding the psychodynamic therapy of affected persons (Krueger, 1988; Lawrence, 1990). It has been observed that CB behavior is not a completely new phenomenon of our consumer society. Indeed the German psychiatrist Emil Kraepelin and the Swiss psychiatrist Eugene Bleuler had already made reference to pathological desire to shop (buying mania) or oniomania (Kraepelin, 1909), which led to extreme levels of debt (Bleuler, 1924).

Like every human behavior, CB ultimately can only be comprehensively elucidated using an integrated approach, i.e., an approach that takes into account the personal, social, and biological causes. The publications of Faber and O'Guinn (1988) and Valence et al. (1988) on CB indicated the necessity for an integrated biopsychosocial approach to explain this behavior, as suggested by the contributions of Donegan, Rodin, O'Brien, and Solomon (1983), Jacobs (1986), Marlatt, Baer, Donovan, and Kivlahan (1988), and Salzman (1981). To date there is a gap in knowledge because of a lack of neurological or biopsychological studies regarding CB. The objective of the present study was to make a contribution toward the eventual filling in of this gap in knowledge.

Compulsive Buying

O'Guinn and Faber (1989) defined CB as chronic, repetitive purchasing behavior that becomes a primary response to negative events or feelings, which is difficult to stop, and results in harmful consequences. These negative consequences are not only economic but also psychological and societal (O'Guinn & Faber, 1989). As an alternative, McElroy et al. (1994) offered an operational definition of CB. The definition recognizes that CB has both cognitive and behavioral components (Black 2001, 18).

In connection with the various definitions of CB (e.g., Black 2001; O'Guinn & Faber, 1989; McElroy et al., 1994; Mittal, Holbrook, Beatty, Raghubi, & Woodside, 2008; Ridgway et al., 2008) the question of its classification as an impulse-control disorder (ICD), obsessive-compulsive disorder (OCD), or addiction (behavioral addiction) remains to be clarified (e.g., Christenson, de Zwaan, Raymond, Specker, Ekern et al., 1994; Gruesser, Poppelreuter, Heinz, Albrecht, & Saß, 2007; McElroy et al. 1994; Frost, Steketee, & Williams, 2002; Scherhorn, 1990; Schlosser, Black, Repertinger, & Freet, 1994; Mueller & de Zwaan, 2008). The research is largely united thus far in regarding CB behavior, as with excessive gambling, as a behavior that can take on a pathological character, thereby maintaining the need for treatments. Since up to now there has been no category for CB behavior in either the Diagnostic and Statistical Manual of Mental Disorders (DSM-IV-TR, 2000) of the American Psychiatric Association (APA) or in the International Statistical Classification of Diseases and Related Health Problems (ICD-10, 2006) of the World Health Organization (WHO), thus far it has been designated as "nothing more specific than a disruption of impulse-control," under the heading 312.30 of DSM-IV-TR and under the heading F63.8 or F63.9 of ICD-10 (Lejoyeux, McLoughlin, & Adès, 2000; McElroy, Hudson, Pope, Keck, & Aizley, 1992; Mueller & de Zwaan, 2008). At present numerous researchers are advancing the view that CB contains elements of both OCD and ICD (Hollander & Allen, 2006; Hollander & Dell'Osso, 2005; Ridgway et al., 2008). For the coming DSM-V a category of obsessive-compulsive spectrum disorders (OCSD) is being considered, wherein CB is placed beside pathological gambling and Internet addiction, among other problems (Dell'Osso, Altamura, Alien, Marazziti, & Hollander, 2006; Hollander, Kim, & Zohar, 2007; Mueller & de Zwaan, 2008). Against this background Ridgway et al. (2008) have defined CB as a consumer's tendency to be preoccupied with buying, such that this is revealed through repetitive buying (characteristic of OCD) and a lack of impulse control overbuying (characteristic of ICD), and have developed a corresponding scale. It is noteworthy that internationally the most commonly used measurement scales are those of d'Astous (1990), Faber and O'Guinn (1992), and Edwards (1993). However, the scale of Ridgway et al. (2008) presents a further procedure for measuring CB. Manolis and Roberts (2008) have made reference to the significance of the theoretical foundation and practical implications of various procedures for measuring CB.

The published prevalence rates to date provide indications of the distribution and growth of CB behavior in society, and as to the relevance of research into this behavior. With regard to the causes of CB and its connection to sociodemographic and psychological factors, there are at present several studies available. Persons affected exhibit increased impulsiveness, a deficit of impulse control (self-control), low self-esteem, depression, social anxiety, money management deficits, disruption of autonomy orientation, and a greater materialistic orientation (e.g., Black, Repertinger, Gaffner, & Gabel, 1998; Faber, 1992, 2004; Faber & Vohs, 2004; Mueller, Mühlhans, Silbermann, Mueller, Mertens, Horbach et al., 2009; Dittmar, 2005a, 2005b; Rose, 2007; Scherhorn, 1990; Scherhorn et al., 1990; Silbermann, Henkel, Müller, & de Zwaan, 2008; Spinella, Yang, & Lester, 2007). The influence of advertising, the significance of consumption in a society, and the use of customer and credit cards have been documented in various studies (e.g., d'Astous & Bellemare, 1989; Faber & O'Guinn, 1989; Faber et al., 1987; Neuner, Raab, & Reisch, 2005a, 2005b; Scherhorn et al., 1990; Raab, 1998). Even taking into consideration more recent studies and possible methodological artifacts, an examination of gender in most studies indicates that women are more often and more intensely afflicted with CB than men (e.g., Kollmann & Kautsch, 2008; Manolis & Roberts, 2008; Neuner et al., 2005a, 2005b; Ridgway et al., 2008). No connection could be substantiated with respect to education, social class, and income (e.g., Neuner et al., 2005a; Scherhorn et al., 1990). The greater prevalence of CB behavior among women, however, apparently has declined or is traceable to research artifacts (e.g., Koran et al., 2006; Reisch & Neuner, 2002; Scherhorn et al., 1990).

The current literature focuses on behavioral, learning theory, sociopsychological, psychoanalytic, and family dynamic models of causality (Mueller et al., 2009; Neuner, Raab, & Reisch, 2008). It is clear that to date there has been no well-substantiated neurological or biopsychological study into the etiology of CB. This is reflected in the finding that the classification remains to be clarified. Also studies thus far conducted and published regarding the effectiveness of medical treatment of CB have yielded contradictory results (e.g., Black, Gabel, Hansen, & Schlosser, 2000; Koran, Chuong, Bullock, & Smith, 2003; Ninan, McElroy, Kane, Knight, Casuto, Rose et al. 2000; Mueller, Reinecker, Jacobi, Reisch, & de Zwaan, 2005). A study of the neural basis and etiology of the behavior can therefore help to answer some of these questions and contribute to a more comprehensive theory of CB.

Neural Basis of Compulsive Buying

As far as the neural foundations and causes of CB are concerned, reference can be made to recent contributions from medicine, psychology, neuroscience, and neuroeconomics. Here of relevance is the observation that in individuals with CB the use of purchased products is not of decisive importance; instead it is the process or act of buying that seems integral to the addiction (d'Astous, 1990, 16; O'Guinn & Faber, 1989). In general the process of acquisition is experienced as positive. This positive factor is, however, set against the negative factor of the price that must be paid. Insofar as the price to be paid represents a loss, and the corresponding lost money cannot be used for other goals, such as the purchase of different products or for saving (Prelec & Loewenstein, 1998). Therefore in learning theory the price is a punishment for purchasing certain products. The fact that purchase decisions involve a tradeoff between the pleasure of buying and the punishment of paying is consistent with recent neuroscientific evidence, which states that distinct neural circuits related to anticipatory affect provide critical input into subsequent decisions (Bechara, Tranel, Damasio, & Damasio, 1996; Clark, Bechara, Damasio, Aitken, Sahakian, & Robbins, 2008; Kuhnen & Knutson, 2005; Knutson, Rick, Wimmer, Prelec, & Loewenstein, 2007). Neuroimaging studies in healthy volunteers and in patients with neuropsychiatric disorders including substance abuse disorders and problematic gambling, as well as studies of patients with brain lesions, suggest that activity in different neural circuits correlates with positive and negative anticipatory affect, and this plays an important role in decision making and behavior (Clark et al., 2008; Paulus, 2007; Knutson et al., 2007; Reuter, Raedler, Rose, Hand, Gläscher, & Büchel, 2005). These studies have underlined the important function of the prefrontal cortex, the insular cortex, the parietal cortex, the amygdala, and the striatum (particularly the nucleus accumbens) (Clark et al., 2008; Clark & Manes, 2004; Ernst & Paulus, 2005; Paulus, 2007; Knutson et al., 2007; Knutson, Wimmer, Kuhnen, & Winkielman, 2008; Krain, Hefton, Pine, Ernst, Castellanos, Klein et al., 2006).

Striatum (Nucleus Accumbens)

In the absence of choice, anticipation of financial gain activates the nucleus accumbens (NAcc) and correlates with self-reported positive arousal, whereas gain outcomes activate the mesial prefrontal cortex (MPFC) (Knutson, Fong, Adams, Varner, & Hommer, 2001). These findings have been interpreted to indicate that NAcc activation correlates with gain prediction, while MPFC activation correlates with gain prediction errors (Knutson, Fong, Bennett, Adams, & Hommer, 2003). Emerging evidence also suggests that activation in these circuits may influence subsequent choice. For example, during an investing task involving a choice of risky or safe alternatives, NAcc activation preceded switching to risk-seeking strategies, in which anticipated gain should outweigh anticipated loss, while insula activation preceded switching to risk-averse strategies, in which anticipated loss should outweigh anticipated gain (Knutson et al., 2008; Kuhnen & Knutson, 2005). Studies of drug addictions also substantiate the important role of the NAcc (Birbaumer & Schmidt, 2006; Carlson, 2004; Volkow, Fowler, Wang, & Goldstein, 2002). It is thereby of particular interest that addictive behavior can also be traced to a growth of incentive salience. Studies have demonstrated that after repeated experiences with a substance, the reaction to the same dose changes. The positive effect or enhancement from the drug declines with time, and a higher dose of the drug becomes necessary to achieve the same positive effect (tolerance). Connected with this development is the achievement of an increased incentive, linked to the associatively entrained intake or activity impulse. This means that the anticipated positive effect of the drug and its associated stimulus lead to an intensified craving for the drug. Here studies of cocaine-addicted subjects using functional Magnetic Resonance Imaging (fMRI) have shown that with the intake of a constant dose over a period of time, there is no increase in NAcc activity, and during the time of dependence there is a lessened activity of the NAcc. Certainly thoughts of using are elicited by the drug and by drug-associated stimuli, e.g., the illustration of a syringe or sight of a cigarette leads to a rise in NAcc activity (Berridge, 2003; Birbaumer & Schmidt, 2006; Robinson & Berridge, 1993; Volkow et al., 1997). This connection is also evinced in studies of gambling addicts using the fMRI (Reuter et al., 2005).

There have also been studies that have a more direct connection to buying behavior, from which it can be concluded that decisions to purchase may engage common anticipatory affective mechanisms. For instance a growing number of fMRI studies have explored neural correlates of product preference. Specifically, men who view pictures of sports cars versus less desirable types of cars show increased mesolimbic activation (NAcc, MPFC) (Erk, Spitzer, Wunderlich, Galley, & Walter, 2002). Both men and women who view pictures of preferred versus nonpreferred drinks show increased MPFC activation (Paulus & Frank, 2003). The same holds true for taste of preferred versus nonpreferred drinks (McClure, Li, Tomlin, Cypert, Montague, & Montague, 2004). Finally men who view pictures of preferred versus nonpreferred brands of beer show increased MPFC activation, and women who view pictures of preferred versus nonpreferred brands of coffee also show increased MPFC activation (Deppe, Schwindt, Kugel, Plassman, & Kenning, 2005). Using fMRI in the context of the simulated purchasing decision, Knutson et al. (2007) were able to show that the purchase of products was associated with an increased activity in the NAcc and in the MPFC. During the presentation of certain products an increased activity in the NAcc was observed, and the corresponding products were also purchased to a significantly greater extent (Knutson et al., 2007).

From the above studies, it can be assumed that individuals with CB derive a positive intensification or satiety from the buying act at the beginning of developing the behavior. Over time this effect dwindles and more must be purchased more often in order to achieve the same effect (tolerance). The development of tolerance presents as CB and can be used as a criterion for the diagnosis of CB (Scherhorn et al., 1990). At the same time the stimulus of shopping increases for individuals with CB. What is evident here is that thoughts of a purchasing act and its associated stimuli, e.g., the perception of certain products lead to increased NAcc activity, and the craving for the purchase results. The question then arises as to why individuals with CB seem not to be able to resist this craving and to control their behavior. An important role in this respect may be played by the ventromedial and ventrolateral prefrontal cortex (vmPFC).

Ventromedial and Ventrolateral Prefrontal Cortex (vmPFC)

Other findings suggest a critical role for the vmPFC in decision making, substance abuse disorders, and behavioral addictions such as pathological gambling (Cato, Crosson, Gokcay, Soltysik, Wierenga, Gopinath et al., 2004; Clark et al., 2008; Reuter et al., 2005). Patients with vmPFC damage commonly display a syndrome that includes poor judgment, socially inappropriate behavior, and impulsivity (Damasio, 1994; Berlin, Rolls, & Kischka, 2004). These patients exhibit maladaptive choices on the Iowa Gambling Task (Bechara, Damasio, Damasio, & Anderson, 1994), where respondents are required to learn the profile of wins and losses associated with four card decks. Two decks (the "risky" decks) yield high immediate wins, but with dramatic occasional losses that result in gradual debt over time. The other two ("safe") decks deliver smaller wins but with minor losses, such that there is an overall profit. While healthy controls rapidly learn to select from the safe decks, patients with vmPFC damage fail to learn this strategy and maintain preference for the risky decks (Bechara et al. 1994, Bechara, Damasio, & Damasio, 2000). Their behavior is driven by the short-term gain associated with the risky decks, without regard for negative consequences. A lessened activity of the vmPFC could also be established in more recent studies using fMRI in patients with stable lesions to the vmPFC (Clark et al., 2008) and in individuals with compulsive gambling (Reuter et al., 2005). It can be inferred from this that individuals with CB display no activity or less activity in the vmPFC during a purchasing decision than those without CB, and thus have difficulty controlling their purchasing behavior. One reason for this could consist of the inability of people with CB to perceive or recognize the negative consequences in a shopping context, such as the price that they must pay for the given product. Controlled decisions and the measuring of positive and negative consequences of the behavior connected with them imply that from the outset the negative aspects and consequences, such as financial loss or the price, are also perceived. In this connection the insular cortex is highly significant.

Insular Cortex

The insular cortex plays an important role in decision making and behavior via its extensive reciprocal connectivity with the vmPFC (Augustine, 1996; Ongur & Price, 2000), as well as the amygdala and the striatum (Reynolds & Zahm, 2005). The somatic marker hypothesis proposes that during decision making bodily states that were previously associated with choice options are retrieved by the vmPFC, and that the somatic and visceral representations themselves are held in the insular and somatosensory cortices (Damasio, 1994; Bechara & Damasio, 2005). Consistent with this theory fMRI studies in healthy volunteers have shown activation of the anterior insular cortex immediately prior to risk-aversive decisions (Kuhnen & Knutson, 2005), the correlates with the uncertainty of monetary reward (Critchley, Mathias, & Dolan, 2001), the overall risk preference (Paulus, Rogalsky, Simmons, Feistein, & Stein, 2003) and the reward variance (Preuschoff, Bossaerts, & Quartz, 2006). Such findings are broadly consistent with a wider role of the anterior insular cortex in signaling the expectancy of aversive outcomes (O'Doherty, Kringelbach, Rolls, Hornak, & Andrews, 2001; Paulus & Stein, 2006), such as in the anticipation of painful stimuli (Ploghaus, Tracey, Gati, Clare, Menon, Matthews et al., 1999) or unpleasant visual stimuli (Simmons, Matthews, Stein, & Paulus, 2004). There is a paucity of lesion data to substantiate these findings from functional imaging in order to demonstrate the necessary role of the insular cortex in decision making (Clark et al., 2008). Further findings suggest that anticipation of pain or punishment activates the insula, among other areas, and that insula activation also correlates with self-reported negative arousal (Buchel & Dolan, 2000; Paulus et al., 2003). Thus insula activation has been hypothesized to play a critical role in loss prediction (Paulus & Stein, 2006) and has been found to play an important role in the process of deciding to buy or not to buy a product (Knutson et al., 2007). In the context of buying, the pain of paying plays an important role in consumer self-regulation (Prelec & Lowenstein, 1998, 4). Various contributions have detailed the significance of the ability to self-regulate, relative to consumption and buying behavior, and to CB (Baumeister, 2002; Faber, 2004; Faber & Vohs, 2004; Hoch & Loewenstein, 1991). Given this background it is assumed that individuals with CB also have greater difficulties controlling their buying behavior because they cannot perceive the negative consequences or do so to a lesser extent than those who do not compulsively buy. This should be born out in lesser insula activity. If this were the case then an important component for controlling of buying behavior would be impaired.

Taken together these findings implicate the important role of neural functioning in the buying process and in CB. Based on these findings our general hypothesis was that interconnected regions of the brain, the striatum (NAcc), and the insular and the prefrontal cortices would show differences in activity between those with and without CB during a simulated buying process. As per Knutson et al. (2007) we have divided a simulated purchase decision process into three phases, in the context of a study using the fMRI: (1) pictorial presentation of products; (2) pictorial presentation of selected products and their respective market prices; (3) pictorial presentation of the selected products and their respective market prices, with the possibility to purchase the presented products or to decline purchasing them (see method). Specifically we predicted the following main hypotheses:

H1: Individuals with CB would evince a significantly higher activity in the striatum (NAcc) than those without CB, in the product presentation phase (Phase One).

H2: Individuals with CB would evince a significantly lower activity in the insula area than those without CB, in the product and price presentation phase (Phase Two).

H3: Individuals with CB would evince significantly lower activity in the vmPFC than those without CB, in the phase involving a decision for or against the purchase of presented products and their prices (Phase Three).

Method

The study was divided into four phases: (1) approach, selection, and recruiting of participants; (2) conducting the study using fMRI; (3) examination of participants using a questionnaire in conjunction with the investigative means of fMRI; (4) analysis of study data.

Participants (Phase One)

In total, 49 women took part in the study; 23 with CB and 26 with normal buying patterns. The limitation to female participants was based on the following points: (1) most studies regarding CB indicate that women are more intensely and more often afflicted with CB than men (e.g., Black, 2007; Dittmar, 2005; Kollmann & Kautsch, 2008; Koran et al., 2006; Manolis & Roberts, 2008; Raab et al., 2005; Ridgway et al., 2008); (2) there are differences between men and women with regard to products they prefer to buy (e.g., Black, 2001; Christenson et al., 1994; Mueller et al., 2009, Scherhorn et al., 1990, 376); (3) to control for gender would have necessitated a corresponding increase in test participants and additional provision of stimulus material for the fMRI study. Women were examined for these reasons only.

Individuals with CB (Experimental Group)   Individuals with CB were recruited and proceeded via notices about the planned study that were placed in various Internet forums, by initiating contact with psycho-therapists and self-help groups for CB, and following media of interviews dealing with the theme of CB (the press, radio, television). Individuals had to be undergoing treatment for their behavior. Thus the formation of the experimental group of individuals with CB did not come about on the basis of the self-diagnosis. Furthermore the participants undergoing psychotherapeutic treatment had to achieve a score of 45 or more on the German Compulsive Buying Scale (GCBS) (Raab et al., 2005; Scherhorn et al., 1990). All individuals achieved a rating exceeding the cutoff score (M = 53.57; SD = 3.84). Data on sociodemographic characteristics including age and income were also collected.

Control Group   The control group was recruited via an advertisement in a regional newspaper. Selection of those individuals depended on their not being in psychotherapeutic treatment on account of their buying behavior, and that they achieved a cutoff score of less than 36 on the GCBS (Raab et al., 2005; Scherhorn et al., 1990). A score of less than 36 characterizes those with noncompulsive buying behavior (Raab et al., 2005). Additionally some sociodemographic data were collected. To avoid the influence of age and income, the control group members were matched on these variables (see Table 5.1). None of the participants in the control group achieved a score of more than 31 (M = 21.50; SD = 4.13). All participants were reimbursed for transportation costs and were given 20 Euros for other expenses.

fMRI Analysis (Phase Two)

fMRI Task   As per with Knutson et al. (2007) participants were scanned while engaging in a novel Saving Holdings or Purchase (SHOP) task, which consisted of a series of trials, identical in temporal structure with jittered

Table 5.1 Characteristics of the Participants with and without CB

Characteristics	Compulsive Buyers	Noncompulsive Buyers
	N = 23	N = 26
German Compulsive Buying Scale (GCBS)[a]	M = 53.57	M = 21.50
	SD = 3.84	SD = 4.13
Age	M = 42.22	M = 41.73
	SD = 12.18	SD = 10.83
Household income (Euro)	M = 2.570	M = 2.585
	SD = 910	SD = 1.030

[a] $p < .001$

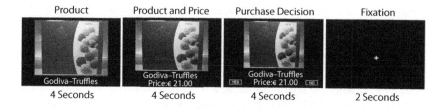

Figure 5.1 Example picture sequence in the simulated buying situation.

intertrial intervals (4–6 s), in which participants could purchase products (see Figure 5.1). Participants viewed a labeled product (4 s); viewed the product's price (4 s); chose either to purchase the product or not by selecting yes or no, as presented randomly on the right or left side of the screen; then fixated on a crosshair (2 s) prior to onset of the next trial. Each participant was presented with a total of 100 products in this manner. The price of the products varied within a range of 1 and 50 Euros. To simulate a buying situation as realistically as possible, each participant received the equivalent of a 50 Euro sum at the outset of the fMRI study. They could opt to spend this on products or not. Upon conclusion of the study one of the products purchased by the participant was selected randomly. The remaining balance was paid to the participant in cash. Thus each test participant could decide with each product viewed to purchase the given product or to keep the corresponding cash. Before the beginning of the fMRI study each participant was informed of this procedure and questioned as to whether they had understood the instructions. All of the questions of the test subjects were answered by the investigators.

The selection of the 100 products proceeded according to the following three criteria: (1) the first related to the product category. The products were selected from six product categories (accessories, drinks, clothing, cosmetics, jewelry, sweets). Products in these categories were preferentially purchased by women with CB according to previous studies (e.g., Black, 2001, 2007; Christenson et al., 1994; García Ureta, 2007; Scherhorn et al., 1990; Schlosser et al., 1994); (2) the second was the expense of the product. Due to the financial expense necessitating provision of a certain monetary amount, the maximum price of a product was limited to 50 Euros; (3) the third related to the selection of the products presented within the product categories mentioned, with regard to the established maximum price. To ensure these were products that would in reality meet with the consumers' interest, data from the product records of a commercial business were consulted. For the study 100 products were randomly selected from a listing of 500 of the most sold products within the 50 Euro price range. Thus product selection was based on real sales numbers and real purchase prices. Afterwards the 100 selected products were photographed and randomly presented to the participants.

fMRI Acquisition and Analysis

Scanning Procedure   Scanning was performed on a 1.5 T Avanto Scanner (Siemens, Erlangen, Germany) using a TIM 8-channel head coil. During the experiment, ~830 echo planar imaging (EPI) scans were acquired. Forty-eight slices covered the whole brain including the cerebellum (slice orientation: C->T30, Figure 5.2). Scan parameters were: slice thickness: 3 mm; interslice gap: 0.66 mm; matrix size: 64 × 64; field of view: 195 × 195 mm; echo time (TE): 50 ms; repetition time (TR): 2.91 s. The task was presented via video goggles (Nordic NeuroLab, Bergen, Norway) using E-prime presentation software (Psychology Software Tools; www.pstnet.com).

fMRI Data Analysis   The fMRI data analysis was performed using Statistical Parametric Mapping 5 (SPM5, www.fil.ion.ucl.ac.uk/spm/). Preprocessing included slice timing, realignment with unwarping, normalization to an EPI-template (resampled voxel size after normalization 3 × 3 × 3 mm), and smoothing with an 8 mm Gaussian kernel. Six vectors of onset times (product, price, and decision (for bought and nonbought decisions)). In order to model the blood oxygen level dependency (BOLD) time course in each voxel these onset vectors were convolved with the SPM5 canonical hemodynamic response function (HRF) and its temporal derivative. For each participant, parameter images of the contrasts of each condition were generated and were then subjected to a second-level random effects analysis using Full Factorial Design with between-participant factor of group (those with CB, control) and within-participant factor buying decision (i.e., subsequently bought versus subsequently nonbought) as a model for each phase (i.e., product, price, decision) separately. An inclusion threshold of p < .001 uncorrected with an extent threshold of at least 10 contiguous voxels was applied. The Anatomical Automated Labeling Tool for SPM (Tzourio-Mazoyer, Landeau, Papathanassiou, Crivello, Etard, Delcroix et al., 2002) was used to label the clusters.

Postscan Analysis (Phase Three)

The participants were surveyed at the conclusion of the fMRI study. Along with questions regarding buying behavior (e.g., products they preferred to buy), brand preference, payment habits, and other questions (e.g., estimated expenditure during the fMRI study), the survey encompassed the following scales:

Self-Esteem. Self-esteem was measured in the study with a 10-item self-esteem scale (Deusinger, 1986), with an internal consistency reliability of .92. This scale has been used in various CB studies in Germany (Scherhorn et al., 1990; Raab et al., 2005).

Self-Control. Self-control was measured with a German version of the 31-item Self-Control Scale (SCS) from Tangney, Baumeister, and Boone (2004), with an internal consistency reliability of .86. The German version was developed in conformance with the present study on the basis of a pretest.

Depression. The extent of depression was measured using the German version of the Basic Depression Scale of the Minnesota Multiphasic Personality Inventory-2 (MMPI-2) (Engel, 2000). The internal consistency reliability for this 57-item scale rated at .80.

Prefrontal dysfunction. Prefrontal dysfunction was measured with a German version of the 46-item Frontal Systems Behavior Scale (FrSBe) from Grace and Malloy (2001). In the present study the internal consistency reliability rated at .91. The German version was developed in conformance with the present study on the basis of a pretest.

Results

fMRI Product Phase Results (Hypothesis One)

During the product phase, we observed a significantly higher activation in the striatum (NAcc) for subsequently bought versus nonbought products in both groups (see Table 5.2). As predicted in hypothesis 1 this effect was significantly higher in the CB group in comparison to the noncompulsive buyers group (see Figure 5.2 and Table 5.2). Furthermore irregardless of whether a displayed product was bought or not, in all 100 of the products presented, higher striatum (NAcc) activity could be observed in the group with CB.

fMRI Price Phase Results (Hypothesis Two)

During the price phase, we observed a significantly stronger activation in the insula and anterior cingulate cortex for subsequently nonbought products when compared to those subsequently bought. This was true for both groups of participants with significantly stronger insula and cingulate cortex activity in the normal buyer group. The significantly lower insula activity in the CB group supports hypothesis two (see Figure 5.3 and Table 5.3). On the whole the indication is that information regarding a product's price is linked with significantly lower insula activity in individuals with CB.

fMRI Decision Phase Results (Hypothesis Three)

In the decision phase we found stronger activity in the ventromedial prefrontal cortex and the dorsolateral prefrontal cortex for bought products versus nonbought products. We were unable to substantiate a lower activity in the prefrontal cortex of individuals with CB, as formulated in hypothesis three. The only significant difference between the two groups

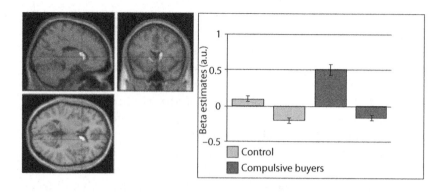

Figure 5.2 Activation during the product presentation phase. Activation for subsequently bought versus subsequently nonbought products during the product presentation phase and differences in activity between normal (gray) and compulsive buyers (black) in the respective region (p < .001; vox thresh: 10).

Table 5.2 fMRI Activations for the Product Phase for Both Groups

Area	MNI Coordinates (X/Y/Z)	Cluster Size	T-Score
Bought versus Nonbought			
R. caudate head[a]	15/12/0	25	4.79
R. post. cingulate cortex[a]	6/–48/21	48	4.62
R. ventromedial frontal cortex[a]	6/42/–12	29	4.23
R. rostral anterior cingulated[a]	–12/30/39	66	4.01
Nonbought versus Bought			
R. precuneus[a]	18/-45/30	14	4.23

[a] p < .001

was evinced in anterior cingulate cortex activity. We were able to register a significantly higher activity especially for bought products in the CB group (see Figure 5.4 and Table 5.4). Moreover, they purchased significantly more products (M_{com} = 34.87, M_{noncom} = 7.58; t = 7.77, df = 29.7; p < .001), spent a higher total average amount (M_{com} = 923.64, M_{noncom} = 166.81; t = 7.15; df = 24.5; p < .001), and also their average expenditure per purchased product was higher than those with normal buying (M_{com} = 25.67, M_{noncom} = 16.89; t = 3.61; df = 36.1; p < .001).

Postscan Results

The post fMRI scan analysis yielded the following results. Individuals with CB reported a significantly lower level of self-esteem (M_{com} = 32.13, M_{noncom} = 47.92; t = –5.66; df = 47; p < .001) and ability to control themselves

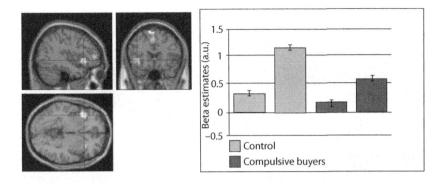

Figure 5.3 Activation during the price phase. Stronger activation during the price phase for subsequently nonbought products compared to products subsequently bought with maximal activity in the insula and differences in activity between normal buyers (gray) and individuals with CB (black) in the respective region with controls showing higher insular activity than those with CB for subsequently nonbought products (p < .001; vox.thresh: 10) (see Table 5.3).

Table 5.3 fMRI Activations for the Price Phase for both Groups

Area	MNI Coordinates (X/Y/Z)	Cluster Size	T-Score
Bought versus Nonbought			
R. precentral gyrus[a]	57/–6/33	20	3.99
Nonbought versus Bought			
Anterior cingulate cortex[a]	–6/24/43	45	6.36
L. anterior insula[a]	39/21/–3	40	5.87
R. anterior insula[a]	36/24/–6	38	4.48
R. DLPFC[a]	45/24/27	47	4.37

[a] p < .001

(M_{com} = 104.39, M_{noncom} = 122.08; t = –3.82; df = 47; p < .001). Suggesting depression and prefrontal dysfunction, they evinced significantly higher values in comparison to normal buyers (M_{com} = 30.26; M_{noncom} = 22.35; t = 4.35; df = 47; p < .001; M_{com} = 115.87, M_{noncom} = 90.69; t = 4.53; df = 47; p < .001).

Discussion

The main goal of the study was to investigate the neural basis and correlates of CB. Like any other human behavior, CB can only be comprehensively explained if one knows the personal, social, and biological causes. Faber and O'Guinn (1988) and Valence et al. (1988) have already pointed out the necessity of a biopsychosocial approach for the elucidate of CB.

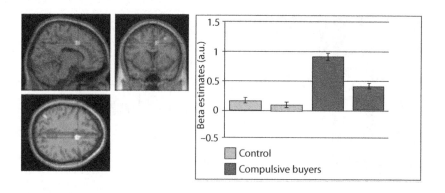

Figure 5.4 Activation during the decision phase. Stronger activity for individuals with CB than for controls during the decision phase in the cingulate cortex and those with CB showing higher ACC activity than controls for bought products (p < .001; vox.thresh: 10) (see Table 5.4).

Table 5.4 fMRI Activations for the Decision Phase for Both Groups

Area	MNI Coordinates (X/Y/Z)	Cluster Size	T-Score
Bought versus Nonbought			
R. VMPFC[a]	6/41/−11	43	5.01
R. DLPFC[a]	45/9/24	25	4.53
Anterior cingulate cortex[a]	6/24/48	35	4.49
R. middle temporal gyrus[a]	57/−41/−9	28	4.02
Nonbought versus Bought			
No sign. activation			

[a] p < .001

Based on this insight, we investigated hypotheses derived from research papers on CB, and from relevant studies in the areas of medicine, the neurosciences, psychology, and neuroeconomics. In accordance with our hypothesis, we were able to substantiate a significantly higher activity in the NAcc in comparison to those with normal buying during the display of products that the participants were able to buy. These results agree with the studies conducted by Knutson et al. (2001, 2007). Moreover, the study results coincide with studies regarding drug dependence and gambling addiction (Berridge, 2003; Birbaumer & Schmidt, 2006; Reuter et al., 2005). The results of these studies demonstrate that images of drugs, associated stimuli, and the potential opportunity to gamble are connected with increased NAcc activity.

While individuals with CB evince a significantly higher NAcc activation than those without CB during the display of products, which is related to a stronger desire and impulse toward purchasing the product, during the presentation of the product and the price, they exhibit a lower insula activity. The insula has been shown to be involved in negative emotional processing and especially in consumer decisions in the evaluation of prices (Knutson et al., 2007). Hence it seems that the anticipated loss of money—in the price condition—does lead to a stronger negative emotional response in healthy participants than in the individuals with CB. As was shown in the study by Knutson and colleagues, higher insula activity was related to a lower probability of a buying decision—the lower insula activity in those with CB would also explain a stronger urge to buy. Finding higher NAcc activity and lower insula activity hints at an imbalance between the "wanting" and the "fear of loss" in the brain of individuals with CB. There is a connection here in that the results substantiate the speculations of Hollander and Allen (2006), Hollander and Dell'Osso (2005), and Ridgway et al. (2008) that CB contains elements of both OCD and ICD.

The results from the purchase decision phase coincide with these findings and speculations. In contrast to our hypotheses, we did not find evidence for differential prefrontal activation between individuals with CB and healthy participants. The observed significantly lower anterior cingulate cortex activity in those with CB, though, substantiates the unbalanced "consuming-network" notion. According to the current state of knowledge, the anterior cingulate cortex is especially active in evaluating the degree of conflict in decisions connected with winning and losing, or response conflict (Bush, Vogt, Holmes, Dale, Greve, Jenike et al., 2002; Pochon, Riis, Sanfey, Nystrom, & Cohen, 2008). It is also noteworthy that a higher anterior cingulate cortex activity has been substantiated in depressed persons (Mayberg, Lozano, Voon, McNeely, Seminowicz, Hamani et al., 2005; Knutson et al., 2007). This is meaningful since various studies indicate that many patients with CB are dealing with depression (Lejoyeux, Tassain, Solomon, & Adès, 1997; Mueller et al., 2009; Schlosser et al., 1994; Scherhorn et al., 1990). The group of subjects with CB we studied also evinced significantly more pronounced symptoms of depression.

The study results have various implications. The greater NAcc activity in individuals with CB makes it clear how meaningful the recommendation is that these individuals avoid situations such as trips to the shopping mall. Furthermore this indicates the responsibility of government and businesses. To what extent government and businesses are prepared to limit purchase-inducing initiatives must be given careful consideration. With regard to the lower insula activity and the related perception of loss, thus namely the price one has to pay in purchasing a product, there are important implications for pricing presentation. It would seem necessary to make the real price and the price labeling of a product completely clear. This poses a challenge to both lawmakers and businesses.

On the whole the study indicates that CB is connected to specific neural activities. Further studies will have to show to what extent the results presented here define CB in relation to other addictions, and whether they support a meaningful, unambiguous classification, such as its classification as OCD and ICD. All this has to be seen in considering limitations of the study. Only women were examined. Even though it is reasonable to assume that the neural correlates would not differ, it nevertheless seems appropriate to do a study with men. Additionally the fact that in purchasing the presented products there were only products within a 1 to 50 Euro price range might have influenced the results. Another critical point is the short time available in this paradigm in presenting the products and the price and the amount of decision time as to whether or not to buy the presented product. Perhaps individuals with CB need more time for making controlled decisions. In this connection it would also be interesting to see what influence mode of payment might have. In the context of this study participants were only given cash as their available amount to spend. The use of cash is steadily declining in the face of credit card use. The higher degree of abstraction and temporarily delayed negative consequences of this form of payment may constitute an encouragement of CB. Apart from these limitations, and from the many open questions regarding the brain's mode of functioning, the integration of neurological insights can contribute to a better understanding of CB. The relevance of such an improved understanding is undeniable in the face of this behavior's prevalence.

Acknowledgment

The study was supported in part by grants from the Klaus Tschira Foundation.

References

Augustine, J.R. (1996) Circuitry and functional aspects of the insular lobe in primates including humans, *Brain Research Reviews*, 22:229–44.

Baumeister, R.F. (2002) Yielding to temptation: Self-control failure, impulsive purchasing, and consumer behaviour, *Journal of Consumer Research*, 28:670–76.

Bechara, A. & Damasio, A.R. (2005) The somatic marker hypothesis: A neural theory of economic decision, *Games and Economic Behavior*, 52:336–72.

Bechara, A., Damasio, H., & Damasio, A.R. (2000) Emotion, decision making and the orbitofrontal cortex, *Cerebral Cortex*, 10:295–307.

Bechara, A., Damasio, H., Damasio, A.R., & Anderson, S.W. (1994) Insensitivity to future consequences following damage to human prefrontal cortex, *Cognition*, 50:7–12.

Bechara, A., Tranel, D., Damasio, H., & Damasio, A.R. (1996) Failure to respond autonomically to anticipated future outcomes following damage to prefrontal cortex, *Cerebral Cortex*, 6:215–25.

Benson, A.L. (2009) *To Buy or Not to Buy: Why We Overshop and How to Stop*, Boston: Shambhala.

Berlin, H.A., Rolls, E.T., & Kischka, U. (2004) Impulsivity, time perception, emotion and reinforcement sensitivity in patients with orbitofrontal cortex lesions, *Brain*, 127:1108–26.

Berridge, K.C. (2003) Pleasures of the brain, *Brain and Cognition*, 52:106–28.

Birbaumer, N. & Schmidt, R.F. (2006) *Biologische Psychologie*, Berlin, Heidelberg: Springer.

Black, D.W. (1996) Compulsive buying: A review, *Journal of Clinical Psychiatry*, 57:50–55.

Black, D.W. (2001) Compulsive buying disorder: Definition, assessment, epidemiology, and clinical management, *CNS Drugs*, 15:17–27.

Black, D.W. (2007) Compulsive buying disorder: A review of the evidence, *CNS Spectrums*, 12:124–32.

Black, D.W., Gabel, J., Hansen, J., & Schlosser, S. (2000) A double-blind comparison of fluvoxamine versus placebo in the treatment of compulsive buying disorder, *American Academy of Clinical Psychiatrists*, 12:205–11.

Black, D.W., Repertinger, S., Gaffner, G., & Gabel, J. (1998) Family history and psychiatric comorbidity in persons with compulsive buying: Preliminary findings, *American Journal of Psychiatry*, 155:960–63.

Bleuler, E. (1924) *Textbook of Psychiatry*, New York: Macmillan.

Bruckheimer, J. (2009) "Confessions of a Shopaholic," Burbank: Touchstone Pictures.

Buchel, C. and Dolan, R.J. (2000) Classical fear conditioning in functional neuro-imaging, *Current Opinion in Neurobiology*, 10:219–33.

Bush, G., Vogt, B.A., Holmes, J., Dale, A.M., Greve, D., Jenike, M.A., & Rosen, B.R. (2002) Dorsal anterior cingulate cortex: A role in reward-based decision making, *Proceedings of the National Academy of Sciences (PNAS)*, 99:523–28.

Carlson, N.R. (2004) *Psychology of Behavior*, Boston: Allyn & Bacon.

Cato, M.A., Crosson, B., Gokcay, D., Soltysik, D., Wierenga, C., Gopinath, K., Himes, N., Belanger, H., Bauer, R.M., Fischler, I.S., Gonzalez-Rothi, L., & Briggs, R.W. (2004) Processing words with emotional connotation: An fMRI study of time course and laterality in rostral frontal and retrosplenial cortices, *Journal of Cognitive Neuroscience*, 16:167–77.

Christenson, G.A., Faber, R.J., de Zwaan, M., Raymond, N.C., Specker, S.M., Ekern, M.D., Mackenzie, T.B., Crosby, R.D., Crow, S.J., Eckert, E.D., Mussell, M.P., & Mitchell, J.E. (1994) Compulsive buying: Descriptive characteristics and psychiatric comorbidity, *The Journal of Clinical Psychiatry*, 55:5–11.

Clark, L. & Manes, F. (2004) Social and emotional decision-making following frontal lobe injury, *Neurocase: Case Studies in Neuropsychology, Neuropsychiatry, and Behavioural Neurology*, 10:398–403.

Clark, L., Bechara, A., Damasio, H., Aitken, M., Sahakian, B.J., & Robbins, T.W. (2008) Differential effects of insular and ventromedial prefrontal cortex lesions on risky decision-making, *Brain*, 131:1311–22.

Critchley, H.D., Mathias, C.J., & Dolan, R.J. (2001) Neural activity in the human brain relating to uncertainty and arousal during anticipation, *Neuron*, 29:537–45.

d'Astous, A. & Bellemare, Y. (1989) Contrasting compulsive and normal buyers' reactions to image versus product quality advertising, in A. d'Astous (ed.), *Proceedings of the Annual Conference of the Administrative Sciences Association of Canada—Marketing Division*, Montréal: Administrative Sciences Association of Canada, 82–91.

d'Astous, A. (1990) An inquiry into the compulsive side of normal consumers, *Journal of Consumer Policy*, 13:15–31.

Damasio, A.R. (1994) *Descartes' Error: Emotion, Reason, and the Human Brain*, New York: G.P. Putnam's Sons.

Dell'Osso, B., Altamura, C.A., Alien, A., Marazziti, D., & Hollander, E. (2006) Epidemiologic and clinical updates on impulse control disorders: A critical review, *European Archives of Psychiatry and Clinical Neuroscience*, 256:464–75.

Deppe, M., Schwindt, W., Kugel, H., Plassman, H., & Kenning, P. (2005) Nonlinear responses within the medial prefrontal cortex reveal when specific implicit information influences economic decision making, *Journal of Neuroimaging*, 15:171–82.

Deusinger, I.M. (1986) *Die Frankfurter Selbstkonzeptskalen (FSKN)*, Handanweisung, Goettingen: Hogrefe.

Dittmar, H. (2005a) Compulsive buying—a growing concern? *British Journal of Psychology*, 96:467–91.

Dittmar, H. (2005b) A new look at compulsive buying: Self-discrepancies and materialistic values as predictors of compulsive buying tendency, *Journal of Social and Clinical Psychology*, 24:806–33.

Donegan, N.H., Rodin, J., O'Brien, C.P., & Solomon, R.L. (1983) A learning theory approach to commonalities, in P.K. Levison, D.R. Gerstein, & D.R. Maloff (eds.), *Commonalities in Substance Abuse and Habitual Behaviour*, Lexington, MA: Lexington Books, 111–56.

Edwards, E.A. (1993) Development of a new scale for measuring compulsive buying behavior, *Financial Counseling and Planning*, 4:67–85.

Engel, R.R. (2000) *MMPI-2TM: Minnesota Multiphasic Personality Inventory-2TM*, Manual, Bern: Huber.

Erk, S., Spitzer, M., Wunderlich, A.P., Galley, L., & Walter, H. (2002) Cultural objects modulate reward circuitry, *Neuroreport*, 13:2499–503.

Ernst, M. & Paulus, M.P. (2005) Neurobiology of decision making: A selective review from a neurocognitive and clinical perspective, *Biological Psychiatry*, 58:597–604.

Faber, R.J. & O'Guinn, T.C. (1988) Compulsive consumption and credit abuse, *Journal of Consumer Policy*, 11:109–21.

Faber, R.J. & O'Guinn, T.C. (1989) Classifying compulsive consumers: Advances in the development of a diagnostic tool, *Advances in Consumer Research*, 16:738–44.

Faber, R.J. & O'Guinn, T.C. (1992) A clinical screener for compulsive buying, *Journal of Consumer Research*, 19:459–69.

Faber, R.J. (1992) Money changes everything: Compulsive buying from a bio-psychosocial perspective, *American Behavioral Scientist*, 35:809–19.

Faber, R.J. (2004) Self-control and compulsive buying, in T. Kasser & A.D. Kanner (eds.), *Psychology and Consumer Culture*, Washington, D.C.: American Psychological Association, 169–89.

Faber, R.J. & Vohs, K.D. (2004) To buy or not to buy? Self-control and self-regulatory failure in purchase behaviour, in R.F. Baumeister & K.D. Vohs (eds.), *Handbook of Self-Regulation*, New York: Guilford Press, 509–24.

Faber, R.J., O'Guinn, T.C., & Krych, R. (1987) Compulsive consumption, in M. Wallendorf & P.F. Anderson (eds.), *Advances in Consumer Research*, Provo, UT: Association for Consumer Research, 132–45.

Frost, R.O., Steketee, G., & Williams, L. (2002) Compulsive buying, compulsive hoarding and obsessive-compulsive disorder, *Behavior Therapy*, 33:201–14.

García Ureta, I. (2007) Addictive buying: Causes, processes, and symbolic meanings: Thematic analysis of a buying addict's diary, *Spanish Journal of Psychology*, 10:408–22.

Grace, J. & Malloy, P.F. (2001) *Frontal Systems Behavioral Scale*, Lutz, FL: Psychological Assessment Resources.

Gruesser, S.M., Poppelreuter, S., Heinz, A., Albrecht, U., & Saß, H. (2007) Verhaltenssucht—Eine eigenständige diagnostische Einheit? *Der Nervenarzt*, 78:997–1002.

Hirschman, E.C. (1992) The consciousness of addiction: Toward a general theory of compulsive consumption, *Journal of Consumer Research*, 19:155–79.

Hoch, S.J. & Loewenstein, G.F. (1991) Time-inconsistent preferences and consumer self-control, *Journal of Consumer Research*, 17:492–507.

Hollander, E. & Allen, A. (2006) Is compulsive buying a real disorder, and is it really compulsive? *American Journal of Psychiatry*, 163:1670–72.

Hollander, E. & Dell'Osso, B. (2005) New developments in an evolving field, *Psychiatric Times*, 22:17.

Hollander, E., Kim, S., & Zohar, J. (2007) OCSDs in the forthcoming DSM-V, *CNS Spectrums*, 12:320–323.

Jacobs, D. (1986) A general theory of addictions: A new theoretical model, *Journal of Gambling Behavior*, 2:15–31.

Knutson, B., Fong, G.W., Adams, C.M., Varner, J.L., & Hommer, D. (2001) Dissociation of reward anticipation and outcome with event-related fMRI, *Neuroreport*, 12:3683–87.

Knutson, B., Fong, G.W., Bennett, S.M., Adams, C.M., & Hommer, D. (2003) A region of mesial prefrontal cortex tracks monetarily rewarding outcomes: Characterization with rapid event-related fMRI, *NeuroImage*, 18:263–72.

Knutson, B., Rick, S., Wimmer, G.E., Prelec, D., & Loewenstein, G. (2007) Neural predictors of purchases, *Neuron*, 53:147–56.

Knutson, B., Wimmer, G.E., Kuhnen, C.M., & Winkielman, P. (2008) Nucleus accumbens activation mediates the influence of reward cues on financial risk taking, *Neuroreport*, 19:509–13.

Kollmann, K. & Kautsch, I. (2008) Kaufsucht in Österreich, http://www.arbeiter-kammer.at/pictures/d85/AKStudie_Kaufsucht.pdf. Accessed 7/19/2010.

Koran, L.M., Chuong, H.W., Bullock, K.D., & Smith, C. (2003) Citalopram for compulsive shopping disorder: An open-label study followed by double-blind discontinuation, *Journal of Clinical Psychiatry*, 64:793–98.

Koran, L.M., Faber, R.J., Aboujaoude, E., Large, M., & Serpe, R.T. (2006) Estimated prevalence of compulsive buying behaviour in the U.S., *American Journal of Psychiatry*, 10:1806–12.

Kraepelin, E. (1909) *Psychiatrie: Ein Lehrbuch fuer Studierende und Aerzte*, Leipzig: Barth.

Krain, A.L., Hefton, S., Pine, D.S., Ernst, M., Castellanos, X.F., Klein, R.G., & Milham, M.P. (2006) An fMRI examination of developmental differences in the neural correlates of uncertainty and decision-making, *Journal of Child Psychology and Psychiatry and Allied Disciplines*, 47:1023–30.

Krueger, D.W. (1988) On compulsive shopping and spending: A psychodynamic inquiry, *American Journal of Psychotherapy*, 42:574–85.

Kuhnen, C.M. & Knutson, B. (2005) The neural basis of financial risk taking, *Neuron*, 47:763–70.

Lawrence, L. (1990) The psychodynamics of the compulsive female shopper, *The American Journal of Psychoanalysis*, 50:67–70.

Lejoyeux, M., Tassain, V., Solomon, J., & Adès, J. (1997) Study of compulsive buying in depressed patients, *Journal of Clinical Psychiatry*, 58:169–173.

Lejoyeux, M., McLoughlin, M., & Adès, J. (2000) Epidemilogy of behavioral dependence: Literature review and result of original studies, *European Psychiatry*, 15:129–34.

Manolis, C. & Roberts, J.A. (2008) Compulsive buying: Does it matter how it's measured? *Journal of Economic Psychology*, 29:555–76.

Marlatt, G.A., Baer, J.S., Donovan, D.M., & Kivlahan, D.R. (1988) Addictive behaviors: Etiology and treatment, *Annual Review of Psychology*, 39:223–52.

Mayberg, H.S., Lozano, A.M., Voon, V., McNeely, H.E., Seminowicz, D., Hamani, C., Schwalb, J.M., & Kennedy, S.H. (2005) Deep brain stimulation for treatment-resistant depression, *Neuron*, 45:651–660.

McClure, S., Li, J., Tomlin, D., Cypert, K.S., Montague, L.M., & Montague, P.R. (2004) Neural correlates of behavioral preference for culturally familiar drinks, *Neuron*, 44:379–87.

McElroy, S.L., Hudson, J.I., Pope, H.G., Keck, P.E., & Aizley, H.G. (1992) The DSM-III-R impulse control disorders not elsewhere classified: Clinical characteristics and relationships to other psychiatric disorders, *American Journal of Psychiatry*, 149:318–27.

McElroy, S.L., Keck, P.E., Pope, H.G., Smith, J.M.R., & Strakowski, S.M. (1994) Compulsive buying: A report of 20 cases, *The Journal of Clinical Psychiatry*, 55:242–48.

Mittal, B., Holbrook, M., Beatty, S., Raghubi, P., & Woodside, P. (2008) *Consumer Behavior: How Humans Think, Feel, and Act in the Marketplace*, Cincinnati: Open Mentis.

Mueller, A. & de Zwaan, M. (2008) Treatment of compulsive buying, *Fortschritte in der Neurologie, Psychiatrie*, 76:478–83.

Mueller, A., de Zwaan, M., & Mitchell, J.E. (2008) *Pathologisches Kaufen*, Köln: Deutscher Ärzte Verlag.

Mueller, A., Mühlhans, B., Silbermann, A., Mueller, U., Mertens, C., Horbach, T., Mitchell, J.E., & de Zwaan, M. (2009) Compulsive buying and psychiatric comorbidity, *Psychotherapie, Psychosomatik, Medizinische Psychologie*, 59:291–9.

Mueller, A., Reinecker, H., Jacobi, C., Reisch, L., & de Zwaan, M. (2005) Pathologisches Kaufen—eine Literaturübersicht, *Psychiatrische Praxis*, 32:3–12.

Neuner, M., Raab, G., & Reisch, L.A. (2005a) Compulsive buying in maturing societies: An empirical re-inquiry, *Journal of Economic Psychology*, 26:509–22.

Neuner, M., Raab, G., & Reisch, L.A. (2005b) Compulsive buying as a consumer policy issue in East and West Germany, in K.G. Grunert & J. Thogersen (eds.), *Consumers, Policy and the Environment: A Tribute to Folke Ölander*, Heidelberg: Springer, 89–114.

Neuner, M., Raab, G., & Reisch, L.A. (2008) Kaufsucht bei Jugendlichen, in M. Klein (ed.), *Kinder und Suchtgefahren. Risiken—Prävention—Hilfen*, Stuttgart: Schattauer, 162–73.

Ninan, P.T., McElroy, S.L., Kane, C.P., Knight, B.T., Casuto, L.S., Rose, S.E., Marsteller, F.A., & Nemeroff, C.B. (2000) Placebo-controlled study of Fluvoxamine in the treatment of patients with compulsive buying, *Journal of Clinical Psychopharmacology*, 20:362–6.

O'Connor, K. (2005) *Addicted to Shopping and Other Issues Women Have with Money*, Eugene, Oregon: Harvest House Publishers.

O'Doherty, J., Kringelbach, M.L., Rolls, E.T., Hornak, J., & Andrews, C. (2001) Abstract reward and punishment representations in the human orbitofrontal cortex, *Nature Neuroscience*, 4:95–102.

O'Guinn, T.C. & Faber, R.J. (1989) Compulsive buying: A phenomenological exploration, *Journal of Consumer Research*, 16:147–57.

Ongur, D. & Price, J.L. (2000) The organization of networks within the orbital and medial prefrontal cortex of rats, monkeys and humans, *Cerebral Cortex*, 10:206–19.

Paulus, M.P. & Frank, L.R. (2003) Ventromedial prefrontal cortex activation is critical for preference judgments, *Neuroreport*, 14:1311–5.

Paulus, M.P. & Stein, M.B. (2006) An insular view of anxiety, *Biological Psychiatry*, 60:383–7.

Paulus, M.P. (2007) Decision making dysfunctions in psychiatry—altered homeostatic processing? *Science*, 318:602–6.

Paulus, M.P., Rogalsky, C., Simmons, A., Feistein, J.S., & Stein, M.B. (2003) Increased activation in the right insula during risk-taking decision making is related to harm avoidance and neuroticism, *NeuroImage*, 19:1439–48.

Ploghaus, A., Tracey, I., Gati, J.S., Clare, S., Menon, R.S., Matthews, P.M., & Rawlins, J.N.P. (1999) Dissociating pain from its anticipation in the human brain, *Science*, 284:1979–81.

Pochon, J.B, Riis, J., Sanfey, A.G., Nystrom, L.E., & Cohen, J.D. (2008) Functional imaging of decision conflict, *The Journal of Neuroscience*, 28:3468–73.

Prelec, D. & Loewenstein, G. (1998) The red and the black: Mental accounting of savings and debt, *Marketing Science*, 17:4–28.

Preuschoff, K., Bossaerts, P., & Quartz, S.R. (2006) Neural differentiation of expected reward and risk in human subcortical structures, *Neuron*, 51:381–90.

Raab, G. (1998) Kartengestützte *Zahlungssysteme und Konsumentenverhalten: eine theoretische und empirische Untersuchung*, Berlin: Duncker & Humblot.

Raab, G., Neuner, M., Reisch, L.A., & Scherhorn, G. (2005) *SKSK. Screeningverfahren zur Erhebung von kompensatorischem Kaufverhalten. Manual*, Goettingen: Hogrefe.

Reisch, L.A. & Neuner, M. (2002) Women and addictive buying: The gender question revisited, in I.G. Ureta & E.O. Fernández (eds.), *El consume y la adicción a las compras diferentes perspectives*, Bilbao: The University of the Basque Country Press, 170–95.

Reuter, J., Raedler, T., Rose, M., Hand, I., Gläscher, J., & Büchel, C. (2005) Pathological gambling is linked to reduced activation of the mesolimbic reward system, *Nature Neuroscience*, 8:147–8.

Reynolds, S.M. & Zahm, D.S. (2005) Specificity in the projections of prefrontal and insular cortex to ventral striatopallidum and the extended amygdala, *The Journal of Neuroscience*, 25:11757–67.

Ridgway, N.M., Kukar-Kinney, M., & Monroe, K.B. (2008) An expanded conceptualization and a new measure of compulsive buying, *Journal of Consumer Research*, 35:622–39.

Robinson, T.E. & Berridge, K.C. (1993) The neural basis of drug craving: An incentive-sensitization theory of addiction, *Brain Research Review*, 18:247–91.

Rose, P. (2007) Mediators of the association between narcissism and compulsive buying: The roles of materialism and impulse control, *Psychology of Addictive Behavior*, 21:576–81.

Salzman, L. (1981) Psychodynamics of the addictions, in S.J. Mule (ed.), *Behavior in Excess*, New York: Free Press, 338–49.

Scherhorn, G. (1990) The addictive trait in buying behaviour, *Journal of Consumer Policy*, 13:33–51.

Scherhorn, G., Reisch, L.A., & Raab, G. (1990) Addictive buying in West Germany: An empirical study, *Journal of Consumer Policy*, 13:355–87.

Schlosser, S., Black, D.W., Repertinger, S., & Freet, D. (1994) Compulsive buying: Demography, phenomenology, and comorbidity in 46 subjects, *General Hospital Psychiatry*, 16:205–12.

Silbermann, A., Henkel, A., Müller, A., & de Zwaan, M. (2008) Der Einsatz von Ecological Momentary Assessment bei Patienten mit pathologischem Kaufverhalten, Psychotherapie, Psychosomatik, *Medizinische Psychologie*, 58:454–61.

Simmons, A., Matthews, S.C., Stein, M.B., & Paulus, M.P. (2004) Anticipation of emotionally aversive visual stimuli activates right insula, *Neuroreport*, 15:2261–5.

Spinella, M., Yang, B., & Lester, D. (2007) Development of the executive personal finance scale, *International Journal of Neuroscience*, 117:301–13.

Tangney, J.P., Baumeister, R.F., & Boone, A.L. (2004) High self-control predicts good adjustment, less pathology, better grades, and interpersonal success, *Journal of Personality*, 72:271–324.

Tzourio-Mazoyer, N., Landeau, B., Papathanassiou, D., Crivello, F., Etard, O., Delcroix, N., Mazoyer, B., & Joliot, M. (2002) Automated anatomical labeling of activations in SPM using a macroscopic anatomical parcellation of the MNI MRI single-subject brain, *Neuroimage*, 15:273–89.

Valence, G., d'Astous, A., & Fortier, L. (1988) Compulsive buying: Concept and measurement, *Journal of Consumer Policy*, 11:419–33.

Volkow, N.D., Fowler, J.S., Wang, G.-J., & Goldstein, R.Z. (2002) Role of dopamine, the frontal cortex and memory circuits in drug addiction: Insight from imaging studies, *Neurobiology of Learning and Memory*, 78:610–24.

CHAPTER 6

Psychiatric Comorbidity and Compulsive Buying

MARTINA DE ZWAAN, MD

Contents

Introduction   87
Compulsive Buying in Psychiatric Samples   94
    Psychiatric Inpatients   94
    Depression   96
    Obsessive-Compulsive Disorder   96
    Compulsive Hoarding   97
    Eating Disorders   98
    Pathological Gambling   98
    Exercise Dependence   99
    Parkinson's Disease and Restless Legs Syndrome   99
References   101

Introduction

It is generally acknowledged that compulsive buying (CB) is associated with high rates of psychiatric comorbidity. The prevalence rates of Axis I disorders are all elevated in comparison to those found in epidemiological samples (Table 6.1) (for depressive episodes in population examples see e.g., Andrade, Caraveo-Anduaga, Berglund, Bijl, de Graaf, Vollebergh et al., 2003). Data from clinical studies show that persons with CB frequently meet lifetime criteria for mood and anxiety disorders, substance use disorders, and eating disorders, primarily binge eating disorder (Christenson, Faber, de Zwaan, Raymond, Specker, Eckern et al., 1994; Mueller, Mühlhans, Silbermann,

Table 6.1 Prevalence Rates (Percent) of Lifetime Psychiatric Disorders in Individuals with Compulsive Buying Disorder (CBD)

	Assessment	Sample Size	Affective Disorders	Major Depression	Anxiety Disorders	Substance Use Disorders	OCD	Eating Disorders	Any Axis I Disorder
			Controlled Studies						
Christenson et al., 1994	SCID	CBD: 24	54	50	50[a]	46[a]	13	21[a]	—
	DSM-III-R	Con: 24	50	46	21	13	0	4	—
Black et al., 1998	SCID	CBD: 33	64[a]	61[a]	42	21	3	15	79
	DSM-III-R	Con: 22	27	27	27	9	0	5	55
Mitchell et al., 2002	SCID	CBD: 19	58	53	53	53[a]	16	5	—
	DSM-IV	Con: 20	50	50	25	10	5	5	—
Mueller et al., 2009a	SCID	CBD: 30	80[a]	57	87[a]	23	40	33[a]	97[a]
	DSM-IV	Con: 30	43	40	40	20	0	3	67

Open Studies

Schlosser et al., 1994	DIS DSM-III-R SCID	CBD: 46	28	28	41	30	4	17	67
McElroy et al., 1994	DSM-III-R DIS	CBD: 20	95	25	80	40	35	35	—
Black et al., 2000	DSM-III-R SCID	CBD: 23 drug tx	—	74	43	22 / 14	—	9 / 10	—
Ninan et al., 2000	DSM-IV	CBD: 42 drug tx	—	45	—	alcohol	10	BED	74

Severity of CBD and Comorbidity

Mueller et al., 2010a		Total (171)	74.3	62.6	57.3	20.5	18.7	19.9	89.5
	SCID	CBD: 107	68.2[a]	57	48.6[a]	15[a]	16.8	15.9	84.1[a]
	DSM-IV	Severe CBD: 64	84.4	71.9	71.9	29.7	26.6	26.6	98.4

Note: CBD = compulsive buying disorder; Con = healthy control subjects; DIS = Diagnostic Interview Schedule; drug tx = drug treatment study; OCD = obsessive-compulsive disorder; SCID = Structured Clinical Interview for DSM Disorders.

[a] = significant difference between CBD and Con ($p < 0.05$)

Müller, Mertens, Horbach et al., 2009a; McElroy, Keck, Pope, Smith, & Strakowski, 1994; Ninan, McElroy, Kane, Knight, Casuto, Rose et al., 2000).

It is important to note that all studies excluded patients whose buying behavior occurred only in the context of hypomanic or manic symptoms. Lifetime bipolar disorder was rarely reported except in the study of McElroy et al. (1994) who found that 70 percent of their patients with CB reported a lifetime bipolar I or bipolar II disorder, whereas only 25 percent reported a lifetime history of major depression. Interestingly buying typically increased during mildly to moderately severe depressive episodes and decreased during hypomanic, manic, and severe depressive episodes.

There are only four controlled studies comparing the psychiatric comorbidity in small samples (n = 19–33) of patients with CB with healthy control subjects (Christenson et al., 1994; Black, Repertinger, Gaffney, & Gabel, 1998; Mitchell, Redlin, Wonderlich, Crosby, Faber, Miltenberger et al., 2002; Mueller et al., 2009a). The differences between patients with CB and controls varied among the four studies as can be seen in Table 6.1. Significant differences for the major groups of psychiatric disorders (affective disorders, anxiety disorders, substance use disorders, and eating disorders) between patients with CB and controls were found for each diagnostic group in at least two studies.

Notably the prevalence of obsessive-compulsive disorder (OCD) was high in most studies. Overall there seems to be an overlap between OCD and CB, even when compulsive hoarding was not counted as an OCD symptom (Mueller et al., 2009a). Mueller et al. (2009a) used a cutoff of 40 on the Savings-Inventory (Frost, Steketee, & Grisham, 2004) to define hoarding and found a frequency of compulsive hoarding of 62 percent in a sample of 63 treatment-seeking individuals with CB. Importantly compulsive hoarding tendencies were a negative predictor for treatment outcome in a psychotherapy trial targeting CB (Mueller, Mueller, Silbermann, Reinecker, Bleich, Mitchell, & de Zwaan, 2008). The same authors reported that in a representative sample of the German general population 39 percent of the participants who screened positive for CB also reported compulsive hoarding (Mueller, Mitchell, Crosby, Glaesmer, & de Zwaan, 2009b). The evidence of the close association between OCD, compulsive hoarding, and CB supports the belief of some researchers that CB falls within the obsessive-compulsive spectrum.

The largest sample investigated so far (Mueller, Mitchell, Black, Crosby, Berg, & de Zwaan, 2010a) is comprised of data from three American samples and one German sample (n = 171). In this study the lifetime prevalence rate of at least one psychiatric disorder was 90 percent in patients with CB. Following a latent profile analysis (LPA) the sample was divided into two groups. Patients with less severe and patients with more severe buying symptomatology separated in the LPA, and it was demonstrated that those with more severe CB had significantly higher psychiatric comorbidity.

In other studies CB has been associated with higher scores on dimensional measures of depression, anxiety, and obsessionality and low on measures of self-esteem (see for example Christenson et al., 1994).

The association between depressive symptoms and CB was also demonstrated in a German population-based sample. The scores on the mood scale of the Brief Patient Health Questionnaire (PHQ-9) were significantly higher (mean 4.82) in 161 participants with CB (SBC-G) compared to 2189 participants without CB (mean 2.26) (Mueller, Mitchell, Crosby, Gefeller, Faber, Martin et al., 2010c).

There is some evidence from two studies that CB runs in families and that within these families Axis I disorders are excessive. McElroy et al. (1994) reported that of 18 individuals with CB, 17 had one or more first-degree relatives with major depression, 11 with substance abuse, and three with an anxiety disorder. The only controlled study (Black, Repertinger, Gaffney, & Gabel, 1998) found significantly higher rates of depression and substance use in 137 first-degree relatives of 33 patients with CB compared to those in a comparison group.

Compared to Axis I disorders little has been published about comorbid personality disorders or traits (Schlosser, Black, Repertinger, & Freet, 1994; Mueller et al., 2008). In an uncontrolled study Schlosser, Black, Repertinger, and Freet (1994) found that nearly 60 percent of 46 subjects with CB met criteria for at least one personality disorder (see Table 6.2). In the only controlled study published so far (Mueller et al., 2009a) 73 percent of a sample of 30 treatment-seeking patients with CB met criteria for at least one personality disorder, compared to 33 percent of a sample of prebariatric surgery patients and 10 percent of a healthy control group. The most commonly identified personality disorders were avoidant (37 percent and 15 percent, respectively) and borderline (20 percent and 15 percent), which generally are highly prevalent in psychiatric outpatients (Zimmermann, Rothschild, & Chelminski, 2005). In both studies surprisingly high rates of obsessive-compulsive (27 percent and 22 percent) and paranoid (17 percent and 11 percent) personality disorders were found compared to psychiatric outpatient samples.

Evaluating personality characteristics Mitchell, Redlin, Wonderlich, Crosby, Faber, Miltenberger et al. (2002) used the Dimensional Assessment of Personality Pathology (DAPP) and found elevated scores in 20 individuals with CB compared with 20 healthy controls on eight of the 18 subscales. They concluded that elevations on the cognitive dysregulation, identity problem, and affective lability scales indicated that individuals with CB may have emotional dysregulation consistent with traits seen in individuals with borderline personality disorder. Elevations on the callousness and conduct problems scales suggested dissocial behavior. The high values on the suspiciousness scale might fit with the observed elevated rates of paranoid personality disorder.

Table 6.2 Personality Disorders in Individuals with Compulsive Buying Disorder (CBD) Compared to Psychiatric Outpatients

	Mueller et al., 2009a N = 30 (CBD)	Schlosser et al., 1994 N = 46 (CBD)	Zimmerman et al., 2005 N = 859 (Psychiatric Outpatients)
Avoidant	37	15	14.7
Depressive	37	—	—
Obsessive-Compulsive	27	22	8.7
Borderline	20	15	9.3
Paranoid	17	11	4.2
Negativistic	10	—	—
Schizoid	10	0	1.4
Histrionic	13	9	1.0
Dependent	7	2	1.4
Narcissistic	7	2	2.3
Antisocial	3	0	3.6
Passive-Aggressive	—	4	—
Any Personality Disorder[a]	73[a]	59	45.5

[a] Significant difference to clinical control group (prebariatric surgery patients) and healthy control group (CBD > Con)

Interestingly there is a large body of literature on the association between personality traits and CB tendencies coming from consumer research. Using the Big Five Model, Mowen and Spears (1999) found that CB was positively associated with neuroticism and agreeableness, and negatively associated with conscientiousness.

DeSarbo and Edwards (1996) conducted a cluster analysis using self-report data from 104 subjects with CB and 101 community control subjects. They found two clusters, both exhibiting high impulsivity. In one cluster CB seemed to be driven by low self-esteem, dependent personality style, and anxiety, whereas in the other cluster CB was linked to materialistic values, escape or avoidance coping style, social isolation, and denial. Finally Rose (2007) found that materialism and impulse control both mediated the association between narcissism and CB.

Mueller, Claes, Mitchell, Wonderlich, Crosby, and de Zwaan (2010b) investigated the relationship between CB and combinations of personality traits, known as personality prototypes, based on the Big Five personality traits (NEO-FFI) in 68 patients with CB who participated in a psychotherapy study. They found two clusters. One was defined as resilient and the other as undercontrolled/emotionally dysregulated. With regard to psychiatric comorbidity, patients in the undercontrolled cluster exhibited higher rates

Table 6.3 Prevalence Rate (Percent) of Lifetime Impulse Control Disorders in Individuals with Compulsive Buying Disorder (CBD) Compared to Psychiatric Inpatients

	Mueller et al., 2009a, N = 30	Christenson et al., 1994, N = 24	Schlosser et al., 1994, N = 46	McElroy et al., 1994, N = 20	Grant et al., 2005, N = 204 (Psychiatric Inpatients)
Compulsive Buying	100	100	100	100	9.3
IED	17	4.2	22	10	6.9
Kleptomania	7	4.2	37	10	9.3
Pathological Gambling	3	8.3	20	5	6.9
Trichotillomania	3	4.2	11	10	4.4
Pyromania	0	0	2	10	5.9
Compulsive Sexual Behavior	—	—	—	10	4.9
Any Impulse Control Disorder	23[a]	20.8[a]	—	—	32.8

Note: IED = Intermittent Explosive Disorder.
[a] Significant differences to healthy control groups (CBD > Con)

of anxiety disorders as well as personality disorders, particularly Cluster B personality disorders.

Disorders of impulse control are also relatively common in individuals with CB (see Table 6.3). Two controlled (Christenson et al., 1994; Mueller et al., 2009a) and two uncontrolled studies (Schlosser et al., 1994; McElroy et al., 1994) have assessed impulse control disorders (ICD) other than CB in subjects with CB. In the two controlled studies 23 percent and 21 percent of the patients with CB met criteria for at least one other ICD, which was significantly higher than the rate in the healthy control groups. The rates are roughly comparable to the 32.8 percent found in a large sample of 204 psychiatric inpatients (Grant, Levine, Kim, & Potenza, 2005). This rate also included CB and compulsive sexual behavior, possibly explaining the apparent higher prevalence. The most common ICDs in the samples with CB were intermittent explosive disorder (IED), kleptomania, and pathological gambling. The prevalence of IED was 17 percent and 22 percent in the two controlled studies, which is much higher than the numbers found in psychiatric inpatients (6.9 percent; Grant, Levine, Kim, & Potenza, 2005) and in epidemiological studies (7.3 percent; Kessler, Coccaro, Fava, Jaeger, Jin, & Walters, 2006). The high prevalence of other ICDs supports the notion that CB is actually an ICD such as pathological gambling. However, it is questionable if the so-called ICDs according to DSM-IV or ICD-10 represent a homogeneous group.

In summary, there is ample evidence that individuals with CB suffer from an excess of other mental disorders. Uncontrolled and controlled studies using structured clinical interviews to assess psychiatric comorbidity have found high rates of Axis I, Axis II, as well as ICDs in clinical samples of patients with CB. The rates were surprisingly high for OCD and obsessive-compulsive personality disorder (OCPD), even after excluding compulsive hoarding behavior as a symptom of OCD and OCPD. In addition the frequencies of paranoid personality disorder and IED were higher than usually found in clinical and community samples. Most importantly we know from psychotherapy trials (Mitchell, Burgard, Faber, Crosby, & de Zwaan, 2006; Mueller et al., 2008) that individuals with CB and comorbid personality pathology show a more severe course, greater psychological distress, and slower recovery.

Major limitations of the reported studies are their small sample sizes and their putative sampling bias. Participants were usually recruited through the media to participate in an assessment study or a treatment study, which may have recruited subjects with elevated levels of distress. On the other hand the small sample sizes may have precluded elucidation of important group differences due to low power. In addition only four studies included a healthy control group, and only one study (Mueller et al., 2009a) included a clinical control group. Diagnostic instruments for assessing CB differed between studies; however, most of the studies relied on clinical interviews rather than self-report instruments. Finally the samples investigated in the different studies might represent heterogeneous groups of patients with CB.

Compulsive Buying in Psychiatric Samples

The prevalence of CB has been assessed in patients with a variety of other psychiatric disorders (see Table 6.4). Since the psychiatric comorbidity is high in patients with CB, CB should also be common in patients with other mental disorders. To fully demonstrate that comorbidity exists, it is also necessary to show that individuals with other disorders are more likely to suffer from CB. Only a few studies included a healthy control group or a clinical control group. Many studies assessed a range of ICDs extending beyond those currently included in the DSM category of ICDs not otherwise classified.

Psychiatric Inpatients

Grant, Levine, Kim, and Potenza (2005) investigated the prevalence of ICDs in a large sample of 204 consecutively admitted adult psychiatric inpatients using the Minnesota Impulsive Disorders Interview (MIDI; Christenson et al., 1994), an instrument frequently used to screen for ICD. Overall 67 (32.8 percent) reported at least one lifetime ICD, with CB being

Table 6.4 Prevalence (Percent) of Compulsive Buying Disorder (CBD) in Patients with Different Psychiatric Disorders

Author	Sample Size	Diagnosis	Setting	Assessment Instrument	Prevalence of CBD (%)
Grant et al., 2005	204	Psychiatric disorders	Inpatients	MIDI	9.3
Grant et al., 2007	102 adolescents	Psychiatric disorders	Inpatients	MIDI	6.9
Lejoyeux et al., 1997	119	Depression	Inpatients	MIDI	31.9
Lejoyeux et al., 1999	52	Depression	Inpatients	McElroy criteria and questionnaire	40.4
Lejoyeux et al., 2002	107	Depression	Inpatients	McElroy criteria and questionnaire	30.8
Du Toit et al., 2001	85	OCD	Outpatients	Newly developed SCID-OCSD	12.9 and 3.5 subclinical
Lejoyeux et al., 2005	60	OCD	Outpatients, general practitioner's office	McElroy criteria and questionnaire	23
Mueller et al., 2009b	105	Compulsive hoarding	General population	CBS-G	61
Frost et al., 2009	653	Compulsive hoarding	Database of hoarders	CAS-buy > 47.8	61.1
Faber et al., 1995	84	Binge eating disorder	Outpatient treatment	CBS	23.8
Fernandez-Aranda et al., 2006	227	Bulimia nervosa	Inpatients	SCID	17.6
Fernandez-Aranda et al., 2008	709	Lifetime eating disorders	Price Foundation Genetic Study	Self-developed interview	11.8
Specker et al., 1995	40	Pathological gambling	Gamblers choice	MIDI	25
Black & Moyer, 1998	30	Pathological gambling	Advertisements	MIDI	23
Frost et al., 2001	36	Pathological gambling	Advertisements	CAS	16.8
Grant et al., 2003	96	Pathological gambling	Advertisements	MIDI	8.3
Lejoyeux et al., 2008	125	Exercise dependence	Fitness center	Self-developed questionnaire	63

Note: CAS-buy = Compulsive Acquisition Scale buying score; CBS = Compulsive Buying Scale; CBS-G = Compulsive Buying Scale-German version; MIDI = Minnesota Impulsive Disorder Interview; SCID-OCSD = SCID for Obsessive Compulsive Spectrum Disorders.

the most common ICD (9.3 percent). Interestingly only four patients met criteria for a prior ICD without evidence of current symptoms, suggesting that ICDs may become chronic if left untreated. Only 1.5 percent of the inpatients were given a diagnosis for an ICD on admission, suggesting that these disorders frequently go unrecognized. Consequently the presence of ICDs should be regularly assessed in psychiatric patients considering that nearly one-third of the patients reported at least one ICD. Interestingly, patients with co-occurring ICD did not significantly differ from those without ICD in the number or type of other psychiatric disorders; however, this analysis was not done for CB separately.

In a subsequent study Grant, Williams, and Potenza (2007) screened 102 consecutive adolescent inpatients with a mean age of 16 years (range 13–18) with a variety of psychiatric disorders for ICDs. Forty-one patients (40.2 percent) were diagnosed with at least one ICD. In contrast, only one patient was diagnosed with an ICD upon admission. In adults (Grant, Levine, Kim, & Potenza, 2005) CB was the most frequently acknowledged ICD, whereas in adolescents, IED was the most common ICD. One explanation for this difference between adults and adolescents might be that adolescents typically have less access to money for buying. The prevalence of CB in adolescents was 6.9 percent, which is comparable to young adults in community samples (Mueller et al., 2010c).

Depression

Lejoyeux, Tassain, Solomon, and Adès (1997) assessed CB in 119 consecutively admitted depressed inpatients and found a prevalence rate of 32 percent. They also found elevated rates of psychiatric comorbidity, other ICDs such as kleptomania, bulimia nervosa, substance dependence disorders, and a high level of impulsivity in the 38 depressed inpatients with CB, compared to depressed inpatients without CB. The authors observed remission of CB in some patients after improvement of depression, leading them to conclude that CB may serve as compensatory behavior that temporarily alleviates depressive symptoms. This is in line with the finding of McElroy et al. (1994) who also found in a small sample of patients with CB that buying temporarily relieved depressive symptoms. In two subsequent studies the authors confirmed their earlier results and found that 40 percent of 52 depressed inpatients (Lejoyeux, Haberman, Solomon, & Adès, 1999) and 31 percent of 107 depressed inpatients (Lejoyeux, Abaretaz, McLoughlin, & Adès, 2002) met criteria for CB. Again the authors found a significant association between CB, other ICDs, and bulimia nervosa.

Obsessive-Compulsive Disorder

Two studies have investigated the prevalence of CB in patients with OCD (du Toit, van Kradenburg, Niehaus, & Stein, 2001; Lejoyeux, Bailly, Moula,

Loi, & Adès, 2005). Using a newly developed interview to estimate the frequency of putative obsessive-compulsive spectrum disorders (OCSD), du Troit, van Kradenburg, Niehaus, and Stein (2001) reported a lifetime rate of CB of 12.9 percent and of an additional 3.5 percent for subclinical CB in 85 OCD patients. CB and IED were the most common comorbid ICDs.

Lejoyeux et al. (2005) found a CB prevalence rate of 23 percent among 60 patients with OCD identified in a general practice office. The authors included a control group of 60 patients also visiting the general practice setting and found a significantly lower prevalence of 6 percent in the control group, which is comparable to the prevalence rates found in general population samples (Mueller et al., 2010c; Koran, Faber, Aboujaoude, Large, & Serpe, 2006). OCD patients with CB presented with a greater number of OCD symptoms, and a higher prevalence of depression and of alcohol use disorder, compared to OCD patients without CB and controls.

It has been suggested that a range of disorders may belong to the so-called OCSD since they share some common features with OCD, such as age of onset, clinical course, comorbidity, response to treatment, brain circuitry, and familial and genetic factors. The DSM-V Work Group on OCSDs also considered the ICDs for grouping within the OCSD. They concluded that even though there are similarities, the ICDs also differ in many ways from OCD. Consequently it has been suggested that CB be included in a new diagnostic category combining behavioral and substance addictions (Hollander, Kim, Braun, Simeon, & Zohar, 2009; Potenza, Koran, & Pallanti, 2009).

Compulsive Hoarding

The prevalence of CB in samples with compulsive hoarding was investigated in two recent studies (Frost, Tolin, Steketee, Fitch, & Selbo-Bruns, 2009; Mueller et al., 2009b). Frost et al. (2009) recruited 653 individuals with compulsive hoarding from a larger database of those with self-identified hoarding and found a prevalence estimate of CB of 61 percent. The authors also stated that many more reported excessive levels of buying without meeting full criteria. In addition excessive acquiring was associated with more severe hoarding and greater psychopathology. This was especially pronounced in patients who engaged in both CB and the acquisition of free things. Mueller et al. (2009b) identified 105 individuals with compulsive hoarding (4.6 percent) in a representative sample of 2307 individuals from the German population. Among those, 61 percent met criteria for CB. The results of both studies are strikingly similar, even though they investigated different samples, and demonstrated that the majority of those with compulsive hoarding also acquire excessively. Frost, Steketee, and Grisham (2009) suggest that CB or excessive acquisition should be considered a central component of compulsive hoarding, which must be addressed in treatment.

Eating Disorders

Faber, Christenson, de Zwaan, and Mitchell (1995) reported estimates of CB of 24 percent in 85 obese patients with binge eating disorder (BED) and of 11 percent in 113 obese patients without BED.

Fernandez-Aranda and colleagues published two studies exploring ICDs in 227 women with bulimia nervosa (Fernández-Aranda, Jiménez-Murcia, Alvarez-Moya, Granero, Vallejo, & Bulik, 2006) and in a large sample of 709 women with a lifetime eating disorder (Fernández-Aranda, Pinheiro, Thornton, Berrettini, Crow, Fichter et al., 2008). The overall prevalence rates of lifetime ICDs were 33.8 percent and 16.6 percent in the two samples. The most frequently reported ICD was CB in both samples, with rates of 17.6 percent and 11.8 percent, respectively. Individuals with bulimia nervosa and ICD exhibited more extreme personality profiles and more general psychopathology, and more closely resembled a group of 42 pathological gamblers than patients with bulimia nervosa without ICD (Fernández-Aranda et al., 2006). In the second study that included patients as well as familial cases with a history of eating disorders ascertained for a genetic study of eating disorders, the authors found that ICD occurred more often in individuals with binge eating subtypes (21.8 percent) and was associated with more eating-related psychopathology, more patho-logical personality traits, and higher psychiatric comorbidity, especially for OCD and other anxiety disorder, depression, substance use dis-order, cluster B personality disorder, and avoidant personality disorder (Fernández-Aranda et al., 2008). Interestingly the onset of the ICD com-monly preceded the onset of the eating disorder. However, no separate analyses were conducted for patients with CB.

Pathological Gambling

Four studies have examined comorbid ICDs in groups of those with path-ological gambling (Grant & Kim, 2003; Specker, Carlson, Christenson, & Marcotte, 1995; Black & Moyer, 1998; Frost, Meagher, & Riskind, 2001). In all of these studies CB was the most frequently reported ICD, with fre-quencies ranging from 8.3 percent to 25 percent, followed by compulsive sexual behavior. It is likely that CB may be the ICD most similar to patho-logical gambling due to shared characteristics of momentary gratification and monetary exchange. Only Specker, Carlson, Christenson, and Marcotte (1995) included a control group, and found CB in only one central subject (1.6 percent). The presence of another ICD was associated with more severe gambling symptoms and higher rates of comorbid major depression.

Exercise Dependence

Lejoyeux, Avril, Richoux, Embouazza, and Nivoli (2008) investigated the comorbidity of 125 fitness center clients with exercise dependency. The rate of CB was 63 percent compared to 38 percent in 175 nonexercise dependent fitness center clients. In addition, bulimia nervosa appeared to be closely associated with CB in this group. The authors assume that CB and eating disorders share common clinical features in that both are concerned with attractiveness and achievement.

In summary the prevalence of ICDs, and CB in particular, has consistently been shown to be higher in patients with a variety of psychiatric disorders compared to the rates found in control groups or in the general population. Frequently the most commonly reported ICD in different samples was CB. The data also suggests that considerable overlap exists among the various ICDs. In addition it has been repeatedly demonstrated that a comorbid ICD is associated with a greater severity of the primary disorder, greater Axis I and Axis II comorbidity, and poorer prognosis. In summary it is important that clinicians inquire about CB and other ICDs, as their presence may have treatment implications.

Parkinson's Disease and Restless Legs Syndrome

Several authors have identified patients who developed an ICD under dopaminergic treatment (see Table 6.5). Systematic prevalence estimates for common ICDs in treated Parkinson's disease (PD) patients are around 14 percent to 17 percent (Isaias, Siri, Cilia, De Gaspari, Pezzoli, & Antonini, 2008; Evans, Strafella, Weintraub, & Stacy, 2009; Weintraub, Siderowf, Potenza, Goveas, Morales, Duda et al., 2006; Weintraub, Koester, & Potenza, 2008; Weintraub, Hoops, Shea, Lyons, Pahwa, Driver-Dunckley et al., 2009). The prevalence rates of newly developed CB (anytime during the neurological illness) range from 1.5 percent to 10 percent, which is definitely lower than in psychiatric samples and closer to population norms. However, their significance lies in the de novo onset after the initiation of dopamine agonist treatment. It is not unusual for a PD patient to develop multiple ICDs. ICD behaviors appear to be underrecognized in clinical practice. In order to ensure their detection, Weintraub et al. (2009) developed and validated a self-assessment screening instrument for a range of ICDs and other compulsive behaviors that occur in PD (QUIP; Questionnaire for Impulsive-Compulsive Disorders in Parkinson's Disease). There is evidence for a dose response relationship between the dopamine agonist dose and the risk for CB, gambling, and sexual behavior (Lee, Kim, Kim, Cho, Lee, Kim et al., 2010). Other risk factors for the development of ICDs are younger age, longer PD duration, and a history of ICD symptoms prior to development of PD. However, the premorbid rates

Table 6.5 Prevalence (Percent) of New Onset Compulsive Buying Disorder (CBD) in Patients with Parkinson' Disease (PD) and Restless Legs Syndrome (RLS)

Author	Sample Size	Diagnosis	Setting	Assessment Instrument	Prevalence of CBD (%)
Weintraub et al., 2006	272	Parkinson's disease	Movement disorder centers	Screening interview (anytime during PD)	1.5
Weintraub et al., 2008	3,090	Parkinson's disease	Patients	—	6
Isaias et al., 2008	50	Parkinson's disease	Patients on dopamine agonists	MIDI	10
Weintraub et al., 2009	157	Parkinson's disease	Movement disorder centers	QUIP (anytime during PD)	6.4
Lee et al., 2009	1,167	Parkinson's disease	Patients	MIDI	2.5
Pourcher et al., 2009	97	Idiopathic RLS	Patients	Questionnaire followed by interview	3.1

Note: QUIP = Questionnaire for Impulsive-Compulsive Disorders in Parkinson's Disease.

of ICDs in patients with PD before dopamine replacement therapy are not known. Others have speculated that dopaminergic treatment might trigger ICD in individuals with specific impulsivity traits because ICDs were associated with high novelty seeking, impulsivity, and a family history of alcohol use disorder. Full remission or clinically significant reductions in symptomatology are usually observed following discontinuation or decreased dosage of the dopaminergic agents (Mamikonyan, Siderowf, Duda, Potenza, Horn, Stern et al., 2008).

Pourcher, Remillard, and Cohen (2009) studied a group of 97 patients with restless legs syndrome and found a prevalence rate of newly developed ICD of 12.5 percent, with 3.1 percent reporting CB. All patients with ICD received dopaminergic treatment.

Even though there is a clear association between dopamine replacement therapy and the de novo onset of ICDs including CB, the underlying neurobiological mechanisms are not fully understood (Voon, Fernagut, Wickens, Baunez, Rodriguez, Pavon et al., 2009). However, the findings underscore the role of dopaminergic mesolimbic stimulation in the reinforcement process of rewarding behaviors, and this might contribute to our understanding of the pathophysiology of ICDs also in individuals without dopaminergic treatment. However, only a small percentage of patients with

PD and restless legs syndrome develop ICD during dopaminergic treatment, and it is unclear what differentiates patients who develop ICDs from patients who do not develop ICDs even if they receive the same medication.

References

Andrade, L., Caraveo-Anduaga, J.J., Berglund, P., Bijl, R.V., de Graaf, R., Vollebergh, W., Dragomirecka, E., Kohn, R., Keller, M., Kessler, R.C., Kawakami, N., Kiliç, C., Offord, D., Ustun, T.B., & Wittchen, H.U. (2003) The epidemiology of major depressive episodes: results from the International Consortium of Psychiatric Epidemiology (ICPE) surveys, *International Journal of Methods in Psychiatric Research*, 12:3–21.

Black, D.W., Repertinger, S., Gaffney, G.R., & Gabel, J. (1998) Family history and psychiatric comorbidity in persons with compulsive buying: preliminary findings, *American Journal of Psychiatry*, 155:960–3.

Black, D.W. & Moyer, T. (1998) Clinical features and psychiatric comorbidity of subjects with pathological gambling behaviour, *Psychiatric Services*, 49:1434–9.

Christenson, G.A., Faber, R.J., de Zwaan, M., Raymond, N.C., Specker, S.M., Ekern, M.D., Mackenzie, T.B., Crosby, R.D., Crow, S.J., Eckert, E.D., Mussel, M.P., & Mitchell, J.E. (1994) Compulsive buying: descriptive characteristics and psychiatric comorbidity, *Journal of Clinical Psychiatry*, 55:5–11.

DeSarbo, W.S. & Edwards, E.A. (1996) Typologies of compulsive buying behavior: a constrained clusterwise regression approach, *Journal of Consumer Psychology*, 5:231–62.

Du Toit, P.L., van Kradenburg, J., Niehaus, D., & Stein, D.J. (2001) Comparison of obsessive-compulsive disorder patients with and without putative obsessive-compulsive spectrum disorders using a structured clinical interview, *Comprehensive Psychiatry*, 42:291–300.

Evans, A.H., Strafella, A.P., Weintraub, D., & Stacy, M. (2009) Impulsive and compulsive behaviors in Parkinson's disease, *Movement Disorders*, 24:1561–70.

Faber, R., Christensen, G., de Zwaan, M., & Mitchell, J.E. (1995) Two forms of compulsive consumption: comorbidity between compulsive buying and binge eating, *Journal of Consumer Research*, 22:296–304.

Fernández-Aranda, F., Jiménez-Murcia, S., Alvarez-Moya, E.M., Granero, R., Vallejo, J., & Bulik, C.M. (2006) Impulse control disorders in eating disorders: clinical and therapeutic implications, *Comprehensive Psychiatry*, 47:482–8.

Fernández-Aranda, F., Pinheiro, A.P., Thornton, L.M., Berrettini, W.H., Crow, S., Fichter, M.M., Halmi, K.A., Kaplan, A.S., Keel, P., Mitchell, J., Rotondo, A., Strober, M., Woodside, D.B., Kaye, W.H., & Bulik, C.M. (2008) Impulse control disorders in women with eating disorders, *Psychiatry Research*, 157:147–57.

Frost, R.O., Meagher, B.M., & Riskind, J.H. (2001) Obsessive-compulsive features in pathological lottery and scratch-ticket gamblers, *Journal of Gambling Studies*, 17:5–19.

Frost, R.O., Tolin, D.F., Steketee, G., Fitch, K.E., & Selbo-Bruns, A. (2009) Excessive acquisition in hoarding, *Journal of Anxiety Disorders*, 23:632–9.

Frost, R.O., Steketee, G., & Grisham, J. (2004) Measurement of compulsive hoarding: saving inventory-revised, *Behaviour Research and Therapy*, 42:1163–82.

Grant, J.E. & Kim, S.W. (2003) Cormorbidity of impulse control disorders in pathological gamblers, *Acta Psychiatrica Scandinavica*, 108:203–7.

Grant, J.E., Levine, L., Kim, D., & Potenza, M.C. (2005) Impulse control disorders in adult psychiatric inpatients, *American Journal of Psychiatry*, 162:2184–8.

Grant, J.E., Williams, K.A., & Potenza, M.N. (2007) Impulse-control disorders in adolescent psychiatric inpatients: co-occurring disorders and sex differences, *Journal of Clinical Psychiatry*, 68:1584–92.

Hollander, E., Kim, S., Braun, A., Simeon, D., & Zohar J. (2009) Cross-cutting issues and future directions for the OCD spectrum, *Psychiatry Research*, 170:3–6.

Isaias, I.U., Siri, C., Cilia, R., De Gaspari, D., Pezzoli, G., & Antonini, A. (2008) The relationship between impulsivity and impulse control disorders in Parkinson's disease, *Movement Disorders*, 23:411–5.

Kessler, R.C., Coccaro, E.F., Fava, M., Jaeger, S., Jin, R., & Walters, E. (2006) The prevalence and correlates of DSM-IV intermittent explosive disorder in the National Comorbidity Survey Replication, *Archives of General Psychiatry*, 63:669–78.

Koran, L.M., Faber, R.J., Aboujaoude, E., Large, M.D., & Serpe, R.T. (2006) Estimated prevalence of compulsive buying behavior in the United States, *American Journal of Psychiatry*, 163:1806–12.

Lee, J.Y., Kim, J.M., Kim, J.W., Cho, J., Lee, W.Y., Kim, H.J., & Jen, B.S. (2010) Association between the dose of dopaminergic medication and the behavioral disturbances in Parkinson disease, *Parkinsonism and Related Disorders*, 16:202–7.

Lejoyeux, M., Avril, M., Richoux, C., Embouazza, H., & Nivoli, F. (2008) Prevalence of exercise dependence and other behavioral addictions among clients of a Parisian fitness room, *Comprehensive Psychiatry*, 49:353–8.

Lejoyeux, M., Bailly, F., Moula, H., Loi, S., & Adès, J. (2005) Study of compulsive buying in patients presenting obsessive-compulsive disorder, *Comprehensive Psychiatry*, 46:105–10.

Lejoyeux, M., Arbaretaz, M., McLoughlin, M., & Adès, J. (2002) Impulse control disorders and depression, *Journal of Nervous and Mental Diseases*, 190:310–4.

Lejoyeux, M., Haberman, N., Solomon, J., & Adès, J. (1999) Comparison of buying behavior in depressed patients presenting with or without compulsive buying, *Comprehensive Psychiatry*, 40:51–6.

Lejoyeux, M., Tassain, V., Solomon, J., & Adès, J. (1997) Study of compulsive buying in depressed patients, *Journal of Clinical Psychiatry*, 58:169–73.

Mamikonyan, E., Siderowf, A.D., Duda, J.E., Potenza, M.N., Horn, S., Stern, M.B., & Weintraub, D. (2008) Long-term follow-up of impulse control disorders in Parkinson's disease, *Movement Disorders*, 23:75–80.

McElroy, S.L., Keck, P.E., Pope, H.G., Smith, J.M.R., & Strakowski, S.M. (1994) Compulsive buying: a report of 20 cases, *Journal of Clinical Psychiatry*, 55:242–8.

Mitchell, J.E., Burgard, M., Faber, R., Crosby, R.D., & de Zwaan, M. (2006) Cognitive behavioral therapy for compulsive buying disorder, *Behaviour Research and Therapy*, 44:1859–65.

Mitchell, J.E., Redlin, J., Wonderlich, S., Crosby, R., Faber, R., Miltenberger, R., Smyth, J., Stickney, M., Gosnell, B., Burgard, M., & Lancaster, K. (2002) The relationship between compulsive buying and eating disorder, *International Journal of Eating Disorders*, 32:107–11.

Mowen, J.C. & Spears, N. (1999) Understanding compulsive buying among college students: a hierarchical approach, *Journal of Consumer Psychology*, 8:407–30.

Mueller, A., Mitchell, J.E., Black, D.W., Crosby, R.D., Berg, K., & de Zwaan, M. (2010a) Latent profile analysis and comorbidity in a sample of individuals with compulsive buying disorder, *Psychiatry Research*. 778:348–53.

Mueller, A., Claes, L., Mitchell, J.E., Wonderlich, S.A., Crosby, R.D., & de Zwaan, M. (2010b) Personality prototypes in individuals with compulsive buying based on the Big Five Model, *Behaviour Research and Therapy*. (Epub ahead of print.)

Mueller, A., Mitchell, J.E., Crosby, R.D., Gefeller, O., Faber, R.J., Martin, A., Bleich, S., Glaesmer, H., Exner, C., & de Zwaan, M. (2010c) Estimated prevalence of compulsive buying in Germany and its association with sociodemographic characteristics and depressive symptoms, *Psychiatry Research*. (Epub ahead of print.)

Mueller, A., Mühlhans, B., Silbermann, A., Müller, U., Mertens, C., Horbach, T., Mitchell, J.E., & de Zwaan, M. (2009a) Compulsive buying and psychiatric comorbidity, *Psychotherapie, Psychosomatik und Medizinische Psychologie*, 59:291–9.

Mueller, A., Mitchell, J.E., Crosby, R.D., Glaesmer, H., & de Zwaan, M. (2009b) The prevalence of compulsive hoarding and its association with compulsive buying in a German population-based sample, *Behaviour Research and Therapy*, 47:705–9.

Mueller, A., Müller, U., Silbermann, A., Reinecker, H., Bleich, S., Mitchell, J.E., & de Zwaan, M. (2008) A randomized, controlled trial of group cognitive-behavioral therapy for compulsive buying disorder: post-treatment and 6-month follow-up results, *Journal of Clinical Psychiatry*, 69:1131–8.

Mueller, A., Mueller, U., Albert, P., Mertens, C., Silbermann, A., Mitchell, J.E., & de Zwaan, M. (2007) Hoarding in a compulsive buying sample, *Behaviour Research and Therapy*, 45:2754–63.

Ninan, P.T., McElroy, S.L., Kane, C.P., Knight, B.T., Casuto, L.S., Rose, S.E., Marsteller, F.A., & Nemeroff, C.B. (2000) Placebo-controlled study of fluvoxamine in the treatment of patients with compulsive buying, *Journal of Clinical Psychopharmacology*, 20:362–6.

Potenza, M.N., Koran, L.M., & Pallanti, S. (2009) The relationship between impulse-control disorders and obsessive-compulsive disorder: a current understanding and future research directions, *Psychiatry Research*, 170:22–32.

Pourcher, E., Remillard, S., & Cohen, H. (2009) Compulsive habits in restless legs syndrome patients under dopaminergic treatment, *Journal of the Neurological Sciences*, epub ahead of print.

Rose, P. (2007) Mediators of the association between narcissism and compulsive buying: the roles of materialism and impulse control, *Psychology of Addictive Behaviors*, 21:576–81.

Schlosser, S., Black, D.W., Repertinger, S., & Freet, D. (1994) Compulsive buying: demography, phenomenology, and comorbidity in 46 subjects, *General Hospital Psychiatry*, 16:205–12.

Specker, S.M., Carlson, G.A., Christenson, G.A., & Marcotte, M. (1995) Impulse control disorders and attention deficit disorder in pathological gamblers, *Annals of Clinical Psychiatry*, 7:175–9.

Voon, V., Fernagut, P.O., Wickens, J., Baunez, C., Rodriguez, M., Pavon, N., Juncos, J.L., Obeso, J.A., & Bezard, E. (2009) Chronic dopaminergic stimulation in Parkinson's disease: from dyskinesias to impulse control disorders, *Lancet Neurology*, 8:1140–9.

Weintraub, D., Hoops, S., Shea, J.A., Lyons, K.E., Pahwa, R., Driver-Dunckley, E.D., Adler, C.H., Potenza, M.N., Miyasaki, J., Siderowf, A.D., Duda, J.E., Hurtig, H.I., Colcher, A., Horn, S.S., Stern, M.B., & Voon, V. (2009) Validation of the questionnaire for impulsive-compulsive disorders in Parkinson's disease, *Movement Disorders*, 24:1461–7.

Weintraub, D., Koester, J., & Potenza, M.N. (2008) Dopaminergic therapy and impulse control disorders in Parkinson's disease: a cross-sectional study of over 3000 patients. 12th International Congress for Parkinson's Disease and Movement Disorders, Chicago, June 22–26.

Weintraub, D., Siderowf, A.D., Potenza, M.N., Goveas, J., Morales, K.H., Duda, J.E., Moberg, P.J., & Stern, M.B. (2006) Association of dopamine agonist use with impulse control disorders in Parkinson disease, *Archives of Neurology*, 63:969–73.

Zimmermann, M., Rothschild, L., & Chelminski, I. (2005) The prevalence of DSM-IV personality disorders in psychiatric outpatients, *American Journal of Psychiatry*, 162:1911–8.

CHAPTER 7

Personality and Compulsive Buying Disorder

LAURENCE CLAES, PHD AND ASTRID MÜLLER, MD, PHD

Contents

Introduction   105
Clinical Samples   106
Nonclinical Samples   107
Personality Typologies   109
Conclusion   110
References   111

Introduction

According to Black (2007), "compulsive buying (CB) is characterized by excessive shopping cognitions and buying behavior that leads to distress or impairment" (p. 14). The lifetime prevalence of CB was estimated to be 5.8 percent in the American (Koran, Faber, Aboujaoude, Large, & Serpe, 2006) and about 7 percent in the German (Neuner, Raab, & Reisch, 2005; Mueller, Mitchell, Crosby, Gefeller, Faber, Martin et al., in press) general population. Clinical trials suggest that 80 percent to 95 percent of persons seeking treatment for CB are women (Black, 2007). However, population-based studies have not confirmed a gender effect (Koran et al., 2006; Mueller et al., in press).

This chapter will focus on personality pathology in those with CB. "The majority of persons with CB appear to meet criteria for an Axis II disorder, although there is no special shopping personality" (Black, 2007, p. 14). Furthermore several researchers (e.g., Mitchell, Burgard, Faber, Crosby,

& de Zwaan, 2006; Mueller, Mueller, Silbermann, Reinecker, Bleich, Mitchell et al., 2008) have shown that individuals with CB and comorbid personality pathology show a more severe illness course, a greater psychological distress, and lower remission rates.

Given the importance of personality features for the course and treatment of these individuals, this chapter will examine both categorical and dimensional personality features in those with CB. We will systematically describe (1) the comorbidity between CB and personality disorders, (2) the relationship between CB and the Big Five personality traits, (3) the association between CB and self-regulation, and (4) the association between CB and personality prototypes (based on combinations of personality traits). Finally we will try to integrate the aforementioned research findings, discuss their implications for CB treatment, and offer some suggestions for future research.

Clinical Samples

Schlosser, Black, Repertinger, and Freet (1994) assessed 46 individuals with CB (80.4 percent female) for comorbid psychiatric Axis II disorders with the Structured Interview for DSM-III-R Personality Disorders (SIDP; Pfohl, Blum, Zimmerman, & Stangl, 1987) and the Personality Disorder Questionnaire-Revised (PDQ-R; Hyler, Reider, Spitzer, & Williams, 1987). A consensus diagnosis was obtained by combining the results of the two instruments. According to the consensus diagnosis, 59 percent of the subjects with CB met criteria for at least one personality disorder. Those observed included obsessive-compulsive (22 percent), borderline (15 percent), avoidant (15 percent), paranoid (11 percent), histrionic (9 percent), schizotypal (4 percent), passive-aggressive (4 percent), narcissistic (2 percent), and dependent (2 percent) personality disorders.

Mueller, Mühlhans, Silbermann, Mueller, Mertens, Horbach et al. (2009) investigated 30 treatment-seeking women suffering from CB, 30 community controls, and 30 bariatric surgery candidates using the German version of the Structured Clinical Interview for DSM-IV personality disorder diagnoses (SCID-II; Wittchen, Zaudig, & Fydrich, 1997). The CB group presented with the highest rates of personality disorders: 73 percent of patients with CB suffered from at least one personality disorder. Those observed included avoidant (37 percent), depressive (37 percent), obsessive-compulsive (27 percent), borderline (20 percent), paranoid (17 percent), histrionic (13 percent), schizoid (10 percent), dependent (7 percent), narcissistic (7 percent), and antisocial (3 percent) personality disorders.

Based on these studies, we can conclude that at least in clinical samples a significant number of individuals with CB meet DSM criteria for Axis II personality disorders, most frequently for cluster C (particularly obsessive-compulsive, avoidant) or cluster B (particularly borderline) personality disorder.

Nonclinical Samples

Mowen and Spears (1999) investigated the association between the Big Five personality traits and CB in two samples of American university students (N = 304/N = 185) by means of structural equation modeling. CB was measured via the Compulsive Buying Scale developed by Faber and O'Guinn (1989, 1992) and the Big Five personality traits via the Five-Factor Model scale developed by Saucier (1994). The results in both samples showed direct positive paths from neuroticism (emotional instability) and agreeableness toward CB; and a direct negative path from conscientiousness toward CB. Extraversion and openness were not directly related to CB. This means that students with CB are characterized by negative emotions such as anxiety, depression, and anger (neuroticism), value getting along with others (agreeableness), and show a preference toward spontaneous rather than planned behavior (lack of conscientiousness) (Costa & McCrae, 1992).

Verplanken and Harabadi (2001) studied the relationship between impulsive buying and the Big Five personality traits in a sample of 144 Norwegian individuals (51.4 percent females). Impulsive buying was measured by a 20-item questionnaire developed by the authors and the Big Five personality traits were measured by means of the Five-Factor Personality Inventory (FFPI; Hendriks, Hofstee, & De Raad, 1999). The results showed that impulsive buying was positively related to extraversion and negatively related to conscientiousness and autonomy.

Sun, Wu, and Youn (2004) investigated the hierarchical relationships between the Big Five personality traits, impulsive buying and CB by means of structural equation modeling in a sample of 224 American university students. Impulsive buying was defined as the degree to which a person is likely to make unintended, immediate, and unreflective purchases. CB was defined as a DSM disorder characterized by excessive and poorly controlled urges or behaviors with respect to shopping and spending. Impulsive buying was measured by means of the Impulsive Buying Tendency Scale (Fisher & Rook, 1995; Weun, Jones, & Beatty, 1997) and CB by means of the 14-item Compulsive Consumption Scale of Faber and O'Guinn (1989). The Big Five personality traits were assessed by means of the 40-item Big Five Personality Scale developed by Saucier (1994). The results showed a positive association between impulsive buying and CB (path coefficient = .59). Neuroticism (emotional instability) showed direct positive paths toward both impulsive and CB. Extraversion and openness were only directly positively related to impulsive buying but not to CB. Finally conscientiousness and agreeableness did not show significant relationships with impulsive and CB. This means that both impulsive and CB are characterized by high levels of neuroticism, which is the tendency to be emotionally reactive and vulnerable to stress. Further, impulsive buying is related to high levels of extraversion (the tendency to seek stimulation and company of others) and high levels of openness (the tendency to appreciate art, adventure, unusual ideas, and a variety of experience) (Costa & McCrae, 1992).

Wang and Yang (2008) investigated the relationships between the Big Five personality traits and CB in a sample of 403 Taiwanese university students (73.7 percent female). CB was assessed by means of an adapted version of Faber and O'Guinn's (1992) Compulsive Buying Scale and the Big Five personality traits by means of Gomez's (2006) 25-item personality traits scale. Comparison of the mean scores on the Big Five personality traits showed that the CB group scored significantly lower on conscientiousness compared to the non-CB group, confirming a negative relationship between CB and conscientiousness. Neuroticism, extraversion, openness, and agreeableness did not differentiate students with and without CB behaviors.

Billieux, Rochat, Rebetez, and Van der Linden (2008) investigated the role of the various components of impulsivity in CB in a sample of 150 (50.7 percent female) undergraduates of the University of Geneva. The French version of the Urgency, Premeditation (lack of), Perseverance (lack of), and Sensation Seeking Impulsive Behavior Scale (UPPS) of Whiteside and Lynam (2001; French version: Van der Linden, d'Acremont, Zermatten, Jermann, Laroi, Willems et al., 2006) was used to assess four different facets of impulsivity: urgency, sensation seeking, (lack of) premeditation, and (lack of) perseverance. CB was assessed by means of the French Questionnaire on Buying Behavior (Lejoyeux, Tassain, Solomon, & Adès, 1997), measuring basic features of CB. The results showed that CB was significantly positively correlated with urgency (tendency to react impulsively under negative affect), lack of perseverance (tendency to get unattended when tasks are boring), and lack of premeditation (tendency to act without thinking). However, CB was not significantly related to sensation seeking (tendency to pursue activities that are exciting). The results of a regression analysis showed that only urgency remained a significant predictor of CB after controlling for gender, age, educational level, and depression. Whiteside and Lynam (2001) based their four impulsivity-related traits on Five Factor Model personality traits: urgency (neuroticism–impulsivity facet), sensation seeking (extraversion–excitement seeking facet), lack of perseverance (conscientiousness-lack of self-discipline facet), and finally, lack of premeditation (conscientiousness-lack of deliberation) (see also in Claes, Vandereycken, & Vertommen, 2005). Therefore we can indirectly conclude that CB was positively related to neuroticism and negatively to conscientiousness and unrelated to extraversion.

Summarizing the results of the aforementioned studies on the relationship between the Big Five personality traits and impulsive/compulsive buying in nonclinical student samples, we can conclude that (1) impulsive buying (to buy on impulse without reflection) is related to extraversion (positive affectivity, sensation seeking; Nigg, 2006), (2) CB is related to neuroticism (emotional instability, negative affect; Nigg, 2006), and (3) both impulsive and CB are related to a lack of conscientiousness (lack of self-regulation or effortful control; Nigg, 2006).

Rose (2007) tested the association between narcissism, materialism, impulse control, and CB in a sample of 238 students (62.2 percent females) at a large Midwestern university. Narcissism was measured by means of the Narcissistic Personality Inventory (NPI; Raskin & Terry, 1988), materialism by means of the Material Values Scale (Richins, 2004), impulse control by means of Goldberg's (1999) 11-item measure from the International Personality Item Pool, and CB by means of the Compulsive Buying Scale (Faber & O'Guinn, 1992). The results showed positive associations between narcissism, materialism, and CB; and impulse control was negatively related to the other variables. Furthermore the results showed that materialism and impulse control mediated the relationship between narcissism and CB; narcissistic persons with high levels of materialism and low levels of impulse control (or low self-regulation) had a higher probability to develop CB.

In three experimental designs, Vohs and Faber (2007) investigated the impact of the depletion of self-regulatory resources (Baumeister & Heatherton, 1996) on impulsive spending responses in American undergraduate students. They found that students whose self-regulatory resources were depleted felt stronger urges to buy, were willing to spend more, and did spend more money in buying situations. Vohs and Faber did not find significant differences in buying between those with impulsive and nonimpulsive buying when their self-regulation was intact. However, after a loss of self-regulatory resources (experimentally induced), those with CB had more problems to control their spending behavior than nonimpulsive buyers.

In the same way, as described at the end of the previous paragraph, the lack of self-regulation or effortful control seems a crucial factor in the presence of CB. Lack of self-regulation/effortful control (low conscientiousness) seems to mediate the relationship between reactive personality traits (e.g., neuroticism) and CB. The results of Vohs and Faber (2007) suggest that only in the absence of effortful control/self-regulation reactive temperamental personality features (e.g., neuroticism) provoke problematic buying behaviors.

Personality Typologies

Finally DeSarbo and Edwards (1996) theoretically differentiated between those with impulsive buying (i.e., unplanned purchasing) and those with CB. They hypothesized that those with impulsive buying are driven by an external trigger (e.g., a product on the shelf) to make a purchase, whereas individuals with CB are motivated by an internal trigger (e.g., anxiety) from which buying is an escape. Although CB may also be driven by impulsiveness, the primary function of CB might be relief from tension. To test their typology theory, they investigated 104 subjects with CB (82 percent female) and 101 normal controls (64 percent female) by means of measures of dispositional (e.g., anxiety, perfectionism, impulsiveness, sensation seeking) and circumstantial (family environment, learned consumption behaviors) factors related to CB. The cluster analysis revealed two clusters. Those in cluster one, the internal CB group (driven by psychological problems), were characterized by impulsiveness, low self-esteem, dependence, and anxiety, whereas those in cluster two, the external CB group (driven by personal circumstances), were characterized by materialism, coping, isolation, denial, and impulsiveness. These findings confirm that those with CB may take alternative routes to their buying behavior. However, impulsiveness was related to both clusters, confirming the idea that lack of impulse control (self-regulation) is common to different subtypes of CB.

Mueller, Claes, Mitchell, Wonderlich, Crosby, and de Zwaan (in press) investigated personality prototypes based on the Big Five factor model in a treatment-seeking sample of 68 individuals with CB. Cluster analysis of the NEO Five-Factor Inventory (NEO-FFI) scales yielded two distinct personality clusters. On the German version of the NEO-FFI (Borkenau & Ostendorf, 1993), participants in cluster two scored significantly higher than those in cluster one on neuroticism and lower on the other four personality traits. Subjects in cluster two reported more severe CB cognitions and behaviors, and were more anxious, interpersonally sensitive, and impulsive than the subjects in cluster one. Furthermore those in cluster two were characterized by higher rates of comorbid anxiety disorders and cluster B personality disorders. The two personality prototypes did not differ with respect to obsessive-compulsive features. Finally those in cluster two reported lower remission rates immediately after a 12-week cognitive behavioral therapy and at 6-month follow-up. Thus patients with higher levels of neuroticism/anxiety and lower levels of conscientiousness (lack of effortful control) seem to have more difficulty in overcoming their CB.

Conclusion

Based on the studies that investigated the relationship between personality and buying behavior we can conclude that (1) impulsive buying (buying without reflection) is positively related to extraversion, (2) CB is positively related to neuroticism, and (3) both impulsive and compulsive buying are related to lack of conscientiousness, lack of self-regulation, or lack of effortful control. Furthermore the study of Vohs and Faber (2007) also suggested that particular personality traits could only trigger pathological buying behavior in the absence of or depletion of self-regulation or effortful control (but not when self-regulation was present). Therefore further research should investigate whether the lack of self-regulation or effortful control moderates/mediates the relationship between reactive personality features (neuroticism, extraversion) and pathological buying. Claes, Vertommen, Smits, and Bijttebier (2009), for example, showed in a sample of 89 Flemish psychiatric inpatients and 162 normal controls that neuroticism and extraversion were only related to, respectively, cluster C and B personality disorders in the absence of effortful control/self-regulation. Thus self-regulation moderated the relationship between personality traits and personality disorders. Ongoing research of Claes and Mueller also focuses on the possible moderating/mediating role of self-regulation/effortful control between reactive personality features (e.g., neuroticism, extraversion) and CB.

As the results of the present review suggest, it appears that CB is driven by neuroticism (anxiety, negative affectivity) and the absence of self-regulation/effortful control or conscientiousness. Therefore treatment of CB certainly needs to include training of self-regulation or effortful control to teach these patients how to deal with their negative affectivity in a way other than CB. Furthermore training in effortful control can also be generalized to deal with other impulsive behaviors (e.g., binge eating, personality disorders) that often go together with CB.

Since most of the studies were conducted in college students or normal consumers, the generalizability of those results is limited. In our opinion there is a strong need for larger studies on individuals with diagnosed CB. Furthermore more effort should be done to collect data from males with CB.

References

Baumeister, R.F. & Heatherton, T.F. (1996) Self-regulation failure: An overview, *Psychological Inquiry*, 7:1–15.

Billieux, J., Rochat, L., Rebetez, M.M.L., & Van der Linden, M. (2008) Are all facets of impulsivity related to self-reported compulsive buying behavior? *Personality and Individual Differences*, 44:1432–42.

Black, D.W. (2007) A review of compulsive buying disorder, *World Psychiatry*, 6:14–8.

Borkenau, P. & Ostendorf, F. (1993) *NEO-Fünf-Faktoren-Inventar*, Göttingen, Germany: Hogrefe.

Claes, L., Vandereycken, W., & Vertommen, H. (2005) Impulsivity-related traits in eating disorder patients, *Personality and Individual Differences*, 39:739–49.

Claes, L., Vertommen, S., Smits, D., & Bijttebier, P. (2009) Emotional reactivity and self-regulation in relation to personality disorders, *Personality and Individual Differences*, 47:948–53.

Costa, P.T. Jr. & McCrae, R.R. (1992) *Revised NEO Personality Inventory (NEO-PI-R) and NEO Five-Factor Inventory (NEO-FFI) Manual*, Odessa, FL: Psychological Assessment Resources.

DeSarbo, W.S. & Edwards, E.A. (1996) Typologies of compulsive buying behavior: A constrained clusterwise regression approach, *Journal of Consumer Psychology*, 5:231–62.

Faber, R.J. & O'Guinn, T.C. (1989) Classifying compulsive consumers: Advances in the development of a diagnostic tool, in T.K. Srull (ed.), *Advances in Consumer Research*, Provo, UT: Association for Consumer Research, 738–744.

Faber, R.J. & O'Guinn, T.C. (1992) A clinical screener for compulsive buying, *Journal of Consumer Research*, 19:459–69.

Fisher, R. & Rook, D. (1995) Normative influences on impulsive buying behavior, *Journal of Consumer Research*, 22:305–14.

Goldberg, L. R. (1999) A broad-bandwidth, public-domain, personality inventory measuring the lower-level facets of several five-factor models, in I. Mervielde, I. Deary, F. De Fruyt, & F. Ostendorf (eds.), *Personality Psychology in Europe*, Tilburg, The Netherlands: Tilburg University Press, 7–28.

Gomez, R. (2006) Gender invariance of the Five-Factor Model of personality among adolescents: A mean and covariance structure analysis approach, *Personality and Individual Differences*, 41:755–65.

Hendriks, A.A.J., Hofstee, W.K.B., & De Raad, B. (1999) The Five-Factor Personality Inventory (FFPI), *Personality and Individual Differences*, 27:307–25.

Hyler, S.E., Reider, R.O., Spitzer, R.L., & Williams, J.B. (1987) *Personality Diagnostic Questionnaire—Revised*, New York: New York State Psychiatric Institute.

Koran, L.M., Faber, R.J., Aboujaoude, E., Large, M.D., & Serpe, R.T. (2006) Estimated prevalence of compulsive buying behavior in the United States, *The American Journal of Psychiatry*, 163:1806–12.

Lejoyeux, M., Tassain, V., Solomon, J., & Adès, J. (1997) Study of compulsive buying in depressed patients, *Journal of Clinical Psychiatry*, 58:169–73.

Mitchell, J.E., Burgard, M., Faber, R., Crosby, R.D., & de Zwaan, M. (2006) Cognitive behavioral therapy for compulsive buying disorder, *Behaviour Research and Therapy*, 44:1859–65.

Mowen, J.C. & Spears, N. (1999) Understanding compulsive buying among college students: A hierarchical approach, *Journal of Consumer Psychology*, 8:407–30.

Mueller, A., Claes, L., Mitchell, J.E., Wonderlich, S.A., Crosby, R.D., & de Zwaan, M. (in press) Personality prototypes in individuals with compulsive buying based on the Big Five Model. *Behaviour Research and Therapy*.

Mueller, A., Mitchell, J.E., Crosby, R.D., Gefeller, O., Faber, R.J., Martin, A., Bleich, S., Glaesmer, H., Exner, C., & de Zwaan, M. (in press) Estimated prevalence of compulsive buying in Germany and its association with sociodemographic characteristics and depressive symptoms, *Psychiatry Research*.

Mueller, A., Mueller, U., Silbermann, A., Reinecker, H., Bleich, S., Mitchell, J.E., & de Zwaan, M. (2008) A randomized, controlled trial of group cognitive behavioral therapy for compulsive buying disorder: Post-treatment and 6-month follow-up results, *Journal of Clinical Psychiatry*, 67:1131–8.

Mueller, A., Mühlhans, B., Silbermann, A., Mueller, U., Mertens, C., Horbach, T., Michell, J.E., & de Zwaan, M. (2009) Compulsive buying and psychiatric comorbidity, *Psychotherapie Psychosomatik Medizinische Psychologie*, 59:291–9.

Neuner, M., Raab, G. & Reisch, L. (2005) Compulsive buying in maturing consumer societies: An empirical re-inquiry, *Journal of Economic Psychology*, 26:509–22.

Nigg, J.T. (2006) Temperament and developmental psychopathology, *Journal of Child Psychology and Psychiatry*, 47:395–422.

Pfohl, B., Blum, N., Zimmerman, M., & Stangl, D. (1987) *Structured Interview for DSM-III Personality Disorders—Revised*, Iowa City, IA: Department of Psychiatry, University of Iowa.

Raskin, R. & Terry, H. (1988) A principal-components analysis of the Narcissistic Personality Inventory and further evidence of its construct validity, *Journal of Personality and Social Psychology*, 54:890–902.

Richins, M.L. (2004) The Material Values Scale: A re-inquiry into its measurement properties and the development of a short form, *Journal of Consumer Research*, 19:303–16.

Rose, P. (2007) Mediators of the association between narcissism and compulsive buying: The role of materialism and impulse control, *Psychology of Addictive Behaviors*, 21:576–81.

Saucier, G. (1994) Mini-markers: A brief version of Goldberg's unipolar big-five markers, *Journal of Personality Assessment*, 63:506–16.

Schlosser, S., Black, D.W., Repertinger, S., & Freet, D. (1994) Compulsive buying: Demography, phenomenology, and comorbidity in 46 subjects, *General Hospital Psychiatry*, 16:205–12.

Sun, T., Wu, G., & Youn, S. (2004) Psychological antecedents of impulsive and compulsive buying: A hierarchical perspective, in A. Cheema, & J. Srivastava (eds.), *The Proceedings of the Society for Consumer Psychology 2004 Winter Conference*, San Francisco, CA: Society of Consumer Psychology, 168–174.

Van der Linden, M., d'Acremont, M., Zermatten, A., Jermann, F., Laroi, F., Willems, S., et al. (2006) A French adaptation of the UPPS Impulsive Behavior Scale: Confirmatory factor analysis in a sample of undergraduate students, *European Journal of Psychological Assessment*, 22:38–42.

Verplanken, B. & Harabadi, A. (2001) Individual differences in impulse buying tendency: Feeling and no thinking, *European Journal of Personality*, 13:307–26.

Vohs, K.D. & Faber, R.J. (2007) Spent resources: Self-regulatory resource availability affects impulsive buying, *Journal of Consumer Research*, 33:537–47.

Wang, C.C. & Yang, H.W. (2008) Passion for online shopping: The influence of personality and compulsive buying, *Social Behavior and Personality*, 36:693–706.

Whiteside, S.P. & Lynam, D.R. (2001) The Five Factor Model and impulsivity: Using a structural model of personality to understand impulsivity, *Personality and Individual Differences*, 30:669–89.

Wittchen, H.U., Zaudig, M., & Fydrich, T. (1997) *Strukturiertes Klinisches Interview für DSM-IV Achse I und II*, Göttingen: Hogrefe.

Weun, S., Jones, M.A., & Beatty, S.E. (1997) A parsimonious scale to measure impulsive buying tendency, in W.M. Pride & G.T. Hult (eds.), *AMA Educators' Proceedings: Enhancing Knowledge Development in Marketing*, Chicago: American Marketing Association, 306–7.

CHAPTER **8**

Hoarding and Compulsive Buying

ASTRID MÜLLER, MD, PHD AND RANDY O. FROST, PHD

Contents

Introduction   115
Hoarding   116
Hoarding and Compulsive Buying   118
Clinical Implications   120
Treating Excessive Acquisition in Hoarding   121
Conclusion   123
References   124

Introduction

Compulsive hoarding is a potentially disabling condition that has been defined as "(1) the acquisition of, and failure to discard a large number of possessions; (2) living spaces sufficiently cluttered so as to preclude activities for which those spaces were designed; and (3) significant distress or impairment in functioning caused by the hoarding" (Frost & Hartl, 1996, p. 341). Individuals who compulsively hoard accumulate a large number of items at their home and/or workplace and keep them in a disorganized manner. They are unable to resist strong urges to collect excessively, to buy compulsively, or to acquire free things. In addition they are reluctant to get rid of possessions, even those with very limited utility or monetary value, because of erroneous beliefs about responsibility, remarkable emotional attachment, and the need to control their possessions (Steketee & Frost, 2003). Individuals with compulsive hoarding feel intense discomfort and anxiety when a stranger touches, moves, or alters possessions without explicit permission and feel as if they had lost control over their environment when they are pressured to get rid of possessions that appear to be useless (Frost, Hartl, Christian, & Williams, 1995; Grisham, Frost, Steketee, Kim, Tarkoff, & Hood, 2009).

Hoarding

Remarkably little attention has been paid to hoarding as a form of psychopathology, but recent research has identified it as a significant public health problem. A survey of health departments found hoarding behaviors to seriously jeopardize the health of the individual and the community (Frost, Steketee, & Williams, 2000). In 6 percent of cases of hoarding investigated by health departments, the hoarding led directly to the person's death from a house fire. Most investigated cases involved unsanitary conditions, significant fire hazards, inhibited access to furniture as well as compromised ability to move throughout the home, maintain proper hygiene, and even prepare food. In addition complaints to health departments typically involved more than one agency and often result in significant costs to the community.

Hoarding poses significant economic and social burden as well. In a large survey of people who self-identified with significant hoarding problems, Tolin, Frost, Steketee, Gray, and Fitch (2008) found greater work impairment among those who hoard than among individuals with anxiety, depression, or substance use. Severity of hoarding was associated with a broad range of chronic and serious medical problems, and a fivefold higher rate of mental health service utilization for problems other than hoarding. Hoarding led to eviction or the threat of eviction in a large percentage (8 percent to 12 percent) of these cases. Hoarding has been identified by other researchers as frequent among the homeless, and in many cases the hoarding directly contributed to their becoming homeless (Mataix-Cols, Grayton, Bonner, Luscombe, Taylor, & van den Bree, submitted). Family members of people with serious hoarding problems experience increased family strain and hold hostile and rejecting attitudes toward the hoarding family member (Tolin, Frost, Steketee, & Fitch, 2008). High levels of disability, depression, and social impairment have been found among hoarding patients as well (Frost, Steketee, Williams, & Warren, 2000; Samuels, Bienvenu, Riddle, Cullen, Grados, Liang et al., 2002).

A standardized questionnaire has been developed to measure hoarding symptoms. The Saving Inventory-Revised (SI-R) is a 23-item self-report questionnaire with three subscales: acquisition problems, difficulty discarding, and clutter (Frost, Steketee, & Grisham, 2004). The subscales are reliable and valid, and evidence suggests that they reflect real and meaningful phenomena related to hoarding. In addition, each of the subscales is sensitive to changes during treatment (Tolin, Frost, & Steketee, 2007).

Using a Likert-type scale from zero to four, typical SI-R total scores for people with compulsive hoarding are 50 points and higher with an average of 62 (Steketee & Frost, 2007).

An interview-based assessment for hoarding has also been developed. The Hoarding Rating Scale-Interview (HRS-I) is a five-question semi-structured interview assessing acquisition problems, difficulty discarding, clutter, distress, and impairment (Tolin, Frost, & Steketee, in press). Each question is rated by the interviewer on a nine-point scale (zero–eight). It has been found to be a reliable and valid measure of hoarding. Preliminary analyses from a controlled trial of cognitive behavior therapy for hoarding suggest that the HRS-I is sensitive to changes during treatment as well (Steketee, Frost, Tolin, Rasmussen, & Brown, 2010). Receiver Operating Characteristic (ROC) curves suggest that scores of 14 and above represent clinically significant hoarding. A self-report version of the HRS (HRS-SR) also appears to be reliable and valid (Tolin, Frost, & Steketee, 2007).

In addition to self-report and interview-based assessment, an observational measure has been developed as well (Clutter Image Rating [CIR]; Frost, Steketee, Tolin, & Renaud, 2008). The CIR contains nine photographs reflecting a room with no clutter to one nearly full. A series of such photographs are included for each of the three main rooms in most people's homes: living room, kitchen, and bedroom. Like the other assessment devices, the CIR has been found to be both reliable and valid as a measure of clutter (Frost, Steketee, Tolin, & Renaud, 2008; Tolin, Frost, & Steketee, 2007).

Hoarding appears in the DSM-IV (APA, 2004) only as a feature of obsessive-compulsive personality disorder (OCPD; "unable to discard worn-out or worthless objects even when they have no sentimental value," p. 729). This definition contradicts recent theory and research since many hoarding people display an excessive attachment to possessions. Indeed the hoarded items are of sentimental or safety signal value for them (Frost, Hartl, Christian, & Williams, 1995; Grisham et al., 2009). Furthermore research confirmed the poor psychometric properties of the OCPD hoarding criterion (Hummelen, Wilberg, Pedersen, & Karterud, 2008).

Since compulsive hoarding is frequently observed in individuals with obsessive-compulsive disorder (OCD; Steketee & Frost, 2003), it also has been considered as a subtype of OCD (Frost, Krause, & Steketee, 1996; Samuels et al., 2002; Steketee & Frost, 2003; Wheaton, Cromer, LaSalle-Ricci, & Murphy, 2008). However, compulsive hoarding correlates only weakly with other OCD symptoms (Wu & Watson, 2005; Abramowitz, Wheaton, & Storch, 2008) and seems not to have a dimensional structure such as washing, checking, obsessing, neutralizing, and ordering (Olatunji, Williams, Haslam, Abramowitz, & Tolin, 2008). In addition some researchers suggested unique genetic and neurobiological features for compulsive hoarding compared to OCD (Saxena, 2007). There is an ongoing discussion about the correct classification of compulsive hoarding, and some authors suggest renaming it "hoarding disorder" and separating it from OCD (Mataix-Cols, Frost, Pertusa, Clark, Saxena, Leckman et al., 2010; Rachman, Elliott, Shafran, & Radomsky, 2009).

Compulsive hoarding seems to be prevalent in the community. Samuels, Bienvenu, Grados, Cullen, Riddle, Liang, and colleagues (2008) estimated the prevalence of compulsive hoarding in 742 participants in the Hopkins Epidemiology of Personality Disorder Study to be nearly 4 percent (5.3 percent, weighted). Mueller, Mitchell, Crosby, Glaesmer, and de Zwaan (2009) examined the point prevalence of compulsive hoarding in a nationally representative sample of the German population (N = 2307) and reported an estimated prevalence rate of 4.6 percent. In the UK, Ierolino, Perroud, Fullana, Guipponi, Cherkas, Collier et al. (2009) reported a prevalence rate of 2.3 percent, while Fullana, Vilagut, Rojas-Farreras, Mataix-Cols, de Graaf, Demyttenaere et al. (2010) reported a European cross-national rate of 2.6 percent.

Hoarding and Compulsive Buying

The excessive acquisition in hoarding involves the collecting of a large number of free objects; e.g., advertisements, newspapers, giveaways, empty plastic bottles, or rubbish. Many such objects would be considered worthless, or at least too numerous to be of reasonable worth, except by the person collecting them. Another form is the uncontrolled excessive buying of items that are not needed and not adequately used after the purchase (Frost, Steketee, & Williams, 2002). This second form of excessive acquisition fulfills the diagnostic criteria for compulsive buying behavior.

Several studies provide evidence that compulsive buying (CB) is associated with compulsive hoarding. Compared to nonhoarding subjects, those self-identified as engaging in hoarding tend to buy more extra items in order not to be caught without a needed thing (Frost & Gross, 1993), and CB is more prominent among people who hoard (Frost, Kim, Morris, Bloss, Murray-Close, & Steketee, 1998). Among a large sample of people with significant hoarding problems (n = 653), 61 percent met diagnostic criteria for CB and a large number (74 percent) reported excessive levels of buying (at least one standard deviation above the mean of community controls). Interestingly 50 percent of hoarders with excessive buying also excessively collected free things.

In CB samples the evidence suggests that people with CB are more likely to save and hoard than those who do not buy compulsively. Frost, Steketee, and Williams (2002) found higher hoarding scores in people meeting criteria for CB (n = 75) than among community controls (n = 85). Strong and significant correlations between hoarding and several measures of CB were also found. Kyrios, Frost, and Steketee (2004) examined symptomatic and cognitive correlates of both compulsive hoarding and buying in the same sample. Those with CB showed maladaptive attachment patterns, erroneous beliefs about the uniqueness of desired items, and decision-making deficits similar to those observed in compulsive hoarding. In our own clinical experience a subset of people who compulsively buy is indeed attached to the purchased items, derives security from purchased things, and experiences fears about losing an opportunity to purchase particular objects.

It should be noted, however, that not all individuals with CB also suffer from compulsive hoarding. For instance, the examination of 66 patients with CB prior to entering a disorder-specific group therapy for CB showed that approximately half of the patients endorsed elevated levels of compulsive hoarding (Mueller, Mueller, Albert, Mertens, Silbermann, Mitchell, & de Zwaan, 2007). Furthermore those with comorbid compulsive hoarding displayed a higher severity of CB symptoms, more psychological distress, more obsessive-compulsive traits, and higher psychiatric comorbidity, especially any current affective, anxiety, and eating disorder. Of interest at least 25 percent did not endorse clinical relevant hoarding symptoms. These results supported the assumption that many but not all individuals with CB are also suffering from compulsive hoarding (Mueller et al., 2007).

Recently the association between CB and compulsive hoarding was confirmed through the investigation of the large German representative sample mentioned above. In this study participants were asked to answer both the Compulsive Buying Scale (CBS; Faber & O'Guinn, 1992) and the German version (Mueller, Crosby, Frost, Bleich, Glaesmer, Osen et al., 2009) of the SI-R (Frost et al., 2004). Both measures were significantly correlated ($r = 0.538$, $p < 0.001$). Thirty-nine percent of the participants with CB also reported clinically relevant compulsive hoarding symptoms. On the other hand, 61 percent of those with compulsive hoarding also reported CB, matching the figure reported by Frost, Tolin, Steketee, Fitch, Selbo-Bruns et al. (2009; see Figure 8.1).

61% (64 of 105) of those with compulsive hoarding   39% (64 of 167) of those with compulsive buying

Figure 8.1 Overlap between compulsive buying and compulsive hoarding in a representative German sample (n = 2307).

Clinical Implications

Those with CB with comorbid compulsive hoarding display greater severity of CB symptoms, more psychological distress, more obsessive-compulsive symptoms, and higher psychiatric comorbidity, especially any current affective, anxiety, and eating disorder (Frost, Steketee, & Williams, 2002; Mueller et al., 2007). Consequently treatment for those with CB who are comorbid for compulsive hoarding may be more difficult. Results of a psychotherapy study in individuals with CB indicated that higher pretreatment hoarding traits as measured with the SI-R (Frost et al., 2004) were significant predictors for poorer outcome (Mueller, Mueller, Silbermann, Reinecker, Bleich, Mitchell, & de Zwaan, 2008). These data ought to be considered when treating CB. Assessing clients' hoarding symptoms is important for treatment planning. Failing to do so can negatively affect the therapy. In our experience patients experience considerable shame regarding the cluttered or even squalid conditions in their home and are uncomfortable reporting them. However, hoarding assessment strategies (e.g., SI-R, HRS) have good discriminating characteristics and have shown little tendency to be influenced by social desirability (Frost et al., 2004; Tolin et al., in press).

The standard exposure-based cognitive behavior therapy designed for obsessive compulsive disorder has not fared well in the treatment of hoarding. Numerous case reports and case series describe treatment failures for compulsive hoarding (Christensen & Greist, 2001; Greenberg, 1987; Savoie, 2008; Seedat & Stein, 2002; Shafran & Tallis, 2006; Winsberg, Cassic, & Koran, 1999). Chief among the reasons cited for these failures was lack of motivation and compliance with treatment requirements (Christensen & Greist, 2001).

In other treatment studies the presence of hoarding has predicted treatment failure. Mataix-Cols, Marks, Greist, Kobak, and Baer (2002) found that high scores on the hoarding factor of the Yale-Brown Obsessive-Compulsive Scale (YBOCS) significantly predicted dropout independent of initial severity. While only 12 percent of OCD patients without hoarding discontinued prematurely, 27 percent of the hoarding patients did so. Only 25 percent of those with hoarding responded to treatment, while 50 percent of those without hoarding did so. Rufer, Fricke, Moritz, Kloss, and Hand (2006) found that hoarding patients were less likely to respond to treatment than OCD patients without hoarding (36.8 percent versus 62.7 percent). Furthermore among the predictors examined, only endorsement of hoarding on the YBOCS significantly predicted poor treatment response after controlling for baseline severity and concurrent medication.

Abramowitz, Franklin, Schwartz, and Furr (2003) compared the treatment outcomes for standard cognitive behavioral therapy (CBT) across five OCD symptom subtypes. While there were no differences among the clusters at pretest, at posttest the hoarding cluster patients had significantly higher YBOCS severity scores than did patients in the harming, contamination, and unacceptable thoughts clusters. A significantly smaller percentage of hoarding patients (31 percent) met stringent criteria for clinically significant change than for patients in each of the other clusters (from 46 percent to 76 percent) (Abramowitz et al., 2003). Since the later range corresponded with reports about the efficacy of exposure and response prevention (ERP) for OCD (62 percent clinically significant change), it would appear that hoarding does not respond well to ERP (Lindsey, Crino, & Andrews, 1997).

Treating Excessive Acquisition in Hoarding

Recent research has focused on creating a treatment for hoarding that is based on the cognitive behavioral model of hoarding (Frost & Hartl, 1996) and targets each of the three manifestations of the problem: clutter, difficulty discarding, and acquisition (Steketee & Frost, 2007). Initial research has indicated that this treatment shows considerable promise as a treatment for hoarding (Hartl & Frost, 1999; Tolin, Frost, & Steketee, 2007; Steketee, Frost, Tolin, Rasmussen, & Brown, 2010). Since excessive acquisition is a major component of hoarding, much of the treatment focuses on gaining control over it (Steketee & Frost, 2007). While some patients who hoard will deny any excessive acquisition, it is imperative that the clinician conduct a thorough investigation of their buying or collecting habits. We have seen patients who claim not to have problems with buying experience severe buying episodes later in treatment when they stop avoiding situations where buying is a problem for them.

Before beginning treatment for CB in hoarding cases it is important to understand the antecedents and consequences of behaviors associated with a buying episode. A functional analysis of moment-to-moment events, emotions, and behaviors usually reveals a sequence of events that begin with an emotional mood state, frequently tied to personal relationships or circumstances. Although this mood state is most often negative (e.g., depression), it is not uncommon for the background mood state to be positive. For instance, one of our patients had a CB episode immediately following an uplifting treatment session that left her in a very good mood. Understanding what kinds of moods are associated with buying episodes is crucial to establishing control over them.

The next part of a typical CB episode involves some kind of trigger or cue for buying. This can include simply driving by a store or even imagining a purchase or object available for purchase. People with CB can sometimes control their buying episodes temporarily by avoiding these cues. We have seen patients who avoid whole sections of town because even driving near a store will trigger a buying episode. While such avoidance may work in the short run, it is not an effective long-term strategy. Buying cues are ubiquitous in current culture, and avoiding them is virtually impossible.

Once exposed to the buying cue, those with CB typically enter what can look like a dissociative state in which their focus of attention is solely on items to be purchased. Anything and everything else in their life is temporarily forgotten (e.g., depressed moods, financial debts, cluttered rooms, etc.). The images produced by these items and their potential acquisition lead to feelings of joy, agency, influence, accomplishment, and even a sense of identity. Any thoughts of not acquiring, if they happen at all, are accompanied by distress and dysphoria and are quickly ignored. Purchasing invariably follows.

Not long after the purchase, however, regret develops and along with it self-criticism that can exacerbate depression that accompanies CB for many clients. For those with CB who do not hoard return of some or all of the items can alleviate some of the problem. However, those with CB who hoard typically become attached to and cannot bring themselves to return the purchased items. Excessive purchases contribute to their growing clutter.

Understanding how such an episode works is crucial for determining how and where to intervene. Among people who hoard we intervene at three points in this process (Steketee & Frost, 2007). The first intervention point is at the cues for buying. It is critical that patients learn to tolerate the urges they experience when exposed to a buying trigger without giving in to them. To do this we ask clients to generate a hierarchy of buying cues from weakest to strongest. Next we implement an exposure and response prevention paradigm by gradually exposing them to increasingly stronger buying cues. The therapist accompanies them on the first of these until they can do them on their own. Similar to a physical conditioning paradigm, we are building their stamina for tolerating the urge to buy and the discomfort that accompanies not buying.

The second intervention point occurs during the dissociative-like state experienced at the sight of a desired object. These states increase buying by blocking any thoughts that would inhibit buying. Most people with CB can easily recite a variety of reasons that they should not buy, but in a buying context, these reasons escape them. A simple strategy we use in treating those with hoarding with acquiring problems is to have them construct a list of questions to ask before making any purchase. These questions are ones most people would ask such as:

Do I have enough money for this?
Do I have enough space for this?
Do I have one or more of these already?

Hoarding and Compulsive Buying • 123

And ones that are more targeted:

Will not buying this help me to solve my hoarding problem?

Clients are asked to carry these questions with them everywhere and answer them whenever they buy anything. We've found that this is almost like having a therapist with them when they are shopping.

Finally we work with hoarders who buy compulsively to return their purchases to the store. This is often the most difficult task in therapy. It requires them to challenge their beliefs about the new possession and to experience a sense of loss when doing so.

Accompanying these efforts are several other therapeutic strategies. For many of those with CB buying represents their major source of pleasure and enjoyment. For people already prone to depression alternative sources of enjoyment must be found and cultivated. In addition a variety of cognitive techniques can be used for those who struggle with the decision to buy, including Socratic questioning, distinguishing need from want, estimating probability, and calculating outcomes (see Steketee & Frost, 2007). Sometimes establishing rules for when it is acceptable to buy can help with decision making (i.e., only buy a shirt if you haven't bought one in six months).

Although hoarding is notoriously difficult to treat (Steketee & Frost, 2003), these strategies have been reasonably successful in treating excessive acquisition in hoarding. Steketee and colleagues (2010) and Tolin, Frost, and Steketee (2007) found more reduction in excessive acquisition during treatment than for any other feature of hoarding.

Units No. 4 and No. 5 of the manual described in this book also address hoarding and include specific assignments. At issue here is whether CB accompanied by compulsive hoarding requires more specialized interventions to engage patients not only to cope with buying urges, impulsivity problems, materialistic values, and money mismanagement, but also with their difficulty to discard hoarded items and to organize their homes. This form of differentiated treatment might include more hoarding-specific interventions following the format suggested by Steketee and Frost (2007), e.g., individual in-home sessions to enable clients to make progress. Thus the number of sessions might vary from the manual published in this book.

Conclusion

Therapists should be aware about potential comorbid compulsive hoarding in clients with CB and address it as appropriate. Considering the higher severity of CB, the higher levels of psychopathology, and the poorer treatment outcome in individuals with CB and comorbid compulsive hoarding, specific therapeutic interventions are necessary. Future research will need to investigate and develop a more differentiated treatment approach to better cope with compulsive hoarding features in a subset of patients with CB.

References

Abramowitz, J.S., Franklin, M.E., Schwartz, S.A., & Furr, J.M. (2003) Symptom presentation and outcome of cognitive-behavioral therapy for obsessive-compulsive disorder, *Journal of Consulting and Clinical Psychology*, 71:1049–57.

Abramowitz, J.S., Wheaton, M.G., & Storch, E.A. (2008) The status of hoarding as a symptom of obsessive-compulsive disorder, *Behaviour Research and Therapy*, 46:1026–33.

APA. (2000) *Diagnostic and Statistical Manual of Mental Disorders*, fourth edition, text revision (DSM-IV-TR), Association AP (ed.), Washington, D.C.

Christensen, D. & Greist, J. (2001) The challenge of obsessive-compulsive disorder hoarding, *Primary Psychiatry*, 8:79.

Faber, R.J. & O'Guinn, T.C. (1992) A clinical screener for compulsive buying, *Journal of Consumer Research*, 19:459–69.

Frost, R.O. & Gross, R.C. (1993) The hoarding of possessions, *Behaviour Research and Therapy*, 31:367–81.

Frost, R.O. & Hartl, T.L. (1996) A cognitive-behavioral model of compulsive hoarding, *Behavior Research and Therapy*, 34:341–50.

Frost, R.O., Hartl, T.L., Christian, R., & Williams, L. (1995) The value of possessions in compulsive hoarding: patterns of use and attachment, *Behaviour Research and Therapy*, 33:897–902.

Frost, R.O., Kim, H.J., Morris, C., Bloss, C., Murray-Close, M., & Steketee, G. (1998) Hoarding, compulsive buying and reasons for saving, *Behaviour Research and Therapy*, 36:657–64.

Frost, R.O., Krause, M., & Steketee, G. (1996) Hoarding and obsessive-compulsive symptoms, *Behavior Modification*, 20:116–32.

Frost, R.O., Steketee, G., & Grisham, J. (2004) Measurement of compulsive hoarding: saving inventory-revised, *Behaviour Research and Therapy*, 42:1163–82.

Frost, R.O., Steketee, G., & Williams, L. (2000) Hoarding: a community health problem, *Health & Social Care in the Community*, 8:229–34.

Frost, R.O., Steketee, G., & Williams, L. (2002) Compulsive buying, compulsive hoarding and obsessive compulsive disorder, *Behavior Therapy*, 33:201–14.

Frost, R.O., Steketee, G., Tolin, D.F., & Renaud, S. (2008) Development and validation of the clutter image rating, *Journal of Psychopathology and Behavioral Assessment*, 30:193–203.

Frost, R.O., Steketee, G., Williams, L., & Warren, R. (2000) Mood, personality disorder symptoms and disability in obsessive compulsive hoarders: a comparison with clinical and nonclinical controls, *Behaviour Research and Therapy*, 38:1071–81.

Frost, R.O., Tolin, D.F., Steketee, G., Fitch, K.E., & Selbo-Bruns, A. (2009) Excessive acquisition in hoarding, *Journal of Anxiety Disorders*, 23:632–9.

Fullana, M.A., Vilagut, G., Rojas-Farreras, S., Mataix-Cols, D., de Graaf, R., Demyttenaere, K., Haro, J.M., de Girolamo, G., Lépine, J.P., Matschinger, H., & Alonso, J. (2010) Obsessive-compulsive symptom dimensions in the general population: results from an epidemiological study in six European countries, *Journal of Affective Disorders*, 124:291–9.

Greenberg, D. (1987) Compulsive hoarding, *American Journal of Psychotherapy*, 41:409–16.

Grisham, J.R., Frost, R.O., Steketee, G., Kim, H.J., Tarkoff, A., & Hood, S. (2009) Formation of attachment to possessions in compulsive hoarding, *Journal of Anxiety Disorders*, 23:351–61.

Hartl, T.L. & Frost, R.O. (1999) Cognitive-behavioral treatment of compulsive hoarding: a multiple baseline experimental case study, *Behaviour Research and Therapy*, 37:451–61.

Hummelen, B., Wilberg, T., Pedersen, G., & Karterud, S. (2008) The quality of the DSM-IV obsessive-compulsive personality disorder construct as a prototype category, *The Journal of Nervous and Mental Disease*, 196:446–55.

Iervolino, A.C., Perroud, N., Fullana, M.A., Guipponi, M., Cherkas, L., Collier, D., et al. (2009) Prevalence and heritability of compulsive hoarding: a twin and genetic association study, *American Journal of Psychiatry*, 166:1156–61.

Kyrios, M., Frost, R.O., & Steketee, G. (2004) Cognitions in compulsive buying and acquisition, *Cognitive Therapy and Research*, 28:241–58.

Lindsay, M., Crino, R., & Andrews, G. (1997) Controlled trial of exposure and response prevention in obsessive-compulsive disorder, *British Journal of Psychiatry*, 171:135–9.

Mataix-Cols, D., Frost, R.O., Pertusa, A., Clark, L.A., Saxena, S., Leckman, J.F., Stein, D.J., Matsunaga, H., & Wilhelm, S. (2010) Hoarding disorder: a new diagnosis for DSM-V? *Depression and Anxiety*. 27:556–72.

Mataix-Cols, D., Grayton, L., Bonner, A., Luscombe, C., Taylor, P.J., & van den Bree, M.B. (submitted) A putative link between compulsive hoarding and homelessness: pilot study.

Mataix-Cols, D., Marks, I.M., Greist, J.H., Kobak, K.A., & Baer, L. (2002) Obsessive-compulsive symptom dimensions as predictors of compliance with and response to behavior therapy: results from a controlled trial, *Psychotherapy and Psychosomatics*, 71:255–62.

Mueller, A., Crosby R.D., Frost, R.O., Bleich, S., Glaesmer, H., Osen, B., Leidel, B., & de Zwaan, M. (2009) Fragebogens zum zwanghaften Horten (FZH)—Validierung der deutschen Version des Saving Inventory-Revised, *Verhaltenstherapie*, 19:243–50.

Mueller, A., Mitchell, J.E., Crosby, R.D., Glaesmer, H., & de Zwaan, M. (2009) The prevalence of compulsive hoarding and its association with compulsive buying in a German population-based sample, *Behaviour Research and Therapy*, 47:705–9.

Mueller, A., Mueller, U., Albert, P., Mertens, C., Silbermann, A., Mitchell, J.E., & de Zwaan, M. (2007) Hoarding in a compulsive buying sample, *Behaviour Research and Therapy*, 45:2754–63.

Mueller, A., Mueller, U., Silbermann, A., Reinecker, H., Bleich, S., Mitchell, J.E., & de Zwaan, M. (2008) A randomized, controlled trial of group cognitive-behavioral therapy for compulsive buying disorder: post-treatment and 6-month follow-up results, *Journal of Clinical Psychiatry*, 69:1131–8.

Olatunji, B.O., Williams, B.J., Haslam, N., Abramowitz, J.S., & Tolin, D.F. (2008) The latent structure of obsessive-compulsive symptoms: a taxometric study, *Depression and Anxiety*, 25:956–68.

Rachman, S., Elliott, C.M., Shafran, R., & Radomsky, A.S. (2009) Separating hoarding from OCD, *Behaviour Research and Therapy*, 47:520–2.

Rufer, M., Fricke, S., Moritz, S., Kloss, M., & Hand, I. (2006) Symptom dimensions in obsessive-compulsive disorder: prediction of cognitive-behavior therapy outcome, *Acta Psychiatrica- Scandanavica*, 113:440–6.

Samuels, J.F., Bienvenu, O.J., Grados, M., Cullen, B., Riddle, M.A., Liang, K.Y., Eaton, W.W., & Nestadt, G. (2008) Prevalence and correlates of hoarding behavior in a community-based sample, *Behaviour Research and Therapy*, 46:836–44.

Samuels, J.F., Bienvenu, O.J., Riddle, M.A., Cullen, B.A., Grados, M.A., Liang, K.Y., Hoehn-Saric, R., & Nestad, G. (2002) Hoarding in obsessive-compulsive disorder: results from a case-controlled study, *Behaviour Research and Therapy*, 40:517–28.

Savoie, D. (2008) Report on a 5-year follow-up of a case of severe hoarding, *Clinical Cases S.*, 7:250–61.

Saxena, S. (2007) Is compulsive hoarding a genetically and neurobiologically discrete syndrome? Implications for diagnostic classification, *The American Journal of Psychiatry*, 164:380–4.

Seedat, S. & Stein, D.J. (2002) Hoarding in obsessive-compulsive disorder and related disorders: a preliminary report of 15 cases, *Psychiatry and Clinical Neurosciences*, 56:17–23.

Shafran, R. & Tallis, F. (1996) Obsessive-compulsive hoarding: a cognitive-behavioral approach, *Behavioural and Cognitive Psychotherapy*, 24:229–31.

Steketee, G. & Frost, R. (2003) Compulsive hoarding: current status of the research, *Clinical Psychology Review*, 23:905–27.

Steketee, G. & Frost, R.O. (2007) *Compulsive Hoarding and Acquiring: Therapist's Guide*, Oxford: University Press.

Steketee, G., Frost, R.O., Tolin, D.F., Rasmussen, J., & Brown, T.A. (2010) Waitlist-controlled trial of cognitive behavior therapy for hoarding disorder, *Depression and Anxiety*.

Tolin, D., Frost, R., & Steketee, G. (in press) A brief interview for assessing compulsive hoarding: the Hoarding Rating Scale, *Psychiatry Research*.

Tolin, D.F., Frost, R.O., & Steketee, G. (2007) An open trial of cognitive-behavioral therapy for compulsive hoarding, *Behaviour Research and Therapy*, 45:1461–70.

Tolin, D.F., Frost, R.O., Steketee, G., & Fitch, K.E. (2008) Family burden of compulsive hoarding: results of an Internet survey, *Behavior Research and Therapy*, 46:334–44.

Tolin, D.F., Frost, R.O., Steketee, G., Gray, K.D., & Fitch, K.E. (2008) The economic and social burden of compulsive buying, *Psychiatry Research*, 160:200–11.

Wheaton, M., Cromer, K., LaSalle-Ricci, V.H., & Murphy, D. (2008) Characterizing the hoarding phenotype in individuals with OCD: association with comorbidity, severity and gender, *Journal of Anxiety Disorders*, 22:243–52.

Winsberg, M.E., Cassic, K.S., & Koran, L.M. (1999) Hoarding in obsessive-compulsive disorder: a report of 20 cases, *Journal of Clinical Psychiatry*, 60:591–7.

Wu, K. & Watson, D. (2005) Hoarding and its relation to obsessive-compulsive disorder, *Behaviour Research and Therapy*, 43:897–921.

PART 2

Treatment

CHAPTER 9

Overview of Treatment for Compulsive Buying

KRISTINE J. STEFFEN, PHARMD, PHD
AND JAMES E. MITCHELL, MD

Contents

Introduction	129
Psychotherapy	129
Pharmacotherapy	132
Genetics and Neurobiology	132
Selective Serotonin Reuptake Inhibitors (SSRIs)	135
Opioid Antagonists	140
Miscellaneous Agents	142
Challenges in Pharmacotherapy Research	142
Future Research	143
References	145

Introduction

Unfortunately, little is known about the treatment of compulsive buying (CB), and the literature can be reviewed succinctly. We will first review the psychotherapy literature before turning to pharmacological approaches.

Psychotherapy

A few case studies of psychotherapy for this condition have appeared (Krueger, 1988; Bernik, Akerman, Amaral & Braun, 1996; Lawrence, 1990). Our group developed a group-based cognitive behavioral treatment

(CBT) for patients with this problem originally described in a book chapter (Burgard & Mitchell, 2000), and subsequently we conducted a pilot study using this manual-based approach (Mitchell, Burgard, Faber, Crosby & de Zwaan, 2006). After this pilot study, a replication study was conducted by colleagues in Germany (Mueller, Mueller, Silbermann, Reinecker, Bleich, Mitchell & de Zwaan, 2008). Since these are the only two available studies systematically addressing psychotherapy, they will be discussed in some detail. The manual included in this book is an update of the manual used in these two trials.

In the first trial, 28 subjects were recruited for active treatment in group psychotherapy sessions and 11 to a waiting list control. Subjects were not randomized but were recruited during different periods of time. At the end of treatment the results showed significant advantages for CBT over the waiting list in terms of reduction in number of compulsive buying episodes and time spent buying, as well as scores on the Compulsive Buying Scale and the Yale-Brown Obsessive Compulsive Scale-Shopping Version. CB episodes decreased from a mean of 10.7 ± 8.3 for the four weeks prior to baseline to a mean of 1.6 ± 3.0 during the last four weeks of treatment, and total time spent buying for the same periods of time decreased from 722.5 ± 778.6 minutes to 133 ± 316.0 minutes. Follow-up data were available on 17 subjects at six months, and the positive results were well maintained with a mean number of compulsive buying episodes in the prior four weeks to the six-month visit of $.59 \pm .07$ episodes with a mean time spent shopping of 47.1 ± 94.9 minutes. There was also significant improvement on the Beck Depression Inventory and on the Social Functioning-36 Scale. At the end of treatment 12 of the 21 patients who completed the group therapy reported no compulsive buying episodes over the last four weeks.

In the second study, conducted in Germany, 31 patients were randomly assigned to the active group CBT and 29 to a waiting list control. Multivariate analysis revealed significant differences between the CBT and waiting list control groups on the primary outcome variables (outcome-by-time-by-group effect, Pillai's trace, $F = 6.960$, $df = 1$, $p = .002$) with good maintenance of treatment outcome at six-month follow-up. The treatment did not affect other psychopathology including compulsive hoarding, impulsivity, or Symptom Checklist 90-Revised (SCL 90-R) scores. Those with worse attendance at group therapy or higher pretreatment hoarding scores were more likely not to respond to the treatment.

The treatment employed in these trials was one in which abstinence from shopping was not the goal. Instead the control of shopping behavior to develop healthy shopping patterns was the goal. There was a strong emphasis on stimulus control techniques, the development of a repertoire of alternative behaviors, and on cognitive restructuring. The therapy can be administered in ten sessions over 10 weeks, with each of the group sessions lasting for an hour and a half. If done in an individual format patients would be seen for 50 to 60 minutes weekly. During the treatment strong emphasis is placed on improving the buying behavior and not on other psychopathology. This sometimes requires redirection. This is particularly true because many patients with CB have psychiatric comorbidity and can end up derailing the group process by attempting to focus on other problems. For that reason therapists may frequently need to say, "Those are important problems, but they really should be dealt with in other treatment or treatment after this group therapy." In the treatment there is much discussion about attitudes toward money, materialism, and consumer culture. The treatment includes an emphasis on certain rules. One is that subjects need to destroy all their credit cards and instead use debit cards, cash, or checks. The approach also includes what is called the "24-hour rule," which means when somebody sees something they want to buy but didn't plan on buying prior to shopping, they must wait at least 24 hours before buying the item. This is underscored as a very important point, but initially patients are very resistant to this, as they are giving up their credit cards.

The group focuses on other shopping rules that include making a list of what you intend to shop for in advance, keeping a budget for special stores, not buying at checkout lines, no impulse buying (the 24-hour rule), and not to use carts or shopping baskets except at the grocery store. Patients are also asked to enter the store through the door closest to the item they wish to purchase, and throw away all catalogs, coupons, and credit card offers without looking at them.

In this CBT approach there is first a strong emphasis on examining cues that trigger problem buying including social cues (e.g., social isolation, boredom), situational cues (e.g., advertisements in magazines), physiological cues (e.g., fatigue), and mental cues (e.g., mental images). There is also a detailed discussion of possible consequences, both negative and positive, with a strong emphasis on differentiating positive consequences, which are usually short term, from negative consequences, which are usually longer term. Examples of positive consequences can be situational (e.g., distraction from aversive tasks), feelings (e.g., relief from tension), and thoughts (e.g., feeling more attractive). Negative consequences can also include social consequences (e.g., lying and lack of trust in relationships), situational (e.g., financial problems), feelings (e.g., depression, guilt), and thoughts (e.g., negative self-evaluation and guilt). Patients also keep detailed records of purchasing behavior including the number of items purchased, the type of items purchased, the value of each item, the total value of the purchases, and where the items are stored or hoarded after buying.

The treatment then progresses to a session on response sets, including an examination of thoughts, feelings, and behaviors. Cues, responses, and consequences are then tied together in chains as illustrated in the treatment manual. There is also a very strong emphasis on the development of alternative behaviors including doing such things as taking a bath or shower, taking a walk, writing a letter, doing relaxation exercises, listening to music, or reading something inspirational. Emphasis is placed on both short-term alternatives that can be engaged in quickly when the person craves shopping (e.g., writing a letter) versus longer-term alternatives that can be planned in advance for problematic times (e.g., planning on going to a movie on Saturday afternoon with a friend).

Pharmacotherapy

CB has received relatively little attention in terms of pharmacotherapy research, despite it first being described by Bleuler and Kraepelin in the early 20th century (Black, 2007). The extant medication literature for CB consists primarily of small case series and uncontrolled trials, along with a small number of controlled trials. The majority of this research has focused on the selective serotonin reuptake inhibitor (SSRI) class of antidepressant medications. Other medications that have been used and reported on in the form of case studies include naltrexone (Kim, 1998; Grant, 2003) and more recently topiramate (Guzman, Filomensky & Tavares, 2007). CB is currently categorized as an impulse control disorder not otherwise specified (ICD NOS) in the DSM-IV and is grouped with other impulse control disorders (ICDs) including pathological gambling, kleptomania, pyromania, and compulsive sexual behavior. Whereas the pharmacotherapy literature for CB is still early in its development, data on other ICDs such as pathological gambling are more advanced. Whether or not it is appropriate to extrapolate the findings of such other literatures to CB is unclear. Thus this other literature will be referred to but not elaborated upon.

The genetic and neurobiological correlates of CB are briefly reviewed relative to potential pharmacotherapeutic approaches that may be considered in future research, although this area has been relatively unexplored. Conducting pharmacological research in CB is associated with several challenges, which will be discussed. Finally, suggestions for future research are proposed.

Genetics and Neurobiology

Given the paucity of research on neurobiology and genetics specific to CB, the ICDs will be discussed together. The ICDs, such as pathological gambling, kleptomania, pyromania, intermittent explosive disorder, trichotillomania, and the other ICD NOS such as problematic Internet use, compulsive skin picking, and compulsive sexual behavior, have been collectively referred to as "behavioral addictions" (Brewer & Potenza, 2008). A review article by Grant, Brewer, and Potenza (2006a) drew parallels between substance addictions and the behavioral addictions on the basis of phenomenology, genetics, and neurobiology. These authors described several commonalities between patients with behavioral and substance addictions, which are summarized as follows:

1. Patients with both types of addiction engage in detrimental behaviors repeatedly and demonstrate diminished control of these behaviors, despite experiencing adverse effects.
2. Both types of disorders are characterized by a state of craving prior to engaging in the behavior, and patients experience hedonic qualities while engaging in the behaviors.
3. Physiological similarities are also apparent, including tolerance, withdrawal, repeated ineffective attempts to decrease the behaviors, and impairment in major areas of functioning.
4. Phenomenological data show that there are high rates of both substance and behavioral addictions during adolescence and young adulthood.
5. Similarly, the "telescoping phenomenon" associated with alcoholism has been observed with pathological gambling, where there is a more rapid progression from initial to problematic behavior in women as opposed to men.
6. Finally, there is substantial comorbidity between substance use and behavioral addiction.

Brewer and Potenza (2008) also reviewed the similarities between the behavioral and drug addictions with a prominent emphasis on their neurobiological commonalities.

Similar to substance addiction, the dopamine system may be implicated in CB. Brain imaging studies have shown that the mesocorticolimbic dopamine system is involved in other behavioral addictions. Brain imaging data obtained in response to a simulated gambling task has shown reduced ventral striatal activation in patients with pathological gambling (Reuter, Raedler, Rose, Hand, Gläscher & Büchel, 2005), and other imaging studies have also demonstrated the involvement of the dopamine system in pathological gambling (Hollander, Pallanti, Baldini, Sood, Baker & Buchsbaum, 2005a; Potenza, Leung, Blumberg, Peterson, Fulbright, Lacadie et al., 2003). Bullock and Koran (2003) reviewed the psychopharmacological, genetic, and neurobiological literature in CB. They suggested that although no studies have looked for dopamine D2 receptor gene (DRD2) abnormalities in CB, they have been observed in alcoholism, drug dependency, obesity, smoking, pathological gambling, and other conditions. Bullock and Koran speculated that the dopaminergic reward pathways are likely to be involved in the pathophysiology of CB. This hypothesis appears consistent with multiple reports in the literature implicating the dopamine agonist medications in compulsive behaviors such as pathological gambling, compulsive eating, sexual behavior, and CB (Lee, Kim, Kim, Cho, Lee, Kim et al., 2009). It should be emphasized that the research in pathological gambling may or may not extend to CB. Whether or not the neurobiological attributes are in fact similar must be determined through additional research.

Devor, Magee, Dill-Devor, Gabel, and Black (1999) examined genetic markers associated with CB. These researchers examined the serotonin transporter gene (5-HTT) in 21 patients diagnosed with CB. When compared to 38 psychiatrically normal controls, no significant polymorphisms were identified. Bullock and Koran (2003) have described this finding as surprising given the high percentage of patients with CB who have mood and anxiety disorders, and suggested that the lack of exclusion criteria in the study may have affected the results.

Several lines of evidence also support potential abnormal serotonin function in impulse control disorders, with the majority of research conducted on those with pathological gambling. For example decreased platelet monoamine oxidase (MAO) activity has been observed in patients with pathological gambling relative to healthy controls (Carrasco, Saiz-Ruiz, Hollander, Cesar & Lopez-Ibor, 1994; Blanco, Orensanz-Muñoz, Blanco-Jerez & Saiz-Ruiz, 1996). A recent crossover study compared the 5HT1B/1D agonist sumatriptan to placebo in 22 patients with pathological gambling versus 19 healthy controls (Pallanti, Bernardi, Allen & Hollander, 2009). All participants denied a lifetime alcohol or substance addiction. The results of the study showed a blunted growth hormone response associated with sumatriptan administration in patients with pathological gambling compared to controls, indicative of downregulation of the 5-HT1B/1D receptors. The investigators concluded that there is serotonin dysfunction associated with pathological gambling analogous to what has been observed in prior studies of patients with alcoholism. A paroxetine platelet membrane binding study has shown a reduction in the maximum binding capacity of the serotonin transporter in pathological gambling patients relative to control participants (Marazziti, Golia, Picchetti, Pioli, Mannari, Lenzi et al., 2008). Increased prolactin response to acute administration of the partial serotonin agonist meta-chlorophenylpiperazine (m-CPP) has also been observed in pathological gambling patients relative to control participants, which also indicates serotonin dysregulation (Pallanti et al., 2006). Although the neurobiology and genetic correlates of CB remain uncertain, progress has been made in other ICDs, particularly pathological gambling.

Selective Serotonin Reuptake Inhibitors (SSRIs)

As mentioned, the SSRI's have been the most extensively studied class of drugs for the treatment of CB. One reason for this is that the presentation of CB has been likened to that of obsessive-compulsive disorder (OCD; Schlosser, Black, Repertinger & Freet, 1994; Grant, 2003; Ravindran, da Silva, Ravindran, Richter & Rector, 2009), for which the SSRIs have demonstrated efficacy. Also, as previously discussed, multiple research studies have shown serotonin dysfunction in other ICDs.

Results in the treatment of CB with the SSRIs have been mixed. While open-label trials, case studies, and open-label lead-in portions of trials have shown benefit (McElroy, Satlin, Pope, Keck & Hudson, 1991; McElroy, Keck, Pope, Smith & Strakowski, 1994; Black, Monahan & Gabel, 1997; Koran, Bullock, Hartson, Elliott & D'Andrea, 2002; Koran, Chuong, Bullock & Smith, 2003; Koran, Aboujaoude, Solvason, Gamel & Smith, 2007) only one controlled trial of citalopram showed benefit during the double-blind discontinuation phase (Koran et al., 2003). This was a two-phase trial, consisting of a seven-week open-label phase followed by a nine-week double-blind discontinuation phase. At the end of the first seven weeks of the trial responders were randomized to either continue the same dose of citalopram or switch to placebo. This study showed a higher rate of relapse among the placebo group than those remaining on citalopram during the double-blind discontinuation phase. A subsequent escitalopram trial (Koran et al., 2007) utilized the same study design and found no benefit for drug over placebo during the double-blind discontinuation phase. Controlled trials of fluvoxamine (Black, Gabel, Hansen & Schlosser, 2000; Ninan, McElroy, Kane, Knight, Casuto, Rose et al., 2000) also produced overall negative results. As shown in Table 9.1, the majority of these trials have included a high percentage of patients with at least one current comorbid psychiatric condition. There has also been considerable heterogeneity in the inclusion criteria across studies with regard to permitting the enrollment of patients with current or lifetime psychiatric diagnoses. Some studies have also allowed patients to participate in ongoing, stable, concomitant psychotherapy and were allowed to enroll in the study provided they stopped their current psychotropic medications shortly before trial commencement. These confounds make it difficult to interpret the drug's efficacy in the treatment of CB apart from its effects on other psychiatric conditions, and amid other concomitant treatments. Some researchers have attempted to control for the psychiatric comorbidity concerns. For example, Black and colleagues (1997) attempted to exclude those with current major depressive disorder (MDD) by requiring a baseline Hamilton Depression Rating Scale (HAM-D) score of less than or equal to 18, in conjunction with a score on the first item of the HAM-D of

Table 9.1 Selective Serotonin Reuptake Inhibitor (SSRI) Studies in Compulsive Buying Disorder

Author and Year	Study Design, Subject Number (N)	Medication and Dose (Maximum and Mean + SD)	N (%) With Psychiatric Comorbidity	Study Duration	Medication Response	Comment
Black et al., 1997	OL N = 10	Fluvoxamine maximum dose: 300 mg/day, mean dose: 205 ± 72.5 mg	N = 6 hx of depression, N = 4 hx of alcohol or other substance abuse N = 2 hx of an eating disorder N = 1: hx panic d/o, ADHD, current specific phobia, GAD, social phobia, OCPD	9 weeks + 1 week SB placebo run-in	N = 9/10 responded (> 50% improvement in YBOCS-SV score) N = 7/10 requested continued medication after the trial had ended Compulsive Buying Scale score at baseline was not significantly correlated with improvement on the YBOCS-SV	Inclusion criteria: CB for > 1 year, HAM-D score < 18 and < 1 on the first item
Black et al., 2000	DB, PC N = 24 randomized N = 18 completed (9 in each group)	Fluvoxamine (Flv) maximum dose: 300 mg/day, mean dose: 220 mg	Lifetime diagnoses: N = 17 MDD N = 5 alcohol/drug use disorder N = 10 anxiety disorder N = 2 eating disorder	9 week trial + 1 week SB placebo lead-in phase	16.7% Flv vs. 54.5% placebo Patients experienced > 50% decline in YBOCS-SV score Improvement on CGI scores: Flv 50% vs. placebo 63.6%	CB for > 1 yr for inclusion No new psychotherapy allowed during trial Psychotropic washout × 2 weeks prior trial Patients kept shopping diaries

Ninan et al., 2000	DB, PC, two-site N = 42 consented N = 23 completed	Flv maximum dose: 300 mg/day; mean dose: 215 ± 76.5 mg/day	74% past or current 60% more than one comorbid diagnosis	12 weeks + 1 week SB placebo lead-in phase	Both conditions improved; no significant differences between drug and placebo	CB for > 6 mo required for inclusion Some patients also received stable psychotherapy No concomitant psychotropic medications Patients kept daily shopping diaries.
Koran et al., 2002	OL N = 24	Citalopram maximum dose 60 mg/day, mean 35.4 ± 21.4 mg/day (6 patients were on < 20 mg/day, 1 patient was on 5 mg every other day)	GAD (N = 5) dysthymia (N = 3) MDD (N = 2) social phobia (N = 2) agoraphobia (N = 2) bulimia (N = 2) PTSD (N = 1) kleptomania lifetime (N = 3) trichotillomania lifetime (N = 2)	12 weeks + 1 year follow-up	YBOCS-SV dropped from 22.6 ± 5.6 at baseline to 7.2 ± 9.5 at endpoint (p < .001) Mean MADRS score dropped from 11.9 ± 6.9 to 4.8 ± 6.5 (p < 0.001)	Required for inclusion: CB for > 1 year and engagement in buying > once/week for the past 3 months Excluded patients on psychotherapy or psychotropic drugs Excluded comorbid OCD, psychotic disorders, substance or alcohol abuse, or dependence within the past 3 months, and several other disorders Patients asked to keep daily shopping log

continued

Table 9.1 (continued) Selective Serotonin Reuptake Inhibitor (SSRI) Studies in Compulsive Buying Disorder

Author and Year	Study Design, Subject Number (N)	Medication and Dose (Maximum and Mean + SD)	N (%) With Psychiatric Comorbidity	Study Duration	Medication Response	Comment
Koran et al., 2003	OL followed by DB DC N = 24	Citalopram maximum dose 60 mg/day Final OL dose was 42.1 ± 15.3 mg/day N = 4 pts on < 20 mg/day	Active comorbid conditions (N = 9; 38%) included MDD (N = 5), dysthymia (N = 3), social phobia, kleptomania, trichotillomania, and pathological gambling (N = 1 each)	7 week OL followed by 9 week DB DC	YBOCS-SV scores decreased from 24.3 ± 4.6 at baseline to 8.2 ± 8.1 at the end of OL treatment (p < .001) N = 15 (63%) of subjects met responder criteria DB phase showed 5/8 assigned to placebo relapsed vs. 0/7 assigned to citalopram (p = .019)	Inclusion: CB for > 1 year, YBOCS-SV of > 17 Excluded substance abuse/dependence within last 3 months, OCD, history of bipolar I or II, and other specific disorders No concomitant psychotherapy or psychotropics allowed Study did not require shopping logs

| Koran, 2007 | OL followed by DB DC N = 26 | Escitalopram 10–20 mg/day | N = 12 (46%) had active comorbid conditions N = 7 MDD N = 4 dysthymia N = 4 social anxiety disorder N = 6 had more than one comorbidity | 7-week OL followed by 9-week DB DC | OL phase demonstrated mean YBOCS-SV reductions from 24.5 ± 3.9 to 9.9 ± 9.3 (mean percent decrease 57.5%, p < 0.001) N = 19 (73%) were considered responders DB phase showed no difference between groups in relapse (6/9 placebo relapsed vs. 5/8 escitalopram) | Required for inclusion: CB for > 1 year and engagement in buying > once/week for the past 3 months, score of > 17 on YBOCS-SV Discontinued all other psychotropics > 1 week prior to study Significantly higher response rate in subjects without depression at baseline |

Note: ADHD = attention deficit hyperactivity disorder; CGI = Clinical Global Impressions Scale; DB = double-blind; DC = discontinuation; d/o = disorder; GAD = Generalized Anxiety Disorder; HAM-D = Hamilton Depression Rating Scale; hx = history of; MDD = Major Depressive Disorder; OCPD = obsessive-compulsive personality disorder; OL = open-label; PC = placebo-controlled; PTSD = posttraumatic stress disorder; SB = single-blind; SD = standard deviation; YBOCS-SV = Yale-Brown Obsessive-Compulsive Scale-Shopping Version.

less than or equal to one, for study entry. Nevertheless, the majority of the patients in the sample had lifetime psychiatric diagnoses, and there were cases of current anxiety disorders and other conditions.

Koran and colleagues (2007) found a differential treatment response with escitalopram in those who had major depression at study entry versus those who did not. This trial included an open-label phase followed by a double-blind discontinuation. Although the sample sizes were quite limited, 6/10 (60 percent) of subjects with depressive disorders at baseline were responders during the open-label phase of the study, in contrast to 13/16 (81 percent) of those without a depressive disorder at baseline. Overall at week seven of treatment, 6/12 (50 percent) of those who had a comorbid condition at baseline responded compared to 13/14 (93 percent) of those without a comorbid condition, which was a statistically significant difference. Koran and colleagues (2002) found that the baseline Yale Brown Obsessive Compulsive Scale-Shopping Version (YBOCS-SV) and Montgomery-Asberg Depression Rating Scale (MADRS) scores were significantly correlated (Pearson $r = 0.56$, $p = 0.005$) and baseline to endpoint changes in the YBOCS-SV and MADRS were also significantly correlated (Pearson $r = 0.58$, $p = .003$). A later study by Koran and colleagues (2003) did not find the YBOCS-SV and MADRS scores to be significantly correlated at baseline (Spearman $r = .318$, $p = .065$), but the change between baseline and endpoint on the YBOCS-SV was significantly correlated with the change on the MADRS (Spearman $r = 0.57$, $p < .01$). Nineteen of the 24 subjects (79 percent) in the citalopram study by Koran and colleagues (2003) had baseline MADRS scores of nine or higher, which the investigators state is indicative of at least mild mood symptoms.

In addition to the small sample sizes and comorbidity, the dosages used in these studies in some cases may have been too low. For example, the study by Koran and colleagues (2002) used doses as low as 5 mg of citalopram every other day with additional patients receiving less than 20 mg/day citalopram. Shopping logs were also used in several studies, which the authors acknowledge may have served as a form of behavioral therapy and contributed to a heightened placebo response rate.

Opioid Antagonists

The opioid antagonist naltrexone has been investigated for the treatment of several conditions and is FDA approved for the treatment of alcohol and opioid dependence (Micromedex, 2009). Naltrexone would theoretically reduce the motivation for buying episodes as well as the pleasure experienced during such episodes. Kim (1998) reported a case of a patient with CB who was successfully treated with 100 mg/day of the opioid antagonist naltrexone. This patient had concurrent bulimia nervosa and a history of cocaine and narcotic abuse. At 100 mg/day of naltrexone the patient's shopping symptoms diminished substantially, and her binge eating and purging symptoms of bulimia nervosa also resolved. A reduction in the patient's urge to shop and binge eat had been sustained for seven months at the time of the report. Kim noted that he has successfully treated an additional three CB patients with naltrexone, which was not described in this report. Grant (2003) has also described three cases where CB patients responded to high-dose naltrexone (100–200 mg/day). The first case described was a 32-year-old patient who had undergone treatment with behavior therapy and psychotherapy for four years without benefit, as well as unsuccessful trials of fluoxetine 80 mg/day for 12 weeks followed by par-oxetine 60 mg/day for 20 weeks. Naltrexone was titrated up to 100 mg/day, and the patient experienced symptom remission for 12 weeks. The patient then discontinued the medication and her shopping urges intensified beyond their pretreatment levels. Upon resuming the naltrexone, her shopping urges stopped again. Similarly, two additional patients with CB who did not have a comorbid Axis I diagnosis were successfully treated with naltrexone. Both of them discontinued the drug temporarily, during which time they experienced relapses of their symptoms. Both patients experienced symptom relief upon restarting the medication.

There have been several controlled trials involving naltrexone or the long-acting opioid antagonist nalmefene, for the treatment of pathological gambling (Kim, Grant, Adson & Shin, 2001; Dannon, Lowengrub, Musin, Gonopolski & Kotler, 2005a; Grant, Potenza, Hollander, Cunningham-Williams, Nurminen, Smits et al., 2006b; Grant, Kim & Hartman 2008a; Toneatto, Brands & Selby, 2009). Results have generally, although not always, supported the efficacy of naltrexone for pathological gambling. Recently, a controlled kleptomania treatment trial has also demonstrated that naltrexone significantly reduced stealing urges and behavior relative to placebo (Grant, Kim & Odlaug, 2009).

Although naltrexone is generally well tolerated, the drug carries a black-box warning regarding hepatotoxicity. This toxicity appears to be dose related, although healthy patients may be able to safely receive higher dosages than the 50 mg/day recommended for alcohol dependence, pro-vided there is adequate monitoring of liver function (Grant, 2003). Doses above 50 mg/day were used in the patients described in the CB case reports; however, an 18-week controlled trial in pathological gambling found 50 mg/day of naltrexone to be as effective as 100 mg/day and 150 mg/day (Grant, Kim, Hollander & Potenza, 2008b). All three doses in this gambling study were reportedly well tolerated. A controlled trial of naltrexone 50 mg/day to 150 mg/day for the treatment of kleptomania found a mean effective dose of 116.7 ± 44.4 mg/day (Grant et al., 2009). Kim and colleagues (2006) showed that prolonged use of high-dose naltrexone (mean of 142 mg/day for 328 days) was safe in a sample of 41 patients, provided that the use of aspirin, acetaminophen, and nonsteroidal anti-inflammatory drugs (NSAIDs) was restricted. Further research is needed to assess the efficacy of naltrexone for CB, and it may be worthwhile to compare the efficacy of lower and higher dosages.

Miscellaneous Agents

Topiramate has been the subject of a recent case study in an individual with CB (Guzman, Filomensky & Tavares, 2007). The patient was started on 50 mg/day of topiramate, which was titrated to 150 mg/day over one month. The patient had comorbid depression and was being treated with venlafaxine when topiramate was added. Symptoms of CB subsided after one month of treatment with topiramate and venlafaxine. Depression remitted after three months. The patient later stopped venlafaxine and tolerated topiramate treatment well. Although this case is the only report in CB to date, there is a randomized, blinded-rater comparison of topiramate and fluvoxamine in pathological gambling (Dannon et al., 2005b) that found both agents to be efficacious. There has also been a case series reported in kleptomania (Dannon, 2003) and an open-label trial in trichotillomania (Lochner, Seedat, Niehaus & Stein, 2006). The mechanism of action of topiramate is not entirely clear, but is thought to include blockage of voltage-dependent sodium channels, antagonism of AMPA/kainate glutamate-receptor subtypes, inhibition of carbonic anhydrase, and augmentation of the activity of GABA at particular GABA-A receptor subtypes (PDR, 2009). Among some of the more common or serious adverse effects associated with topiramate are weight loss (6 percent to 21 percent), taste perversion (3 percent to 15 percent), confusion (3 percent to 14 percent), dizziness (8 percent to 32 percent), paresthesia (2 percent to 51 percent), somnolence (9 percent to 29 percent), and nephrolithiasis (1 percent to 3 percent) (Micromedex, 2009).

Challenges in Pharmacotherapy Research

Suggestions for future pharmacotherapy research in CB are discussed, although several factors present obstacles to carrying out controlled medication trials in CB. First, adequately powered controlled medication trials are extremely expensive to conduct. Large government funding agencies in the United States generally have not supported trials in this area. For-profit businesses and foundations are also unlikely to fund this work, since consumer spending engenders business and benefits the economy. Currently, CB is classified as an ICD NOS in the DSM-IV-TR. Pharmaceutical companies may be reluctant to support research in pursuit of new indications for disorders that do not have full diagnostic status in the DSM. Second, there is continued debate regarding whether CB constitutes a distinct disorder or represents a behavioral manifestation of an underlying Axis I psychopathology. In particular, high co-occurrence rates suggest that the separation between CB and mood and anxiety disorders may often be blurred. In patients with CB, coexisting mood disorders are reported in 21 percent to 100 percent, anxiety disorders in 41 percent to 80 percent, substance use disorders in 21 percent to 46 percent, eating disorders in 8 percent to 35 percent, an Axis II disorder in approximately 60 percent (most commonly obsessive-compulsive, avoidant, and borderline), and frequently other disorders of impulse control as well (Black, 2007). Thus the results of pharmacotherapy trials with CB patients can be difficult to interpret since many of the drugs are also effective for multiple Axis I conditions. For example, most of the CB pharmacotherapy literature involves the SSRIs. Various agents in this class have received FDA approval for a wide range of disorders including major depressive disorder, generalized anxiety disorder, social anxiety disorder, OCD, panic disorder, posttraumatic stress disorder, as well as other disorders. As shown in Table 9.1, the majority of pharmacotherapy studies have included a large proportion of patients with comorbid psychiatric conditions. Thus even with rigorous patient assessment it is difficult to determine whether the drug has an independent effect on CB symptoms that can be distinguished from its effects on mood, anxiety, and other conditions. Finally, despite a prevalence rate of approximately 5.8 percent (Koran et al., 2006) for CB, it is often unrecognized by health care providers who are in a position to prescribe medications or refer patients to research protocols offering pharmacotherapy. Similarly, patients may be more likely to seek financial counseling for debt resulting from CB than to view their situation as a mental health concern and seek guidance from a health care professional or pursue research related treatments. Finally, a placebo response rate of up to 64 percent has been observed in CB pharmacotherapy trials (Black, 2007). This remarkably high placebo response rate makes it difficult for a medication to show statistically significant efficacy beyond placebo in controlled trials.

Future Research

Despite the aforementioned challenges to conducting research in this area, there are several areas in which the pharmacotherapy literature in CB could be expanded. Perhaps of greatest significance is the need to better characterize the neurobiology of CB. This information would help guide the selection of appropriate pharmacological agents for future research. The most extensive research has been conducted with the SSRI antidepressants, and the data have been mixed. To conclusively determine whether SSRIs are efficacious for CB disorder, research will need to address several points. First, it is unclear whether the drugs treat CB disorder symptoms specifically or whether they reduce CB behavior by improving comorbid mood, anxiety, or other disorders. The trials to date have been limited in sample size and have included substantial percentages of patients with at least one comorbid psychiatric disorder. Indeed, some of these trials have found significant correlations between improvements in symptoms of CB and of mood. Although one small trial made efforts to exclude patients with comorbid mood disorders (Black, Monahan & Gabel, 1997), this practice may pose a significant detriment to study recruitment given the substantial overlap of these conditions. A valid argument could also be made that the generalizability of study findings would be reduced by excluding CB patients who have comorbid conditions. A trial comparing SSRI response between patients with CB who have a coexisting mood disorder and CB patients with no history of a mood disorder may be informative.

Second, the SSRI trials have generally permitted significant variability in the dose of the medication. Although the mean SSRI doses have generally fallen within what would be considered the therapeutic range, a notable proportion of patients in some of the trials have been on very low doses, which may have been subtherapeutic. For example, one trial allowed patients to remain in the trial on as little as 5 mg of citalopram every other day (Koran et al., 2002), although the overall results of this trial were positive. It is possible that subtherapeutic dosing in trials could weaken the observed efficacy of the drug relative to placebo. It has been proposed that CB may represent a compulsive spectrum disorder related to OCD (Grant, 2003; Ravindran et al., 2009). Treatment of OCD with an SSRI typically requires higher dosages than for mood or other anxiety disorders (Bloch, McGuire, Landeros-Weisenberger, Leckman & Pittenger, 2009). Therefore it may be worthwhile to investigate the efficacy of higher dosages of the SSRIs for the treatment of CB and to withdraw patients from the trial who cannot tolerate a reasonable minimum daily dose.

Finally, as discussed by several authors, requiring the patients to keep shopping logs during the trials may represent a form of behavioral therapy and may make it more difficult to observe a drug effect. Coupled with this, placebo-response rates have tended to be high, which also makes it more difficult to observe a drug effect.

Several drugs in addition to the SSRIs and opioid antagonists have been investigated for the treatment of pathological gambling, such as bupropion SR (Black, 2004; Black et al., 2007; Dannon et al., 2005a; Dannon et al., 2007), lithium carbonate (Pallanti, Quercioli, Sood & Hollander, 2002; Hollander, Pallanti, Allen, Sood & Baldini Rossi, 2005b), valproate (Pallanti, Quercioli, Sood & Hollander, 2002), carbamazepine (Black, Shaw & Allen, 2008), olanzapine (McElroy, Nelson, Welge, Kaehler & Keck, 2008), nefazodone (Pallanti, Baldini, Rossi, Sood & Hollander, 2002), and n-acetyl cysteine (Grant et al., 2007). While some of these reports showed positive results and others were negative, these data may be informative for pharmacotherapy research in CB.

Larger trials exploring the opioid antagonist naltrexone would add to the literature, as would controlled trials exploring topiramate and other anticonvulsants. Given the significant parallels observed between addictive disorders and ICDs, it may be worthwhile to examine compounds beyond the opioid antagonists that have shown efficacy for substance or alcohol addiction. Likewise, drugs that have been useful for OCD may be worth investigating. As has been the case with several other psychiatric conditions, it is also possible that medication monotherapy will be insufficient. Trials comparing medication to cognitive behavioral treatment (CBT) and trials examining the combination of medication and CBT are warranted. Combinations of medications may also be more effective than single-drug therapy, although it may be premature to pursue this given the current developmental phase of this literature.

References

Bernik, M.A., Akerman, D., Amaral, J.A. & Braun. (1996) Cue exposure in compulsive buying (letter), *Journal of Clinical Psychiatry*, 59:159–64.

Black, D.W., Monahan, P. & Gabel, J. (1997) Fluvoxamine in the treatment of compulsive buying, *Journal of Clinical Psychiatry*, 58:159–63.

Black, D.W., Gabel, J., Hansen, J. & Schlosser, S. (2000) A double-blind comparison of fluvoxamine versus placebo in the treatment of compulsive buying disorder, *Annals of Clinical Psychiatry*, 12:205–11.

Black, D.W. (2007) A review of compulsive buying disorder, *World Psychiatry*, 6:14–18.

Black, D.W. (2004) An open-label trial of bupropion in the treatment of pathologic gambling, *Journal of Clinical Psychopharmacology*, 24:108–10.

Black, D.W., Arndt, S., Coryell, W.H., Argo, T., Forbush, K.T., Shaw, M.C., Perry, P. & Allen, J. (2007) Bupropion in the treatment of pathological gambling: a randomized, double-blind, placebo-controlled, flexible-dose study, *Journal of Clinical Psychopharmacology*, 27:143–50.

Black, D.W., Shaw, M.C. & Allen, J. (2008) Extended release carbamazepine in the treatment of pathological gambling: an open-label study, *Progress in Neuropsychopharmacology & Biological Psychiatry*, 32:1191–4.

Blanco, C., Orensanz-Muñoz, L., Blanco-Jerez, C. & Saiz-Ruiz, J. (1996) Pathological gambling and platelet MAO activity: a psychobiological study, *American Journal of Psychiatry*, 153:119–21.

Bloch, M.H., McGuire, J., Landeros-Weisenberger, A., Leckman, J.F. & Pittenger, C. (2009) Meta-analysis of the dose-response relationship of SSRI in obsessive-compulsive disorder, *Molecular Psychiatry*, epub ahead of print.

Brewer, J.A. & Potenza, M.N. (2008) The neurobiology and genetics of impulse control disorders: relationships to drug addictions, *Biochemical Pharmacology*, 75:63–75.

Bullock, K. & Koran, L. (2003) Psychopharmacology of compulsive buying, *Drugs Today*, 39:695–700.

Burgard, M. & Mitchell, J.E. (2000) Group cognitive-behavioral therapy for buying disorder, in A. Benson (ed.), *I Shop, Therefore I Am: Compulsive Buying and the Search for Self*, New York: Jason Aronson.

Carrasco, J.L., Saiz-Ruiz, J., Hollander, E., Cesar, J. & Lopez-Ibor, J.J. Jr. (1994) Low platelet monoamine oxidase activity in pathological gambling, *Acta Psychiatrica Scandinavica*, 90:427–31.

Dannon, P.N., Lowengrub, K., Musin, E., Gonopolski, Y. & Kotler, M. (2005a) Sustained-release bupropion versus naltrexone in the treatment of pathological gambling: a preliminary blind-rater study, *Journal of Clinical Psychopharmacology*, 25:593–6.

Dannon, P.N., Lowengrub, K., Gonopolski, Y., Musin, E. & Kotler, M. (2005b) Topiramate versus fluvoxamine in the treatment of pathological gambling: a randomized, blind-rater comparison study, *Clinical Neuropharmacology*, 28:6–10.

Dannon, P.N. (2003) Topiramate for the treatment of kleptomania: a case series and review of the literature, *Clinical Neuropharmacology*, 26:1–4.

Dannon, P.N., Lowengrub, K., Musin, E., Gonopolsky, Y. & Kotler, M. (2007) 12-month follow-up study of drug treatment in pathological gamblers: a primary outcome study, *Journal of Clinical Psychopharmacology*, 27:620–4.

Devor, E.J., Magee, H.J., Dill-Devor, R.M., Gabel, J. & Black, D.W. (1999) Serotonin transporter gene (5-HTT) polymorphisms and compulsive buying, *American Journal of Medical Genetics*, 88:123–5.

Grant, J.E. (2003) Three cases of compulsive buying treated with naltrexone, *International Journal of Psychiatry in Clinical Practice*, 7:223–5.

Grant, J.E., Brewer, J.A. & Potenza, M.N. (2006a) The neurobiology of substance and behavioral addictions, *CNS Spectrums*, 11:924–30.

Grant, J.E., Potenza, M.N., Hollander, E., Cunningham-Williams, R., Nurminen, T., Smits, G. & Kallio, A. (2006b) Multicenter investigation of the opioid antagonist nalmefene in the treatment of pathological gambling, *American Journal of Psychiatry*, 163:303–12.

Grant, J.E., Kim, S.W. & Odlaug, B.L. (2007) N-acetyl cysteine, a glutamate-modulating agent, in the treatment of pathological gambling: a pilot study, *Biological Psychiatry*, 62:652–7.

Grant, J.E., Kim, S.W. & Hartman, B.K. (2008a) A double-blind, placebo-controlled study of the opiate antagonist naltrexone in the treatment of pathological gambling urges, *Journal of Clinical Psychiatry*, 69:783–9.

Grant, J.E., Kim, S.W., Hollander, E. & Potenza, M.N. (2008b) Predicting response to opiate antagonists and placebo in the treatment of pathological gambling, *Psychopharmacology*, 200:521–7.

Grant, J.E., Kim, S.W. & Odlaug, B.L. (2009) A double-blind, placebo-controlled study of the opiate antagonist, naltrexone, in the treatment of kleptomania, *Biological Psychiatry*, 65:600–6.

Guzman, C.S., Filomensky, T. & Tavares, H. (2007) Compulsive buying treatment with topiramate, a case report, *Revista Brasileira de Psiquiatria*, 29:380–4.

Hollander, E., Pallanti, S., Baldini, R.N., Sood, E., Baker, B.R. & Buchsbaum, M.S. (2005a) Imaging monetary reward in pathological gamblers, *World Journal of Biological Psychiatry*, 6:113–20.

Hollander, E., Pallanti, S., Allen, A., Sood, E. & Baldini Rossi, N. (2005b) Does sustained-release lithium reduce impulsive gambling and affective instability versus placebo in pathological gamblers with bipolar spectrum disorders? *American Journal of Psychiatry*, 162:137–45.

Kim, S.W. (1998) Opioid antagonists in the treatment of impulse-control disorders, *Journal of Clinical Psychiatry*, 59:159–64.

Kim, S.W., Grant, J.E., Adson, D.E. & Shin, Y.C. (2001) Double-blind naltrexone and placebo comparison study in the treatment of pathological gambling, *Biological Psychiatry*, 49:914–21.

Kim, S.W., Grant, J.E., Yoon, G., Williams, K.A. & Remmel, R.P. (2006) Safety of high-dose naltrexone treatment: hepatic transaminase profiles among outpatients, *Clinical Neuropharmacology*, 29:77–9.

Koran, L.M., Bullock, K.D., Hartson, H.J., Elliott, M.A. & D'Andrea, V. (2002) Citalopram treatment of compulsive shopping: an open-label study, *Journal of Clinical Psychiatry*, 63:704–8.

Koran, L.M., Chuong, H.W., Bullock, K.D. & Smith, S.C. (2003) Citalopram for compulsive shopping disorder: an open-label study followed by double-blind discontinuation, *Journal of Clinical Psychiatry*, 64:793–8.

Koran, L.M., Aboujaoude, E.N., Solvason, B., Gamel, N.N. & Smith, E.H. (2007) Escitalopram for compulsive buying disorder: a double-blind discontinuation study, *Journal of Clinical Psychopharmacology*, 27:225–7.

Koran, L.M., Faber, R.J., Aboujaoude, E., Large, M.D. & Serpe, R.T. (2006) Estimated prevalence of compulsive buying behaviour in the United States, *American Journal of Psychiatry*, 163:1806–12.

Krueger, D.W. (1988) On compulsive shopping and spending: a psychodynamic inquiry, *American Journal of Psychotherapy*, 42:574–84.

Lawrence, L. (1990) The psychodynamics of the compulsive female shopper, *American Journal of Psychoanalysis*, 50:67–70.

Lee, J.Y., Kim, J.M., Kim, J.W., Cho, J., Lee, W.Y., Kim, H.J. & Jeon, B.S. (2009) Association between the dose of dopaminergic medication and the behavioral disturbances in Parkinson disease, *Parkinsonism & Related Disorders*, Dec. 15, epub ahead of print.

Lochner, C., Seedat, S., Niehaus, D.J. & Stein, D.J. (2006) Topiramate in the treatment of trichotillomania: an open-label pilot study, *International Clinical Psychopharmacology*, 21:255–9.

Marazziti, D., Golia, F., Picchetti, M., Pioli, E., Mannari, P., Lenzi, F., Conversano, C., Carmassi, C., Catena Dell'Osso, M., Consoli, G., Baroni, S., Giannaccini, G., Zanda, G. & Dell'Osso, L. (2008) Decreased density of the platelet serotonin transporter in pathological gamblers, *Neuropsychobiology*, 57:38–43.

McElroy, S.L., Keck, P.E., Pope, H.G., Smith, J.M.R. & Strakowski, S.M. (1994) Compulsive buying: a report of 20 cases, *Journal of Clinical Psychiatry*, 55:242–8.

McElroy, S.L., Nelson, E.B., Welge, J.A., Kaehler, L. & Keck, P.E. Jr. (2008) Olanzapine in the treatment of pathological gambling: a negative randomized placebo-controlled trial, *Journal of Clinical Psychiatry*, 69:433–40.

McElroy, S.L., Satlin, A., Pope, H.G., Keck, P.E. & Hudson, J.J. (1991) Treatment of compulsive shopping with antidepressants: a report of three cases, *Annals of Clinical Psychiatry*, 3:199–204.

Micromedex˚ Healthcare Series (n.d.) Retrieved December, 2009, from http://www.thomsonhc.com, Greenwood Village, CO: Thomson Healthcare.

Mitchell, J.E., Burgard, M., Faber, R., et al. (2006) Cognitive behavioral therapy for compulsive buying disorder, *Behavior Research & Therapy*, 44:1859–65.

Mueller, A., Mueller, U., Silbermann, A., Reinecker, H., Bleich, S., Mitchell, J.E. & de Zwaan, M. (2008) A randomized, controlled trial of group cognitive-behavioral therapy for compulsive buying disorder: post-treatment and 6-month follow-up results, *Journal of Clinical Psychiatry*, 69:7.

Ninan, P.T.N., McElroy, S., Kane, C.P., Knight, B.T., Casuto, L.S., Rose, S.E., Marsteller, F.A. & Nemeroff, C.B. (2000) Placebo-controlled study of fluvoxamine in the treatment of patients with compulsive buying, *Journal of Clinical Psychopharmacology*, 2:362–6.

Pallanti, S., Quercioli, L., Sood, E. & Hollander, E. (2002) Lithium and valproate treatment of pathological gambling: a randomized single-blind study, *Journal of Clinical Psychiatry*, 63:559–64.

Pallanti, S., Baldini Rossi, N., Sood, E. & Hollander, E. (2002) Nefazodone treatment of pathological gambling: a prospective open-label controlled trial, *Journal of Clinical Psychiatry*, 63:1034–9.

Pallanti, S., Bernardi, S., Quercioli, L., DeCaria, C. & Hollander, E. (2006) Serotonin dysfunction in pathological gamblers: increased prolactin response to oral m-CPP versus placebo, *CNS Spectrums*, 11:956–64.

Pallanti, S., Bernardi, S., Allen, A. & Hollander, E. (2009) Serotonin function in pathological gambling: blunted growth hormone response to sumatriptan, *Journal of Psychopharmacology*, Oct. 13. epub ahead of print.

PDR˚ Electronic Library TM (Internet database) Greenwood Village, CO: Thomson Reuters (Healthcare) Inc. Updated periodically.

Potenza, M.N., Leung, H.C., Blumberg, H.P., Peterson, B.S., Fulbright, R.K., Lacadie, C.M., Skudlarski, P. & Gore, J.C. (2003) An fMRI Stroop task study of ventromedial prefrontal cortical function in pathological gamblers, *American Journal of Psychiatry*, 160:1990–4.

Ravindran, A.V., da Silva, T.L., Ravindran, L.N., Richter, M.A. & Rector, N.A. (2009) Obsessive-compulsive spectrum disorders: a review of the evidence-based treatments, *Canadian Journal of Psychiatry*, 54:331–43.

Reuter, J., Raedler, T., Rose, M., Hand, I., Gläscher, J. & Büchel, C. (2005) Pathological gambling is linked to reduced activation of the mesolimbic reward system, *Nature Neuroscience*, 8:14–18.

Schlosser, S., Black, D.W., Repertinger, S. & Freet, D. (1994) Compulsive buying: demography, phenomenology and comorbidity in 46 subjects, *General Hospital Psychiatry*, 16:205–12.

Toneatto, T., Brands, B. & Selby, P. (2009) A randomized, double-blind, placebo-controlled trial of naltrexone in the treatment of concurrent alcohol use disorder and pathological gambling, *American Journal of Addiction*, 18:219–25.

CHAPTER **10**

Case Examples

APRIL BENSON, PHD, LISA A. PETERSON, MA,
TROY W. ERTELT, MA, AND AIMEE ARIKIAN, MA

Contents

Introduction	149
Sarah	150
Deborah	151
Ron	153
Nora	155
Amanda	157
References	158

Introduction

Compulsive buying (CB) is characterized by shopping and buying behavior that causes marked distress, impairment in social and occupational functioning, and financial problems. Though it may seem to be a relatively new phenomenon, Kraepelin (1909) and Bleuler (1923) described these behaviors as "oniomania" about a century ago. More recently, specific criteria for CB have been offered. These include a preoccupation with buying, the sense of irresistible, unwanted, or unnecessary urges to buy, frequently buying unneeded items or more than one can afford, shopping for longer periods of time than intended, and experiencing adverse consequences in terms of interpersonal, occupational, and financial problems (McElroy, Keck, Pope, Smith & Strakowski, 1994).

These criteria can lead to various adverse consequences including frequent feelings of guilt or remorse, excessive debt, family problems, divorce or relationship dissolution, and the exacerbation of other psychiatric

149

illness. In fact, CB is commonly comorbid with other disorders, particu-larly mood and anxiety disorders, substance use disorders, eating disorders, pathological gambling, and other impulse control disorders (Black, Gabel, Hansen & Schlosser, 2000; Faber, Christenson, de Zwaan & Mitchell, 1995; Frost, Kim, Morris, Bloss, Murray-Close & Steketee, 1998; McElroy, Keck, Pope, Smith & Strakowski, 1994; Ninan, McElroy, Kane, Knight, Casuto, Ross et al., 2000; Schlosser, Black, Repertinger & Freet, 1994). The follow-ing case vignettes illustrate several examples of individuals with CB. All identifying information has been changed to protect client confidentiality.

Sarah

Sarah was a 55-year-old widowed female who participated in a 10-week group cognitive-behavioral treatment for CB. She appeared quite guarded initially, and for the first several sessions only participated in group discussion when specifically asked to do so; however, she became a more active participant as the treatment progressed. When Sarah contributed to group discussion her comments were insightful and beneficial to the other group members.

Over the first two sessions, Sarah identified as her problematic buying behaviors various impulsive purchases, going shopping without an item in mind, returning items, and storing items without ever using them. She reported being most at risk for problem buying behaviors in the evenings, after daily visits with her mother who had recently moved to a long-term care facility. She also reported feeling happy and satisfied when she felt as though she had found a great bargain, and identified a local designer dis-count store as her most high risk place to shop. She indicated that she went browsing in this store nearly every evening after leaving the visits with her mother, and spent much more time than she planned on each occasion.

Sarah reported feeling as though she had engaged in CB behaviors most of her adult life. She discussed financial hardships in her family of origin and indicated she liked to treat herself, because she was financially able to do so as an adult. Sarah did not report significant debt or other financial consequences as a result of her buying behavior. However, she reported choosing shopping over socializing with friends and family members, and frustration over spending her money on things she did not usually need or use, instead of saving for travel or items more useful or valuable to her.

In identifying reasons for and against changing her buying behavior, Sarah had a difficult time with the idea of giving up treating herself, the enjoyable aspects of browsing, and the positive feelings associated with having found a good deal. The question of what constitutes normal or healthy buying behavior plagued Sarah throughout treatment. She appreciated the group's response that normal was for her to decide and occasionally treating herself by purchasing useful, desired items within her budget would be consistent with healthy buying. Instituting the 24-hour rule (see Treatment Manual in Chapter 12) was also helpful for her in distinguishing healthy buying from more maladaptive behaviors.

During sessions focused on delineating thoughts and feelings associated with maladaptive buying behaviors, Sarah identified as precursors to buying episodes loneliness and feelings of guilt about her mother having to move to a long-term care center. Scheduling opportunities to socialize with friends and family members in the evenings and immediately following visits with her mother were very successful alternative activities for Sarah. Interestingly, Sarah did not disclose until the eighth week that her husband had died less than two years prior to her joining the group. She became very emotional while discussing her feelings about his death, and it appeared that her thoughts and feelings about the death had exacerbated her shopping behavior.

Sarah appeared to benefit greatly from increasing her socialization with friends and family. By her report, she demonstrated almost immediate improvements in her buying behavior and did not report significant problematic buying episodes during the course of treatment. She also decreased the time she spent browsing and the number of days per week she did so at the outset of treatment, and maintained this progress over the 10-week treatment period. Addressing her grief seemed very important and likely contributed to the sustained reduction of her CB behavior. It was recommended that she seek grief counseling or similar services following the buying treatment.

Deborah

Deborah was a 48-year-old married female who also participated in a 10-week group. She was an active participant in the group beginning in the first session; however, her comments were, at times, overly detailed and focused on irrelevant aspects of her behavior rather than the topic of group discussion. This improved as she appeared to become more willing to address her shopping behavior, but redirection from facilitators was often necessary.

During the first two sessions, Deborah identified impulse purchases, multiple purchases, returning items, and hoarding as problematic buying behaviors. She reported feeling most at risk for buying episodes immediately after leaving work for the day. Deborah indicated she had difficulty making decisions about purchases, which often resulted in buying multiple different types of the same item, and not always being able to return unnecessary items. She also described herself as a bargain hunter and reported satisfaction from using coupons, finding the cheapest version of a particular item, or finding items on sale. She believed this stemmed from financial concerns within her family of origin. Deborah did not report significant financial hardship or debts as a result of her behaviors, but did identify as consequences problems in her relationship associated with never being at home in the evenings due to shopping, and not having money for more desired and useful purchases. She also stated her hoarding behaviors had adversely affected her social life and that of her family in that they did not feel comfortable having guests in their home because of the clutter.

In examining the thoughts and feelings associated with her buying behaviors, Deborah discussed feeling self-conscious about her social skills, her apparent inability to make friends, and the resulting loneliness as precursors to buying episodes. She was less willing to discuss her relationship with her husband, but did report feeling anxious about going home after work because she thought that he often did not like the meals she prepared.

Throughout the group sessions, Deborah demonstrated a number of characteristics associated with obsessive-compulsive personality disorder, including rigid beliefs, excessive attention to detail, perfectionism that interfered with task completion, and preoccupation with work and productivity to the detriment of socialization. These traits appeared to contribute to her buying behaviors in that she spent large amounts of time looking for the perfect version of the item she had in mind at the perfect price, which led to multiple purchases and the inability to make decisions and leave stores in a timely manner. There also was a general lack of self-confidence. Deborah also had difficulty pinpointing potentially satisfying alternative behaviors and often felt she had to tackle other projects, such as cleaning out her home during her free time, rather than taking time to socialize or pursue a hobby. She also discussed ways in which rigid beliefs and unrealistically high expectations for others had negatively impacted her ability to make friends and to socialize.

During treatment Deborah demonstrated some improvements in the time she spent in stores, her ability to decide on one item, and her overall maladaptive spending. However, she reported several instances during the treatment of wandering around stores seemingly aimlessly. She also reported buying three different pairs of work gloves and two shovels on one occasion, and on another ordering two different sets of curtains "in case one wasn't right." She continued to report difficulty planning alternative behaviors. Through her participation in the group Deborah generally appeared to gain insight into her behaviors and the painful emotions she used buying to avoid. Perhaps the most helpful aspects of group participation for Deborah were the support and positive feedback she received from other group members.

Ron

Ron was a 51-year-old man who lived alone in a single-family home. He had never been married and had no children. Ron had an advanced degree in anthropology and had spent much of his professional life working on archaeological digs in various parts of the world.

Approximately six years before being seen, Ron was hurt badly during a dig. He fell into an open excavation pit, broke his right leg, and seriously injured his back. His injuries required a number of invasive surgeries in order to correct some of the damage done to his spinal column, but Ron continued to have limited range of motion and constant dull pain as a result of the accident. Ron had not worked since the accident; however, he successfully sued his employer for negligence in preparing the worksite where his accident occurred. He received a large settlement that was being paid out to him as a monthly annuity, and Ron used this money to cover his expenses.

After his accident and subsequently being homebound, Ron experienced a rather serious major depressive episode during which he considered committing suicide on a number of occasions. Ron had derived much of his identity from his professional accomplishments, and he felt as though his life no longer had a purpose once he was no longer able to work in archaeology. Ron had no siblings and both of his parents had been dead for 10 years. Since Ron invested so much time in his career, he had never married and never had any children. All of Ron's friends were also his coworkers, and not being able to see them during the normal work week or during expeditions made him feel isolated from the outside world. Ron's only social support during this time was from a physical therapist who visited him three times a week to help improve his physical functioning and from a housekeeper who worked at his home every other day. Eventually Ron's mood improved somewhat, and his depressive episode remitted without any professional help.

During the time that Ron was depressed, he began buying DVDs through online retailers. Going shopping at traditional retailers became quite difficult for Ron, and he found that online shopping helped him pass his time during the day. Additionally, Ron was impressed by the wide selection available through online retailers. After a few months, Ron was amassing an extensive collection of DVDs and took great satisfaction in his collection. He also found that watching the DVDs helped distract him from thinking about his accident and resulting career changes. As time went on Ron began buying increasingly sophisticated electronic items such as Blu-ray players and widescreen televisions. Since Ron was receiving large sums of settlement money, he was able to purchase high-end electronics without significant financial consequences. Ron also found additional social support from online friends he met in message forums and chat rooms dedicated to entertainment electronics and movies. Ron remained, however, homebound and generally isolated from his previous peer group.

Ron's CB behavior continued to grow for several years. He eventually expanded into purchasing expensive home décor items and gourmet cooking utensils as he developed new hobbies that he could engage in while at home. Ron was aware that his CB behavior was getting out of control, but he did not experience untoward financial consequences from the behavior due to his settlement money. Ron saw an online advertisement for a randomized trial of cognitive-behavioral therapy for CB disorder. Ron completed the intake and qualified for inclusion in the study.

During the first week of intervention Ron presented as pleasant and affable. He had no difficulty disclosing his CB behavior. Although his apparent openness to treatment generally seemed to be a positive predictor of Ron's success, it quickly became apparent that Ron was glamorizing his excessive purchases and was looking for a reaction from the therapist in order to confirm his beliefs that his purchasing power was beyond that of other people and his taste in expensive goods was better than that of others. The therapist remained cognizant of these somewhat narcissistic and materialistic attributes throughout therapy and attempted to avoid providing any reinforcement for the behaviors, but also tried to avoid any overt punishment so as not to trigger a narcissistic reaction. Instead the therapist tried to remain task oriented and redirect Ron to the material from the manual.

Ron's glamorizing behavior persisted into the third week of treatment, and the therapist remained goal oriented. This was particularly challenging because Ron was a sophisticated individual with strong verbal abilities, and he was able to redirect conversations into inappropriate territory as quickly as the therapist could redirect the conversation into discussion of the week's manual section. During the third week, Ron reported that he had two separate buying episodes at online retailers. Ron was encouraged to continue trying to use the 24-hour waiting period rule.

Ron reported no CB episodes during the previous week at the week six group session. He reported that writing down his purchases was helping him to see that his buying behavior was out of control; however, Ron was quick to emphasize that his buying behavior did not cause him financial consequences. Ron's glamorizing behavior was less evident during this session and appeared to be extinguished due to lack of reinforcement.

During session eight, Ron reported that he continued to be abstinent from CB episodes. Ron also reported that he had identified some hoarding tendencies in himself after reading material from the compulsive hoarding section of the CB manual and decided to liquidate some of his DVD collection, which numbers around 1000 DVDs. Ron reported that he was feeling very positive about overcoming his CB behavior.

During the final session, Ron reported continued abstinence from CB episodes. He communicated appropriately with the therapist and other group members and did not engage in glamorizing behavior. Overall Ron felt that the treatment was successful for him.

Overall, the most helpful treatment strategies in reducing Ron's CB behavior were implementing the 24-hour waiting period rule and writing down all purchases in the purchasing recall. Although Ron knew his compulsive buying behavior was becoming excessive and problematic, seeing his week's purchases written down in one place helped him to fully recognize the severity of his problem. Throughout the treatment the self-monitoring aspects of using the weekly purchasing recall helped Ron to make more appropriate purchasing choices.

Ron had difficulty with some of the interventions in the manual such as implementing alternative behaviors. Since he was generally home-bound, Ron's behavioral alternatives were somewhat restricted; however, Ron identified that he began reading more about archaeology as he was spending less time in shopping activities online and watching home shopping channels.

Nora

Nora was a 27-year-old female who reported struggling with CB as well as with comorbid anxiety, depression, physical health problems, and a history of anorexia nervosa. She participated in a 10-week cognitive-behavioral therapy group for CB. Her goals for treatment were stated as building the confidence to change her shopping behavior and understanding the connection between her thoughts about CB and her CB behavior. She said that although she had been in therapy before, she never had the opportunity to concentrate on exploring her CB behavior. Nora described some of her specific CB patterns as relating to art projects and materials, as she was an artist by profession, and beauty products and apparel.

During one of the first group sessions, Nora described that she had bought a pair of expensive jeans and realized that she did not need another addition to the number of jeans that she already owned. After a group discussion of reasons for and against stopping CB she made it a goal to return the jeans in the next week. During the next group session Nora hesitated to say she was successful when she returned the jeans, reporting that on her way out of the mall she bought an expensive hairstyling tool. She described how she tried to walk past the kiosk but was pulled in by a salesperson who, although Nora resisted and questioned the purchase, eventually convinced her to buy the item. The group was able to help Nora define her successes and areas for improvement regarding this scenario. She identified that because she spent so much time deliberating about returning the jeans she felt she was extra vulnerable to the salesperson's techniques.

Nora and other group members talked about the complicated and analytical thoughts about purchases that were part of their buying behavior. Nora especially described that it was typical for her to deliberate about purchases for days before making a purchase. She described her process of rumination about justifying purchases as disruptive, evidenced by her limited ability to complete art projects, job hunt, and spend time socializing. It seemed helpful for Nora when the group therapist defined CB as inclusive of both cognitive compulsions as well as impulsive purchases. Talking about these CB characteristics helped Nora realize that buying episodes, such as buying the styling tool, were ultimately related to the lengthy compulsive thought patterns she described. Therefore Nora began to apply the 24-hour rule to her disorder by employing it as a thought-stopping technique. Nora seemed to be doing a great job of being aware of her thoughts and behaviors and beginning to realize how they were connected.

During sessions that focused on thought restructuring and behavior chain exercises, she later realized that her hairstyling tool purchase was representative of some of the core feelings at the root of her CB behavior. Nora shared an example with the group about her reactions to a Thanksgiving holiday meal. Key phrases she used to describe the event were how planning and preparing for the family meal was overly stimulating, and afterward she kept thinking, "What now?" She said she felt that after she returned to her apartment "something was missing." As group members and the therapist urged her to name thoughts, feelings, and behaviors related to this example, she went on to explain that it was hard for her to connect with her family, a group of overachievers, and she often felt inadequate in comparison. The group praised Nora for acknowledging her feelings and reaching out for support. She reported that instead of making purchases to fill up the void that she felt, she ended up spending time with a friend and watching a movie.

In a subsequent session Nora shared with the group that she was going through a difficult relationship breakup. She reported, though, that she felt she was learning and growing from the experience. She reported that in hindsight her apparel and hairstyling purchases were directly related to her feelings of wanting to hold on to her relationship. She said that she had noticed her boyfriend spending time with another woman, who had "fabulous hair." She talked about thinking at that time that her hairstyling purchase "would make (her) better, or fill a void she needed to fill." She also talked about how this really was representative of chronic behaviors and feelings for her.

After discussing the above behavior chain Nora came to the last few group sessions reporting marked improvement. She talked about gaining awareness into her shopping behavior and simultaneously taking better care of herself. She reported that one of the biggest tools she gained from the CB treatment was the belief that "I have this choice between (buying) this thing over buying groceries or paying rent on time." She talked about finding that her guilt over CB was even deeper than she realized, and it represented the "core of my self-worth, because (having) a love affair with this thing is preventing me from having a love affair with myself." Nora realized that time spent ruminating about and desiring material things to counteract feelings of loneliness or inadequacy were in fact preventing her from enjoying experiences. She reported less spending as a result of her efforts to be more aware of her thoughts and feelings in the moment.

Amanda

Amanda was in her middle 40s when she came for help. She'd been over-buying clothing as well as books and magazines for six years—ever since she'd begun serious weekend work on a novel. The book was to be light, a woman's story of life in the big city. But it was slow going. Her frustrations with the writing process had led her to cultivate procrastination, and eBay, with its unparalleled variety, 24/7 instant access, excellent prices, and auction-generated excitement, had quickly become her procrastination method of choice.

Unlike most long-time overshoppers, Amanda hadn't yet found herself in debt. With a decent salary, no children, and a two-income family, she'd been managing to pay for the cavalcade of packages that made regular stops at her front door. Amanda shopped on the Internet daily—"I think about it constantly, from the moment I get up in the morning until late at night"—still believing on some level that she could get whatever she wanted. On weekends, when her novelistic hunt for words became difficult, she'd escape to eBay.

Amanda told the group in her first session that "although I don't smoke, I think I take an Internet shopping break the way someone else takes a cigarette break—except I don't have to go outside to do it." She began to acknowledge how deeply she dreaded the mental and emotional frustrations of her workday job and of her weekend writing; for the first time, she discovered that these negative feelings were triggering her shopping impulses. She also came to see her obsessive acquisition of clothes as a resonance of other negative feelings, reinforced by our appearance-obsessed society.

Amanda's openness to new ideas was matched by her openness to other people. One week, a group member had a significant overshopping episode, failed to do the reading or writing assignments and, filled with shame and trepidation, came to the group 30 minutes late. Amanda lauded her bravery, implored her never again to think twice about coming, and told her how important she was to the group. This marked a turning point for the tardy group member, and it gave other group members the courage to report on their embarrassing difficulties.

Advancing beyond the middle of the 12-session group, Amanda was making progress. Her goal for that week was to avoid all Internet shopping, and she was prepared to achieve it. If her motivation flagged, she told us, she'd remind herself that she'd bought no fewer than 22 items on eBay in the two months before the group.

Two weeks later, she took a vacation to visit one of her sisters; her parents were flying in as well. Such gatherings always involved movies and malls, and Amanda was keenly aware of the shopping risks. Her success on this trip was one of several she could now look back on. And she was making real progress with her writing.

There were slips. One week, Amanda bought several becoming outfits for ice skating, an activity she enjoyed with her husband. It was overshopping, and she knew it. Instead of precipitating an all-out spree, however—which can easily happen once you step across the line of disciplined self-denial—the event sobered her.

As she neared the end of the group, she was solidly controlling her shopping, not catastrophizing the occasional slip, and holding to an even, mindful course.

In her final session, Amanda reported that she hadn't bought anything on the Internet for several weeks. It was almost, she said, "like back in 2002, when shopping wasn't a big deal." She identified the most critical single agent of this change as the recognition "that my shopping behavior was not congruent with my values."

References

Black, D.W., Gabel, J., Hansen, J. & Schlosser, S. (2000) A double-blind comparison of Fluvoxamine versus placebo in the treatment of compulsive buying disorder, *Annals of Clinical Psychiatry*, 1:205–11.

Bleuler, E. (1923) *Lehrbuch der Psychiatrie*, Berlin: Springer.

Faber, R.J., Christenson, G.A., de Zwann, M. & Mitchell, J. (1995) Two forms of compulsive consumption: Comorbidity of compulsive buying and binge eating, *Journal of Consumer Research*, 22:296–304.

Frost, R.O., Kim, H.J., Morris, C., Bloss, C., Murray-Close, M. & Steketee, G. (1998) Hoarding, compulsive buying, and reasons for saving, *Behavior Research and Therapy*, 36:657–64.

Kraepelin, E. (1909) Psychiatrie, *Ein Lehrbuch für Studierende und Ärzte I. Band Allg. Psychiatrie*, Leipzig: Johann Ambrosius Barth.

McElroy, S.L., Keck, P.E., Pope, H.G., Smith, J.M.R. & Strakowski, S.M. (1994) Compulsive buying: A report of 20 cases, *Journal of Clinical Psychiatry*, 55:242–8.

Ninan, P.T.N., McElroy, S., Kane, C.P., Knight, B.T., Casuto, L.S., Ross, S.E., et al. (2000) Placebo-controlled study of Fluvoxamine in the treatment of patients with compulsive buying, *Journal of Clinical Psychopharmacology*, 20:362–6.

Schlosser, S., Black, D.W., Repertinger, S., & Freet, D. (1994) Compulsive buying: Demography, phenomenology, and comorbidity in 46 subjects, *General Hospital Psychiatry*, 16:205–12.

CHAPTER 11

Therapist's Guide to the Treatment Manual

JAMES E. MITCHELL, MD

Contents

Session One—Content 161
Session Two—Identifying Problem Buying Behaviors and
Their Consequences 163
Session Three—Cues and Consequences 164
Session Four—Cash Management, Hoarding 164
Session Five—Responses "Thought, Feeling, and Behavior" 165
Session Six—Restructuring Your Thoughts 165
Session Seven—Cues and Chains 165
Session Eight—Self-Esteem 166
Session Nine—Exposure 166
Session Ten—Stress Management and Problem Solving 167
Session Eleven—Relapse Prevention 167
Session Twelve—Summary and Outlook 167

Session One—Content

This session is designed to set the stage for the complete treatment program. In the introduction the therapist discusses that the goals of treatment are to interrupt the compulsive buying (CB) behavior and instead to establish healthy purchasing patterns. Other goals include identifying and restructuring maladaptive thoughts and feelings, as well as developing healthy coping skills and communication patterns, and learning relapse prevention techniques. The therapist also discusses the issue of group expectations, particularly focusing on the need for confidentiality. There is also a brief discussion about the involvement of family and friends, and patients are urged to involve family and friends in their recovery process.

The treatment program overview discusses the difficulty in overcoming the problematic behavior pattern and the role of the group in overcoming the compulsive behavior. There is then a general discussion as to what constitutes CB including clinical characteristics, cognitive and emotional factors, social factors, and behavioral factors, as well as psychosocial and psychological factors. Homework includes completing the Purchasing Record, reading over and signing the treatment contract, reading "Myths about Compulsive Buying," and reading the material for the next session. Patients are also asked to define their problem areas, particularly the stores that are problematic, and the types of items that they purchase in a problematic way. Patients are instructed about the need to give up credit cards and the need to institute a 24-hour rule, wherein if they see something they want to buy but didn't plan on buying prior to shopping they must wait at least 24 hours. These concepts, particularly giving up credits cards and the 24-hour rule, are stressed.

It is also important to remember certain stylistic issues when working with groups, and potentially with individuals if an individual approach is used as well. Much of this treatment is akin to taking a class in that there are reading assignments, homework assignments, and a clear expectation to master the material. Particularly when using a group format it is very important for the therapist to be responsible for the progress of the group. Not uncommonly subgroups of patients, particularly those with Cluster B Axis II personality disorders, may attempt to derail the process of the group. Also patients may attempt to switch the process to focus on other issues such as depression or relationship issues. The therapist needs to be able to say, "Those are important problems, but we don't have time to focus on them in this group. Our focus is on compulsive buying and you may need to work on those in some other therapy context." If the therapist establishes this precedent early on this will be very helpful for group members in developing the expected cadence and direction of the treatment.

The general format for each session will be a review of the homework assignments followed by group discussion of the material, closing with assigning homework for the next session. Generally it is helpful for the therapist to focus on patients who are having some success and are doing the required reading and homework assignments. To focus on problem patients will slow the group down. Patients who have difficulty with the reading and homework typically will accelerate their progress if it is clear that that is the expectation that is rewarded by the therapist with group time. It is also important for the therapist to be clear that there are certain rules that patients are expected to adopt, such as giving up credit cards and the 24-hour rule. These are not things for patients to consider but are inherently important parts of the treatment, and this not uncommonly needs to be stressed repeatedly.

Another issue of great importance is using a "go around" when discussing homework assignments. For example, if one is focusing on specific issues such as the sort of items that people purchase when they are engaging in CB, go around the group and have each person contribute his or her items; sometimes going left to right and sometimes right to left. If some subjects have difficulty speaking up in the group and being part of the process the therapist should make sure that they are included by specifically calling on them and asking them to contribute.

Session Two—Identifying Problem Buying Behaviors and Their Consequences

First, the homework should be reviewed in the group context, again using the go-around technique whenever feasible. For the readings, such as the "Myths" reading, it is good to ask subjects about their understanding of the material. It is also good to review the Purchasing Records and in particular focus on patients who have done a good job in order to illustrate the proper way to do the homework. It is important again to stress the need to do the homework faithfully and to set aside a bit of time every day, perhaps 30 minutes in the evening, to work with the manual and to complete the homework assignments. It is also important to review that subjects are making a commitment to change by signing the treatment contract.

The focus can then switch to recognizing and identifying problematic buying and specific problematic buying behaviors. Emphasis should be placed on the fact that such behaviors can be both impulsive and compulsive, but that many times they are not planned ahead, and that most of the time patients purchase things they really do not need. The habitual nature of the problem should be stressed. There is also discussion of when patients are most likely to engage in problem buying. For many individuals this will be during the weekend, on their lunch break, or during the evening. Discussion should also focus on the consequences, both positive and negative, and the shopping rules should be reviewed in detail. Emphasis should be placed on making a list in advance of shopping, getting rid of all credit cards, substituting debit cards, and the necessity for the 24-hour rule.

Patients should also articulate and list reasons for and against unhealthy buying habits. The main message here is that there are reasons against stopping as well as reasons for stopping, and dealing with this ambivalence directly can be very helpful for patients. Assignments include the Purchasing Records, reading "What to Expect as You Change Your Buying Behavior," the material for the next session, and a reminder about the 24-hour rule and getting rid of credit cards.

Session Three—Cues and Consequences

In this session we introduce cues and the response set as well as further discuss consequences. Cues are things that stimulate or precede CB behavior, and consequences are what results from the CB behavior. Cues should be discussed in detail and individualized. It is important to note that probably the most important cue for most people is simply boredom. Consequences should be reviewed in terms of both positive consequences, which are usually short term, and negative consequences, which are usually longer term. There should then be discussion about strategies for change focusing on the cues, using such techniques as avoidance, restricting the stimulus field, and strengthening cues for desired behavior. In terms of changing responses to cues there should be discussion about building in a pause, and the great importance of alternative behaviors. There is also further discussion about consequences, both mental and material. Rewards are discussed, as is the need to rearrange consequences. Assignments include Purchasing Records, the Cues and Consequences Worksheet, the Rearranging Cues and Changing Responses Worksheet, and the development of a list of alternative behaviors, as well as reading about warning signs and reading the material for the next session.

Session Four—Cash Management, Hoarding

First, each of the homework assignments should be reviewed. Strong emphasis should be placed on the development of alternative behaviors. These should include short-term things that can be done when one is faced with the sudden impulse to buy, and longer term alternatives that are things one can plan to do in advance during high-risk periods, such as a Saturday afternoon, if that is a prime shopping time. The warning signs allow patients to look at a number of issues that have developed in their lives because of the CB.

In session four it is good to again discuss getting rid of credit cards (and hopefully many patients will have done so by this time), as well as offering suggestions for cash management. There is also discussion about what is included in healthy buying behavior and a discussion about hoarding. Patients are asked to list the types of items they buy and hoard, the number of items that they have hoarded, the approximate value of each item, the approximately total value, and where things are stored. It is important for the therapist to remember that many patients with CB do not open or use what they compulsively buy but will store or hoard the items, give them away, or take them back. Many people have very significant problems with the amount of things they are hoarding. Assignments include completing Purchasing Records and the hoarding assignment, and reading of the next session's material.

Session Five—Responses "Thought, Feeling, and Behavior"

A great deal of emphasis should be placed on reviewing the hoarding material and encouraging patients to develop plans to return or in some way get rid of the hoarded items. This initially can be very difficult for patients, but nonetheless this is a key part of addressing an essential problem for many of them.

In the session the response set proper is dealt with in greater detail, looking at the separation of thoughts, feelings, and behaviors. Some patients are very good at identifying thoughts but not feelings, and vice versa. Most commonly people will identify feelings and will have difficulty articulating the underlying thought.

Relative to maladaptive styles of thinking, overgeneralization, catastrophizing, dichotomous thinking, self-fulfilling prophecy, and overreliance on the opinions of others are all mentioned. However, for many patients the terminology is much less important than simply articulating their thoughts, often automatic thoughts, about buying. Assignments include completing Purchasing Records and the Restructuring Thoughts Worksheet, and reading the next session.

Session Six—Restructuring Your Thoughts

Following the discussion of the homework, this session focuses on techniques for restructuring thoughts. Various methods are discussed including challenging maladaptive thoughts by questioning them or by prospectively testing them. This is a difficult area for some patients. Some will take to cognitive restructuring quite readily, while other patients have a great deal of trouble with it and tend to be quite concrete. It is up to the therapist to decide how much to push these concepts. They can be very helpful for many patients; however, other patients seem to benefit better from more clearly behavioral rather than cognitive strategies, and that is quite acceptable as well. Assignments include completing Purchasing Records and Restructuring Thoughts Worksheets, and reading the next session.

Session Seven—Cues and Chains

As was mentioned previously in the session on restructuring thoughts, some patients take very readily to the material in this session as well including cues and chains, while others have more difficulty. The emphasis here is placed on seeing how patterns of behavior emerge over time and how things that happened earlier in the day can result in CB behavior later in the day. Emphasis is on interrupting the chain as early as possible, such as engaging in alternative behaviors, rearranging consequences, and if the chain involves maladaptive cognitions, restructuring thoughts. Assignments for the next session include completing the Purchasing Records and the Behavioral Chain Worksheets, and reading the next session.

Session Eight—Self-Esteem

This is an excellent time to go to a whiteboard and draw out cues and chains based on problems that patients have experienced in the last week. Again it is often very useful to focus on patients who have had some success, such as those who were able to interrupt the chain earlier. Some emphasis can be given to helping patients who are struggling, but by this point in therapy a lot of emphasis needs to be on the expectation that changes are being made and that patients are showing improvement. Stories of what was helpful for individual patients who have been successful can be quite useful in the group. Whenever possible, encourage group members to provide the material, such as what is the next step in the chain. Assignments include completing the Purchasing Record and the Self-Concept Inventory, and reading over the next session.

Session Nine—Exposure

Begin by reviewing the self-esteem homework. The self-concept inventory is very difficult for people. Group members generally will know each other well enough that they can help each other; for example, suggesting something positive about the physical appearance of the other patient that is attractive or how they relate to others in the group. It is difficult for patients to talk openly about this since they are really talking about themselves, but again it is quite worthwhile to spend time having individual patients, with the help of others in the group, go through this material and also the revision form. Relative to exposure, this is controversial. One of the editors of this book thinks that exposure and response prevention are very useful for many patients with CB (Astrid Müller); the other thinks that exposure is too risky in that for most patients simply avoiding places where they compulsively shopped is preferable (James Mitchell). You as a therapist, based on your background and experiences and your theoretical orientation, will have to decide how to approach this. From a theoretical standpoint a case can be made for exposure and response prevention; however, in reality most people can buy what they need without going into certain stores, and one of us feels that that is a preferable strategy. If this is to be pursued the steps outlined in this session can be quite useful. Assignments include completing the Purchasing Record, going shopping in exposure and response prevention paradigm if used, and reading the material for the next session.

Session Ten—Stress Management and Problem Solving

As always Purchasing Records should be reviewed early in the session. First the homework is reviewed. If exposure has been used, patient's exposure in the last week should be discussed in detail. What was successful should be the focus, or problems should also be discussed but more briefly. If an exposure paradigm is not being used much of the discussion can be used on what stores people need to avoid on a permanent basis. This is important since most people focus on a few specific stores, often clothing stores.

The material on stress management is limited and probably insufficient for many patients. Because of this additional material may be useful depending on the patient or patients in the group. Behavioral problem solving is quite useful for most patients and many will take to it quickly. Other stress management techniques may be less easily grasped. Assignments include completing the Purchasing Records, a stress reduction experiment, and reading the next session.

Session Eleven—Relapse Prevention

The stress reduction experiment should be reviewed along with the buying records. Again emphasis should be placed on patients who were able to successfully complete the experiment, and others should be encouraged to follow along.

It is very important for patients to understand the differences between lapse and relapse. The idea that they have completely relapsed if they have a single buying episode is antithetical to the theoretical model of the program. Lapses or slips should be seen as opportunities to learn. It should be stressed that lapses should be thought about and studied, and then the patient needs to move on. Assignments include completing the Purchasing Records and the Lapse and Relapse Plan, and reading the session material for the last session.

Session Twelve—Summary and Outlook

Lapse and relapse plan should be reviewed in detail. Patients should be encouraged to copy things in other people's plans that they would find useful as well. This is also a good opportunity to discuss that the risk of relapse is highest in the first six months after treatment, and that patients should consider devoting time to rereading the manual and practicing the skills that have been useful for them for a few minutes each day for the next several months. Hopefully patients will be able to list a number of positive changes they have observed and that others have observed and then also to examine other goals they would like to meet in the future. This is also an opportunity to talk about people who may have come forth with other sorts of problems (marital issues, interpersonal conflict with their boss) and how they might find other ways, including additional therapy, to work on these problems as well.

CHAPTER **12**

Compulsive Buying Disorder Group Treatment Manual*†

JAMES E. MITCHELL, MD

Contents

Introduction   171
   Goals of Treatment   171
   Group Expectations   171
   Group Reminders   171
   Involvement of Family and Friends   171
Unit 1: Treatment Program Overview   173
   What Is Compulsive Shopping?   174
Assignments   175
   Myths About Compulsive Buying   179
Contract for Compulsive Buying Disorder Treatment   181
   Making a Commitment to Change   181
Unit 2: Identifying Problem Buying Behaviors and Their
Consequences   183
   Shopping Rules   185
   Reasons For and Against Changing Unhealthy Buying Habits   187
Assignments   189
   What to Expect as You Change Your Buying Behavior   193

169

Unit 3: Cues and Consequences   195
  Possible Consequences That Result from Problem Buying
  Behaviors   196
  Strategies for Change—Focusing on the Cue   196
  Alternative Behaviors   197
  Strategies for Change—Focusing on Consequences   199
  Rearranging Consequences—Goal Setting and Self-Rewards   199
Assignments   200
  Maximizing Healthy Behaviors and Minimizing Buying Behaviors   205
  Alternatives to Problem Buying Behaviors   207
Unit 4: Cash Management, Hoarding   209
  Credit Cards   209
  Cash Management Suggestions   209
  What Is Healthy Buying?   210
  Hoarding   211
Assignments   212
Unit 5: Responses: Thoughts, Feelings, and Behaviors   215
  Introduction   215
  Thoughts, Feelings, and Behaviors   215
  Maladaptive Styles of Thinking   217
  Self-Fulfilling Prophecy   218
Assignments   218
  Becoming Aware of Your Responses   223
Unit 6: Restructuring Your Thoughts   225
  Introduction   225
  Method 1: Challenging Maladaptive Thoughts by Questioning Them   225
  Method 2: Challenging Maladaptive Thoughts by Testing Them   226
Assignments   227
  Restructuring Your Thoughts   231
Unit 7: Cues and Chains   235
Assignments   237
  Identifying Behavioral Chains Worksheet   241
  Identifying Behavioral Chains Worksheet   243
  Identifying Behavioral Chains Worksheet   245
Unit 8: Self-Esteem   247
Assignments   247
  Self-Concept and Self-Esteem   251
  Revision   257
Unit 9: Exposure   259
Assignments   260
Unit 10: Stress Management and Problem Solving   263
  Introduction   263
Assignments   266

Stress Reduction Experiment   269
Unit 11: Relapse Prevention—Lapse and Relapse Plans   271
    Lapse   271
    Relapse   271
Assignments   273
Unit 12: Summary and Outlook   277
    Goal Setting   278

Introduction

Goals of Treatment

1. Interrupt buying disorder behaviors.
2. Establish healthy purchasing patterns.
3. Identify and restructure maladaptive thoughts and negative feelings associated with shopping and buying.
4. Develop and use healthy coping skills.
5. Develop healthy communication patterns.
6. Develop and use relapse prevention techniques.

Group Expectations

1. Attendance at all groups is required. If you are unable to attend, please call your therapist indicating the reason for your absence. Please arrive on time.
2. The Buying Disorder Treatment Program is not appropriate for everyone. For example, a person demonstrating any of the following thoughts or behaviors (persistent suicidal thoughts, self-damaging behavior [cutting, overdosing], misuse of alcohol or drugs) might not benefit from this program and may be referred to another, more appropriate treatment alternative.
3. Please respect confidentiality. Anything said in the group should not be discussed with individuals outside of the group.

Group Reminders

Checking In   Please allow sufficient time for parking and checking in.

Involvement of Family and Friends

People with compulsive buying disorder often find it hard to talk to family and friends about their shopping and buying problems and find it difficult to ask for help. Many fear being misunderstood or ridiculed. Others may think that compulsive buying disorder is a problem they should solve by themselves and view asking for support as a weakness. Many individuals find that conflicts with family and friends stem from financial problems associated with excessive spending.

Think over your own situation. Would you like more support from and communication with family and friends? Are there things that you are reluctant to discuss with them?

Some reasons for involving family and friends in your treatment program include:

1. to be involved with others;
2. to be exposed to different perspectives or ways of thinking;
3. to validate your feelings or check-out your perceptions with people whose feedback you trust and respect;
4. to have access to information and other resources;
5. to provide an opportunity to practice specific skills (such as being assertive and giving rewards);
6. to receive hope and encouragement for your behavior change process.

Unit 1: Treatment Program Overview

1. Buying Disorder is difficult to overcome for several reasons:
    A. The habitual buying pattern very closely resembles that of dependence on chemicals but, unlike chemical dependency where use of the chemical can be given up, usually one cannot avoid shopping or buying.
    B. The behavior presents immediate rewards that reduce motivation to stop. Many people who engage in excessive shopping and buying find that the shopping and buying themselves are stress reducing or in some way reinforcing. The behavior may reduce unpleasant feelings.
    C. Many people with compulsive buying disorder have had previous failures in attempting to stop their behaviors and fear failing in treatment.
    D. When excessive buying behaviors are discontinued, individuals often experience emotional ups and downs and other unpleasant feelings. Without a clear understanding of such symptoms, stopping the behavior may become exceedingly stressful.

However, there are reasons to be hopeful. You can successfully stop all excessive buying and shopping and begin to approach necessary shopping appropriately.

This program is based on treatment concepts that have helped others recover with problems similar to excessive buying. Recovery is a lot of hard work and needs to be your top priority. You increase your chances for success if you make your treatment the No. 1 priority in your life for now.

We strongly encourage you to begin to rapidly decrease your excessive buying behaviors early in treatment. Even though you may be convinced that you cannot do this, a positive attitude is essential, and problem shoppers can decrease their behaviors if properly prepared and offered support. The homework assignments, daily plans, and therapy sessions are designed to help you stop and regain control over your behavior.

2. The role of group in changing problem buying behavior: Several attributes of group therapy offer specific benefits for the treatment of compulsive buying disorder. Group treatment may provide sufficient structure and support to:
    A. Permit interruption of the chronic, habitual nature of the behavior;
    B. Promote reduction of the shame that accompanies the behavior;
    C. Increase the number of people offering insight and support;
    D. Permit group members to increase their own self-esteem through providing support for other group members.

What Is Compulsive Shopping?

I. Clinical characteristics of compulsive buying disorder
   A. Occurrence
      1. Mainly female
      2. Common co-occurrence with mood disorders, anxiety disorders, substance abuse, and problems with impulsivity
   B. Diagnostic criteria for compulsive buying disorder
      1. Feeling irresistible impulses, loss of control
      2. Social, occupational impairment
      3. Financial consequences
   C. Negative consequences
      1. Cognitive and emotional
         a. Depression
         b. Irritability
         c. Problems concentrating
         d. Anxiety
         e. Low self-esteem
      2. Social
         a. Financial-loss of savings, borrowing from friends
         b. Family and friends—isolation
         c. Work and school—lack of advancement, poor attendance
         d. Legal—arrests for bad checks, shoplifting, forging checks
      3. Behavioral
         a. Lying
         b. Impulsive behaviors

II. Factors important to our understanding of compulsive buying disorder
   A. Psychosocial factors
      1. Social and cultural context
         a. Preoccupation with material goods
         b. Emphasis on youth and fashion
         c. Pressures to succeed and appear successful
         d. Money and purchasing as symbols of power
      2. Psychological
         a. Sense of self-worth
         b. Ability to cope with stressful situations
         c. Influence mood
         d. Reduce loneliness
   B. Different factors may perpetuate the symptoms once they start (as it becomes reinforcing)

Assignments

1. Complete "Purchasing Record."

   Keep track of your purchasing habits. For each day, use a blank Purchasing Record form to record:

   a. The time of day you shop/buy;
   b. The items you buy;
   c. The amount of money you spent;
   d. Your thoughts and feelings that are linked with your shopping/ buying;
   e. The time spent planning or thinking about shopping and buying and the time spent shopping and buying.
   f. In the last column mark the buying episode with + (healthy buying), – (impulsive buying), or +/– (undecided).

   Please record your purchase every time you buy something— whether it is a necessary purchase or not.

   You will be using your completed records at the next session. At that session, you will be evaluating how your current purchasing compares to what is considered normal and responsible shopping.
2. Read over and sign your treatment contract.
3. Read "Myths About Buying Disorder"
4. Read next session.
5. Define your problem areas!

   a. What stores?_____
   _____
   _____

   b. What items? _____
   _____
   _____

6. Need to give up credit cards!
   Many people are very resistant to this, but this is very important. You need to substitute debit cards for credit cards.

   List of credit cards:

   _____   _____
   _____   _____
   _____   _____
   _____   _____
   _____   _____

7. Institute the 24-hour rule!

Whenever you see something you want to buy, but didn't plan on buying prior to shopping, you must wait 24 hours! This is very important.

Purchasing Record

Date	Time	Items[a]	Cost	Thoughts/Feelings	+/−

How much time did you spend shopping/buying today? _____ min.

How much time did you spend planning or thinking about shopping/buying today? _____ min.

[a] Indicate if by television (TV) or Internet (IN)

Myths About Compulsive Buying

1. **Myth:** Compulsive buying disorder is a financial problem that will respond to a financial solution.

   Reality: Compulsive buying disorder is a psychologically and socially based problem that will respond to the psychological and social techniques you will learn about in this program. Financial information—e.g., budgeting and goal-setting—is important, but it is not enough in itself. Chances are you already know how to set financial goals and devise budgets—but you are still buying compulsively.

2. **Myth:** Compulsive buying disorder is the same for every compulsive buyer.

   Reality: People differ in why they buy compulsively. Some people buy primarily for psychological reasons—for instance, because buying helps them feel special or successful, because it gives them a high, or because it helps them feel more like they think they should feel. Other people buy primarily for social reasons—e.g., because buying gives them a way to be with people who are important to them (like mother, sisters, children, and friends). For most people, compulsive buying comes from combinations of these psychological and social factors.

   Session 3 will help you distinguish psychological and social reasons for compulsive buying and identify cues that are connected with your buying behavior.

3. **Myth:** American culture discourages compulsive buying.

   Reality: American society is not clear. It tells you compulsive buying is bad. But it encourages you to try to get whatever gratification you want whenever you want it. In addition popular culture glamorizes buying, wealth, and acquisition of material goods. Money and buying are also associated with power in many images seen in popular culture.

4. **Myth:** People have no control over compulsive buying disorder.

   Reality: No matter how strong your inclination to buy compulsively, you can control these behaviors. You can find other, less problematic ways to feel special or successful, happy or high. And you can find less problematic ways to feel close to the important people in your life. Maybe you can't "just say no" to compulsive buying, but you can control the problem by figuring out why you buy and when you buy, and by using coping strategies to change your behavior patterns.

Contract for Compulsive Buying Disorder Treatment

Making a Commitment to Change

I agree to attend the compulsive buying disorder treatment program on a regular basis for the duration of my assigned group. I will attend the sessions, read the required materials, complete the required assignments, and make every effort to participate actively in the group therapy. I will try very hard to bring my problems into the group and to follow the basic principles of the program. I agree to make treatment the #1 priority in my life for now.

Signed: _____   Date: _____

Witness: _____

Unit 2: Identifying Problem Buying Behaviors and Their Consequences

A. How do I recognize problem buying?

It is not always easy to draw a line between problem buying and healthy shopping.

1. Problem buying is often impulsive or compulsive!
2. Problem buying is usually not planned ahead of time!
3. Problem buying might give you a rush!
4. Purchases are not needed!

B. Identifying problem buying **BEHAVIORS**

1. Problem buying is a habit (Note: A habit is a network of thoughts, feelings, and behaviors that operates automatically in response to a cue.)
2. Excessive buying behaviors can occur in response to specific environmental cues or triggers.
3. What are your excessive buying **BEHAVIORS**? (check all that apply to you)

   Impulse purchases
   Multiple purchases
   Going shopping without an item in mind
   Credit card abuse
   Returning items
   Storing/hiding items
   Buying to please/impress others
   Buying for collections I have
   Garage/rummage sales
   Catalogue shopping
   TV shopping
   Internet shopping

4. When are you most at risk of engaging in problem buying behaviors? (e.g., time of day, when feeling angry, etc.)

   1. _____

   _____

   2. _____

   _____

   3. _____

   _____

C. Identify the consequences of your problem buying behaviors.

1. _____

   _____

2. _____

   _____

3. _____

   _____

4. _____

   _____

5. _____

   _____

6. _____

   _____

Shopping Rules

- Make a list of what you need in advance. Write it down.
- If an item is not on the list, don't buy it (even though this might be inconvenient). Don't step outside the list.
- If necessary, keep a running list of items you need.
- Keep a budget for special stores. Decide on the amount of money you want to spend.
- Don't buy at the checkout.
- Don't buy impulsively because it is on sale. *Remember the 24-hour rule!*
- Don't use a cart or shopping basket (except at the grocery store).
- Enter the store through the door closest to the item you want to purchase.
- Throw away catalogues, coupons, and credit card offers that come by mail. Don't even look at them.
- If you want to buy something that is not on your list, build in a pause before you give in. Think about it for at least 24 hours and then decide again.
- Write an emergency card and keep it in your wallet or somewhere else close to you. Write down five reasons why you want to give up problem buying. Read the card whenever you feel tempted to buy impulsively.
- *Remember the 24-hour rule!*
- Do not rationalize.
- Give up all your credit cards. Use debit cards!

Have you found other rules to be helpful?

_____

_____

_____

_____

_____

Reasons For and Against Changing Unhealthy Buying Habits

In the left-hand column list your reasons for stopping your unhealthy buying habits. In the right-hand column list your reasons against stopping your unhealthy buying habits.

Reasons for Stopping	Reasons Against Stopping
Examples: Excessive debt	Examples: Ability to buy whatever & whenever I want
Conflict at home	Provides some security to me

Assignments

1. Complete Purchasing Record.
2. Read "What to Expect as You Change Your Buying Behavior."
3. Read next session.
4. Have you changed your credit cards for debit cards?
5. *Remember the 24-hour rule!*

Purchasing Record

Date	Time	Items[a]	Cost	Thoughts/Feelings	+/−

How much time did you spend shopping/buying today? _____ min.

How much time did you spend planning or thinking about shopping/buying today? _____ min.

[a] Indicate if by television (TV) or Internet (IN)

What to Expect as You Change Your Buying Behavior

The following is a brief list of changes that you can expect to experience as you change your buying behaviors. For some people these changes will be very mild; for others they will be more troublesome. If these changes present a problem for you, please bring your concerns to the group's attention.

1. Changes in Thoughts and Feelings For many people buying and other shopping behaviors serve to "stuff" or numb unpleasant or inappropriate thoughts and feelings. When the buying behavior stops, so do the anesthetic qualities of these behaviors.

As a result, you will probably become more aware of these unpleasant thoughts and feelings. Common changes to expect include feeling demoralized and becoming increasingly more aware of emotional pain, anger, loss, and confusion. This confusion is often associated with being unclear about how you feel and what you want for yourself.

These unpleasant thoughts and feelings will decrease as you learn healthy responses to replace them.

2. More Change in Thoughts and Feelings: Questioning Uncertainty and Anxiety Whenever you are faced with something new, you can expect to experience some anxiety and to question the outcome. This is especially true when you are learning a behavior where the outcome is uncertain— that is, when you have never experienced the outcome or you are unsure of the outcome.

This same anxiety and questioning is often linked with learning to manage your buying behaviors.

Another way to help you overcome this anxiety is to remind yourself of the reasons for learning this new skill. These reasons include:

a. being able to control many of the cues that trigger your unhealthy buying habits;
b. having a flexible framework for controlling your buying behavior;
c. the positive consequences that will follow.

Unit 3: Cues and Consequences

Our responses are cued by what happens before them. The word **CUE** refers to events that occur before responses—thoughts, feelings, or behaviors.

Our responses are encouraged or discouraged by their results, or by those things that occur after the responses. The word **CONSEQUENCE** refers to events occurring after responses.

Cues and consequences can be grouped into the categories shown in Figure 12.1. For the time being, think of responses as Problem Buying **BEHAVIORS**.

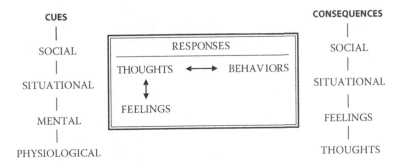

Figure 12.1

Possible Cues That Trigger Problem Buying Behaviors

Categories	Cues	
Social		1. Social isolation (boredom and loneliness)
		2. Interpersonal conflict (anger, frustration, self-blame)
		3. Watching friends engage in shopping behavior
		4. Social holiday and celebrations
		5. Observing others shop excessively
Situational		1. Advertisements in magazines, on TV, etc.
		2. Passing by a shop window
		3. Seeing a Sale or Clearance sign
		4. Necessary shopping
Physiological		1. Fatigue
Mental		1. Memory
		2. Mental image

Possible Consequences That Result from Problem Buying Behaviors

Consequences may be similarly separated into categories. Your unhealthy buying responses result in some positive consequences, or they would not be maintained, and in negative consequences, or there would be no need to change. It is helpful to specify these differences as follows:

Categories	Positive Consequences	Negative Consequences
Social	1. Avoiding anger and frustration	1. Social withdrawal
	2. Social reinforcement for appearing attractive, well off	2. Lying and lack of trust in relationships
Situational	1. Distraction from aversive tasks	1. Occupational problems
	2. Avoiding responsibility or independence	2. Financial problems
Feelings	1. Relief from tension, stress, anger, sadness	1. Depression, guilt, shame
	2. Relief from boredom	2. Tendency to overreact emotionally
	3. Emotional numbing	3. Inability to cope with feelings directly
	4. Feeling nurturance, pleasure, or comfort	
Thoughts	1. Thoughts about looking attractive, getting a bargain	1. Increase in negative self-evaluation or guilt-related thoughts

The problem buying behaviors are maintained because positive consequences resulting from buying are more immediate than the negative consequences and, therefore, more reinforcing.

Strategies for Change—Focusing on the Cue

A major goal of treatment is to change your unhealthy buying habits. One way to change these habits is to take control of the cue by breaking up the relationship between the cue and your buying responses. This is done by: (a) rearranging cues, and (b) changing your responses to cues. Some methods for breaking up the cue-to-response relationship are listed below.

Rearranging Cues

1. **AVOIDANCE:** The simplest method of rearranging cues is to avoid the cue entirely. If a particular cue is a potent trigger for problem buying behaviors you can restructure your environment to remove that cue. For example, if driving by the mall on the way home from work is a cue, take an alternate route home.

2. **RESTRICT THE STIMULUS FIELD**: If you wish to reduce the frequencies of problem buying behaviors, restrict the cues that trigger the behaviors. For example, only shop in specific stores.
3. **STRENGTHEN CUES FOR DESIRED BEHAVIOR**: Expose yourself to existing cues that lead more frequently to healthy behavior. For example, if you are less likely to shop when you are with friends, spend more time with friends.

Changing Your Response to Cues

1. **BUILD IN A PAUSE—DELAY THE RESPONSE**: Building in a pause allows time to pass and breaks up the cue from the automatic buying response. Remember the 24-hour rule!
2. **ALTERNATIVE BEHAVIORS**: Replace a maladaptive behavior with a competing behavior that is adaptive. This method allows a more adaptive behavior to be associated with the high-risk cue (see following section).

Alternative Behaviors

A very powerful way to avoid compulsive buying is to engage in alternative behaviors. This happens in several ways:

1. You can plan alternative behaviors to engage in later during times when it is likely that you will go shopping. Such a time for many people would be in the evening after work or on a Saturday or Sunday afternoon (long-term plans).
2. You can plan alternative behaviors for when you feel the impulse to go shopping (short-term plans). Many times if you engage in alternative behaviors for a fairly brief period of time the urge to shop will decrease.

It is important to establish a list of alternative behaviors for both types of situations:

Planning for High-Risk Times These are the behaviors that many times you need to plan for in advance. For example, if shopping on Saturday afternoon is a common behavioral pattern for you, then earlier in the week you need to decide on what you will be doing on Saturday, and if possible make arrangements with your family or a friend to accompany you. For example:

- Outdoor activities:
  1. swimming
  2. biking
  3. ice skating
  4. hiking

    5. skiing

    6. camping

    7. grilling out

- Indoor activities:

    1. bowling

    2. museums

    3. health club

    4. crafts

    5. movies

    6. plays

    7. restaurants

    8. concerts

Now go back over the list and circle the things which you already do occasionally and enjoy; afterwards go through the above list and put a star (*) by things that you are not now doing but would like to try to do.

Plan some activities from the above categories that you would like to engage in during the next few weeks. Try to include things you have already tried and enjoy and things that you have not tried, but think you might enjoy. Plan to do them at the times you usually go shopping.

Times when you might typically compulsively shop. Be specific—what are the times during the next two weeks when you would be at high risk for shopping? (e.g., tomorrow evening, Tuesday evening)	Alternative behavior in which you would like to involve yourself during that time. Make this a concrete plan and do it.

It is also important to have a list of alternative behaviors ready for times when you have a sudden impulse to shop. Continue to add to this list as you think of other ideas.

Strategies for Change—Focusing on Consequences

Another goal of treatment is to rearrange consequences of behavior so that appropriate behaviors are rewarded and inappropriate behaviors are not. Some methods for using consequences to manage your own behavior are listed below:

Guidelines for the Use of Rewards
    a. The reward must follow rather than precede the behavior.
    b. The reward must be contingent on the occurrence of the behavior (no behavior, no reward).
    c. The reward should follow the behavior as quickly as possible.
    d. Reward behavior in small steps.

There Are Two Types of Rewards: Mental and Material or Activity

Mental Rewards   It is important to congratulate yourself when you are making progress toward your goal. Tell yourself that you are succeeding, that you are doing a good job. Be sure to do this whenever you score even a minor victory. Telling yourself that you are making progress (when you are) can help you continue your gradual success.

Mental rewards are things that you imagine or say to yourself. They can be:

    1. Compliments about something you have done.
    2. Reminding yourself of some characteristics of yourself that you value.

In other words, mental rewards involve saying something positive to yourself *about* yourself.

Mental rewards are useful because:

    1. They can be used anytime, anywhere.
    2. They can be totally tailor-made because they come directly from you.
    3. They can be given immediately after you accomplish a goal.

Material or Activity Rewards   Treat yourself to something fun or pleasurable when you have accomplished your goal. Select activities that are easily obtainable and tailor-made for you. Some examples might include visiting a favorite museum, getting a manicure, or taking a leisurely walk by a lake.

Rearranging Consequences—Goal Setting and Self-Rewards

Self-rewards are an excellent way to encourage healthy behaviors. Setting up an effective reward system involves the following steps:

1. Define the goal behavior that you would like to achieve. Be specific in describing this goal behavior. Also it is important to spell out when and how frequently you will want to accomplish this goal. Remember to keep the goal simple.

   Illustration: My goal behavior is to go grocery shopping with my husband without purchasing any nonessential items.

   _____

   _____

   _____

2. Specify the reward for meeting your goal.

   Illustration: If I meet my goal, then I will take a bubble bath.

   _____

   _____

   _____

Assignments

1. Complete Purchasing Record.
2. Cues and Consequences associated with problem buying behaviors.
3. Rearranging Cues and Changing Responses.
4. List of alternative behaviors.
5. Warning signs.
6. Read next session.

Purchasing Record

Date	Time	Items[a]	Cost	Thoughts/Feelings	+/−

How much time did you spend shopping/buying today? ____ min.

How much time did you spend planning or thinking about shopping/buying today? ____ min.

[a] Indicate if by television (TV) or Internet (IN)

Cues and Consequences		
Cues	Problem Buying Behaviors	Positive and Negative Consequences

Maximizing Healthy Behaviors and Minimizing Buying Behaviors

Rearranging Cues and Changing Your Responses to Cues   Think of three cues that are frequently associated with problem buying behaviors. Then consider strategies that you can use to rearrange the cue to minimize the occurrence of the problem shopping behaviors. Refer to **Strategies for Change**.

Cue: _____

Strategy: _____

_____

_____

_____

Cue: _____

Strategy: _____

_____

_____

_____

Cue: _____

Strategy: _____

_____

_____

_____

Alternatives to Problem Buying Behaviors

1. Call a group member or friend. Keep calling until you reach someone.
2. Write the purchase instead of actually buying it.
3. Take a bath or shower.
4. Take a walk.
5. Do a non-shopping-related activity outside shops. Stay out of the mall.
6. Write a letter.
7. Do a relaxation exercise or meditation.
8. Distract yourself with a craft project, book, or TV program.
9. Write out thoughts and feelings.
10. Go to a movie, museum, or play.
11. Read something inspirational.
12. Listen to music.
13. _____
14. _____
15. _____
16. _____
17. _____
18. _____
19. _____
20. _____

It is important that you choose alternatives that you enjoy. It is also important that there are alternatives to choose that are readily available. For instance, if reading a book is an alternative, make sure you have one available that is interesting and, even better, difficult to put down.

There may be times when you find it necessary to try several alternatives before the urge to shop/buy diminishes. There also may be times when you try everything and the urge to shop/buy remains strong. On these occasions you may need to hold on to your chair or simply go to sleep. You will feel better the next day, especially after having made it through a very difficult period.

Unit 4: Cash Management, Hoarding

In the last session, we discussed cues and consequences of excessive shopping. When people have problems with compulsive buying they often describe themselves as acting impulsively and feeling out of control of their behavior.

You should consider decreasing the availability of buying by reducing the number of or giving up credit cards.

Credit Cards

We encourage you to take the opportunity in group today to give up or destroy your credit cards if you have not done so yet. This process can be frightening and painful, but it is extremely helpful in limiting excessive buying because credit cards are a powerful cue for most individuals with these problems. The decision to give up your credit cards is a difficult one, but we suggest you take this step in the way that it will be most helpful to you.

Take a few minutes to evaluate your current credit card status and to decide on an elimination strategy that will work best for you.

How many credit cards do you own? (List) _____

_____

What will be the advantages of giving up credit cards?

1.

2.

3.

4.

What will be the disadvantages of this?

1.

2.

3.

4.

Cash Management Suggestions

1. For two weeks, keep track of every cent you spend, including petty cash.
2. Pay yourself first, by putting about 10 percent of your net income into savings.
3. Build an emergency fund; 3–6 months take-home pay.
4. Set up an escrow fund to pay for periodic payments such as car insurance.

5. Use automatic payroll deposit, savings deposit, and bill payment.
6. Leave your checkbook at home.
7. Carry only as much cash as you can afford to lose.
8. Pay off your credit cards. This may take some time.
9. Buy no nonessential items until you have made a satisfactory payment on your debts.
10. Put any tax refund or other windfall into savings immediately.
11. Balance your checkbook every month or hire someone to do it for you.

What Is Healthy Buying?

Healthy buying is using money in a thoughtful way for past, present, and future purposes. Thoughtful buying means allocating money in ways that reflect priorities you establish to enable you to live the kind of life you want to live.

Thoughtful buying for past purposes means gradually paying off bills you've already accumulated. Thoughtful buying for present purposes means spending the right amount of money—neither too much nor too little—on life's necessities, that is, shelter, clothing, food, fun, and taxes. Thoughtful buying for future purposes means setting aside the right amount of money—again, neither too much nor too little—for future needs, that is, emergency, retirement, educating children, helping elderly parents. "The right amount of money" obviously depends on your income and obligations as well as on your values. But all of these—income, obligations, and values—are influenced by what money means to you.

For some people money means *success*. These people use money as a signal to themselves and others that they are successful, that they are competent, that they are up to the task, whatever the task might be. For other people money means *affection*. These people use money, and the things money can buy, to try to attract other people, to draw them closer, and hold on to them. For still others money means expression. These people use money to express themselves, to show that they are distinctive, special. And for still other people money means *security*. They hold on to it, save it eagerly, buy it cautiously, keep it under control at all times. Many of us use money for two or more of these purposes.

There is nothing wrong with using money for any or all of these purposes. It is good to be successful. It is good to attract people. It is good to express yourself. And it is good to be planful and cautious.

What is not so good, though, is using money for these different purposes without recognizing that that is what you are doing—to buy more and more symbols of success, affection, expression, and security without recognizing that that is what we are doing. The deeper our needs to tell other people and ourselves that we are successful or attractive or distinctive or cautious, the more desperately we may use money for those purposes, and the further we will be from thoughtful buying.

Hoarding

Many times people with compulsive buying disorder buy things they don't really need, and at times they don't even unwrap these things but will store or hoard them. At other times they will give them away or take them back to the store.

Some people with compulsive buying disorder therefore have a number of things, never used, that they have stored or hoarded somewhere in their house or have rented a storage place. If you have such things then list them below:

Type of Item	Number of Them	Approx. Value Each Item	Approx. Value Total	Where Stored or Hoarded
Example: Shoes	20 pairs	$50	$1000	Closet in upstairs hall

It's time to "clean house." If you have designated spaces where you store or hoard things you are not going to use, it is time to get rid of them. There are several ways to do this:

1. Simply throw them out.
2. If they are valuable you can give them away to a worthy cause. If you give things like this away you can take a tax deduction as a donation to charity.
3. You can take things back to the store.
4. You can give them away to family or friends as gifts or presents.

Whatever your plan, it is important to stop storing or hoarding things that you do not want to use or cannot use. Therefore for each of the items above repeat the name of the group of items below, and indicate what you intend to do with them. Check off when you have completed your plan.

Group of Item	How Will You Get Rid of Them?	When Will You Get Rid of Them?	Check Off When Done
Example: 20 pairs of shoes	Give 10 to free store; take 10 back	Next Monday	

Assignments

1. Complete Purchasing Record.
2. Hoarding Assignment.
3. Read session material for next session.

Purchasing Record

Date	Time	Items[a]	Cost	Thoughts/Feelings	+/−

How much time did you spend shopping/buying today? _____ min.

How much time did you spend planning or thinking about shopping/buying today? _____ min.

[a] Indicate if by television (TV) or Internet (IN)

Unit 5: Responses: Thoughts, Feelings, and Behaviors

Introduction

In Unit 3 we discussed how specific cues trigger problem buying responses that lead to specific consequences. Cues trigger *external* and *internal* responses. External responses are the **BEHAVIORS** (actions you do that are observed by others). Internal responses are the **THOUGHTS** and **FEELINGS** that are usually "private" and are often difficult for you to identify or for others to observe. Thoughts are particularly important in determining how a person reacts to a situation or cue. That is, the thoughts you have regarding a particular situation or cue can influence your feelings and behaviors. In this session we will focus on how your thoughts about a situation or cue are linked to your feelings and behaviors (Figure 12.2).

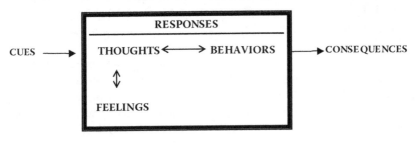

Figure 12.2

Thoughts, Feelings, and Behaviors

You may have observed that different people react to the same cue in a variety of ways. The various ways that people react to a cue are linked with their thoughts about the situations. For example, let's say there are two people passing by a shop window after a stressful day at work. One person has a history of problem buying, whereas the other person does not have a history of problem buying. These two people may have very different reactions to this shop. It is very likely that the person without a history of problem shopping may either pay no attention to the shop or stop briefly and browse. In contrast the person with problem shopping may feel tense, experience an urge to buy, then begins to buy several items with little thought. Thus the two people have reacted to the same cue differently. The difference in their reaction is primarily due to the thoughts they have had with regard to the shop. The person without problem shopping may have thought, "Maybe I'll take a look before I go home." On the other hand, the person with problems shopping may have thought, "I have been having a rough day. I deserve new clothes."

Feelings   There are no right or wrong feelings—feelings just are. What you feel is okay. Everyone experiences many feelings during the day. At times it may be difficult to put a finger on what you are feeling. If you are not used to identifying or experiencing your feelings, it may be difficult to understand exactly what you are feeling. By taking time to think about what has happened, and to get in touch with your feelings, you will be able to do something about the way you feel. It may be that you need to confront someone because you are angry or hurt; or that you are happy and need to express it; or that you are lonely and need a hug; or maybe need to do something fun with someone. Every emotion you feel does not need to be identified and acted upon. The ones that you feel intensely and are causing a change in your behavior are the emotions that may need attention.

Your feelings are determined by your thoughts. If your thought is, "I look unattractive," you might be feeling anxious and upset. If you think, "I am an interesting person," then you might feel calm and relaxed.

Automatic Thoughts   You may not always be aware of some of your thoughts in response to certain situations. For example, have you sometimes driven a car and couldn't remember how you got from one place to another? Obviously you were thinking, otherwise you could not have reached your destination, but you were not aware of the behaviors and thoughts associated with the driving. Similarly you may find that you are upset or anxious, but may not be aware of the thoughts that led to these feelings. If you are responding in a way that is maladaptive, such as with problem buying, it is important to first become aware of your thoughts and then to change these thoughts that lead to maladaptive feelings and behaviors. We will describe how to challenge these thoughts in the next session.

How would you react to the following situation?

Cue: You just bought two pairs of shoes that weren't on your purchasing plan.

What are your **thoughts** associated with this situation? What are you saying to yourself? Think of as many thoughts as you can. It's helpful to ask yourself: "If I think this thought, then what would I think?" If you have difficulty coming up with thoughts, try to guess what you might think. Some examples are:

_____

_____

_____

_____

What are your **feelings** associated with this situation? (Usually one-word descriptions such as depressed, angry, anxious, etc.)

_____

_____

_____

_____

How might you **behave** in this situation? What do you do or say? (Can include shopping behaviors.)

_____

_____

_____

_____

Maladaptive Styles of Thinking

With time you may become aware that you have developed particular styles of thinking. There are some styles of thinking that may lead to problem shopping responses. The following are examples of maladaptive styles of thinking that may contribute to your shopping behaviors.

Overgeneralization   Extracting a rule on the basis of one event and applying it to other situations. Watch for key words—"always," "never."

   a. Nobody likes me.
   b. I'm never going to be able to control my shopping and buying.
   c. I always feel like shopping.

Catastrophizing   Embellishing a situation with surplus meaning that isn't supported by objective evidence. Seeing certain situations in an extreme way.

   a. I've made more purchases than are on my purchasing plan—I'm a failure.
   b. I'm going to be late—this is terrible.
   c. I splurged while shopping. I've spoiled everything I've done in treatment.

Dichotomous   All or nothing, black-or-white thinking.

   a. I've already gone over my budget; I might as well buy these extra things.

  b. I've bought one item I didn't plan; the entire day is downhill from here.

  c. I'm either in complete control or totally out of control.

Self-Fulfilling Prophecy

Making predictions about the outcome of one event and acting in ways to ensure it will come to pass.

  a. I won't be able to control my spending on Saturday.

  b. I'll always be in debt.

Overreliance on the Opinions of Others

  a. The saleswoman told me that this dress was meant for me.

It is important to begin recognizing your particular maladaptive styles of thinking in response to situations and to begin challenging these thoughts. List below some maladaptive thoughts you frequently have in relation to your compulsive buying disorder.

1. _____

2. _____

3. _____

4. _____

5. _____

Assignments

1. Complete Purchasing Record.
2. Restructuring Thoughts Worksheet 1.
3. Read next session.
4. Have you given up credit cards for debit cards?

Purchasing Record

Date	Time	Items[a]	Cost	Thoughts/Feelings	+/−

How much time did you spend shopping/buying today? ____ min.

How much time did you spend planning or thinking about shopping/buying today? ____ min.

[a] Indicate if by television (TV) or Internet (IN)

Restructuring Thoughts Worksheet 1

Cue	Responses		Consequences
	Thoughts	Behaviors	
	Feelings		

Becoming Aware of Your Responses

Step 1: IDENTIFY the Problem   Think of a **CUE** that usually leads to problem shopping behaviors. Use the following questions to identify the cue, thoughts, feelings, behaviors, and consequences. Write your answers to each question on the top half of the Restructuring Thoughts Worksheet.

   a. What is the situation or **CUE** that is triggering your problem buying responses? Refer to the previous session for examples of cues.
   b. How are you responding to this cue? (Complete in any order.)
      • How are you **FEELING**? Are you feeling anxious, depressed?
      • What are you telling yourself about this cue? What are your **THOUGHTS**? Remember to list as many thoughts as you can.
      • What are you doing or saying? What **BEHAVIORS** are triggered by this cue? Do you make inappropriate purchases?
   c. Now consider the **CONSEQUENCES** to your responses. List these consequences in the last column. The consequences can be positive or negative. Refer back to the previous session for examples of consequences.

Unit 6: Restructuring Your Thoughts

Introduction

In the previous session you learned the *first step* in how to restructure your thoughts that are linked with problem buying behaviors—that is, to become aware of your thoughts, feelings, and behaviors that are triggered by a particular cue and result in specific consequences.

The *second step* is to evaluate your thoughts to determine whether they are accurate or reasonable. There are two ways that you can determine the accuracy of your thoughts. The first way is to challenge your thoughts by questioning them. The second way is to set up experiments that test for the accuracy of your thoughts.

Method 1: Challenging Maladaptive Thoughts by Questioning Them In other words, ask yourself if your thoughts are really accurate. The primary questions that will help you to evaluate your thoughts are:

1. What is the *evidence* to support or refute my thoughts?
2. What are the *implications* of my thoughts? In other words, what if the thoughts are really true?
3. What are *alternative* explanations for my thoughts?

The *third step* is to change your thoughts based on the new information you uncovered through your questions.

The *fourth step* is to evaluate how your revised thoughts will change your feelings, behaviors, and consequences.

EXAMPLE:
Step 1. Identify the problem.

Cue:	Stressful morning at work.
Thoughts:	"I can't deal with work. I have to go shopping at lunch to get through the day."
Feelings:	Guilty
Behaviors:	Engage in excessive buying
Consequences:	Self-disgust, more depressed, more distracted at work because of concerns about personal finances.

Step 2. Evaluate your thoughts. **What is the evidence?**

Supports	(none)
Refutes	I am having a difficult day at work but there is no evidence that I *can't deal* with it. Also, shopping usually makes me feel worse rather than better afterwards.

What are the implications?

If I really am having problems with work, I can consult my boss or co-worker for help and advice.

What are the alternative explanations?

None.

Step 3. Change your thoughts. **What are the revised thoughts?** It's been a difficult morning, but I've handled challenging situations at work successfully in the past. I'll feel worse if I shop at lunch; seeking support from my colleague at lunch will end up helping me more.

Step 4. Determine the effects of your revised thoughts. **What are the revised feelings?** Less anxious, less depressed, more confident.

What are the revised behaviors? No shopping; spend time with friend.
What are the revised consequences? Sense of achievement, sense of being in control, able to concentrate at work, not feeling guilty.

Method 2: Challenging Maladaptive Thoughts by Testing Them

Another method of challenging thoughts is to test them by setting up experiments to determine their accuracy.

How can you test the following thought: "I couldn't possibly survive without my credit cards."

_____

_____

_____

Are there any maladaptive thoughts that you can test? What are these?

_____

_____

_____

How can you go about testing these thoughts?

_____

_____

_____

It is possible that in testing some of these thoughts, they are, in fact, accurate. In that case it may be helpful to evaluate the implications of these thoughts.

Example: People will notice me more if I'm wearing expensive clothes.

Implication: That may be true in some cases; however, what if they don't notice me? That does not mean that something is wrong with me. It's not necessary to be noticed by others in order to feel good about myself.

Assignments

1. Complete Purchasing Record.
2. Restructuring Thoughts Worksheet.
3. Read next session.

Purchasing Record

Date	Time	Items[a]	Cost	Thoughts/Feelings	+/−

How much time did you spend shopping/buying today? _____ min.

How much time did you spend planning or thinking about shopping/buying today? _____ min.

[a] Indicate if by television (TV) or Internet (IN)

Restructuring Your Thoughts

Instructions: Using the Restructuring Thoughts Worksheet on the next page:

1. Copy the specific **CUE** that you have listed in Step 1 of the last session's assignment, as well as the **THOUGHTS, FEELINGS, BEHAVIORS,** and **CONSEQUENCES.**

2. Challenge your thoughts using the three questions mentioned. Write in these new **THOUGHTS** in the Revised Thoughts column.

    You may ask yourself the first question and gather enough new information so that it is not necessary to ask the other two questions.

3. Now imagine yourself in the same situation (listed under the first column). Write in your new Revised **FEELINGS** and **BEHAVIORS** in the appropriate column. What would be the revised **CONSEQUENCES** to these new responses?

Cue	Responses			Consequences
	Thoughts	Feelings	Behaviors	
	Revised Thoughts	Revised Feelings	Revised Behaviors	Revised Consequences

Unit 7: Cues and Chains

In the previous sessions, we have talked about the occurrence of behavior consisting of five components. The **cue** often leads to responses consisting of **thoughts, feelings**, and **behaviors** that lead to specific **consequences** (see Figure 12.3).

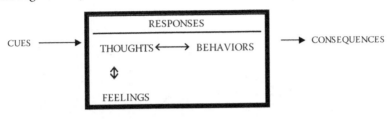

Figure 12.3

The occurrence of behavior often does not involve only these five components. Most of the time the occurrence of behavior consists of a series of components where each part represents one link in a long behavioral chain. For example, a cue triggers responses (thoughts, feelings, behaviors) which become a cue that triggers *another* set of responses, and so on until the final consequence occurs. Writing out a behavioral chain is a helpful strategy for understanding how a particular behavior came about. You may discover that a chain started in the morning or even the previous day that resulted in the final consequence. Or your chain may be a series of cues, thoughts, feelings, etc., that occurred in a period of three hours. The following illustrates a behavioral chain that eventually triggered a problematic buying episode (see Figure 12.4).

It is very important for you to determine your chain of behavior so that you can break the chain early in the cycle. The earlier the chain is broken, the easier it is to prevent the occurrence of buying behavior.

The same strategies for behavior change which were described in previous sessions can be used for breaking a behavioral chain. To review, these strategies include:

Rearranging Cues:	Avoid the cue
	Restrict your stimulus field
	Strengthen cues that promote healthy behaviors
Changing Responses to Cues:	Build in a pause—delay the response
	Alternative behaviors
Rearranging Consequences:	Structuring rewards for your success
Restructuring Thoughts:	What is the evidence?
	What are the implications?
	What are the alternative explanations?

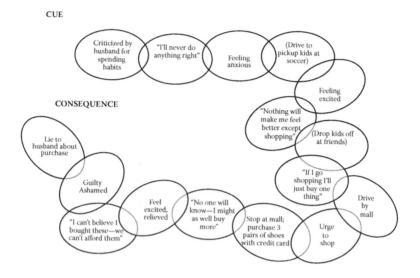

Figure 12.4 Behavioral chain.

Using the previous example, consider what techniques you would use to break the chain at the following places:

1. "I never do anything right":

_____

_____

2. Feeling agitated:

_____

_____

3. "If I go shopping, I'll just buy one thing":

_____

_____

4. Drive by mall:

_____

_____

5. "No one will know; I might as well buy more":

_____

_____

Assignments

1. Complete Purchasing Record.
2. Complete Behavioral Chain Worksheets.
3. Read next session.

Purchasing Record

Date	Time	Items[a]	Cost	Thoughts/Feelings	+/−

How much time did you spend shopping/buying today? _____ min.

How much time did you spend planning or thinking about shopping/buying today? _____ min.

[a] Indicate if by television (TV) or Internet (IN)

Identifying Behavioral Chains Worksheet

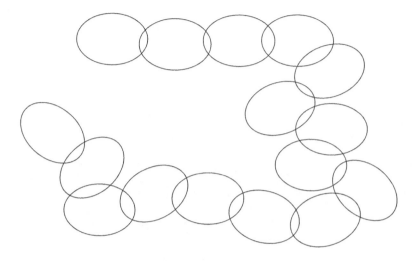

1. Identify three places where you would break this behavioral chain by placing a line between two links.
2. What strategies would you use at these breaks in the chain?

_____

_____

_____

Identifying Behavioral Chains Worksheet

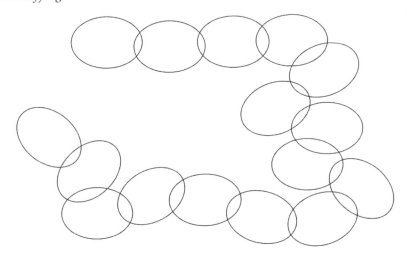

1. Identify three places where you would break this behavioral chain by placing a line between two links.
2. What strategies would you use at these breaks in the chain?

_____

_____

_____

Identifying Behavioral Chains Worksheet

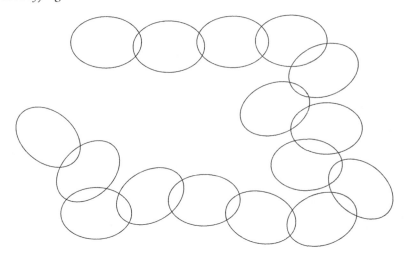

1. Identify three places where you would break this behavioral chain by placing a line between two links.
2. What strategies would you use at these breaks in the chain?

_____

_____

_____

Unit 8: Self-Esteem

We define self-esteem as the way in which an individual evaluates herself/himself. Self-esteem is one aspect of self-concept, which is a more general term for how an individual defines herself/himself.

Many individuals with buying problems have low self-esteem; they tend to evaluate themselves in a negative, self-critical manner. Specifically they exaggerate their weaknesses and minimize their strengths. Self-esteem problems often contribute to buying problems, since many individuals end up shopping to make themselves feel better or as a form of self-punishment. After excessive spending, individuals usually end up feeling even worse about themselves.

The techniques used for evaluating the accuracy of your thoughts that lead to excessive buying can also be used to challenge and test thoughts that contribute to low self-esteem. The first step is to identify the types of "cognitive errors" you tend to make in evaluating yourself.

Here are some examples of dysfunctional thoughts related to low self-esteem:

Thought	Type of Thinking Error
"I'm no good."	Overgeneralizations
"I'm a failure."	
"I never do anything right."	
"I'm worthless."	
"I can't do it—I'll never do it right."	Catastrophizing
"I did it well, but I should have done it better."	Minimization
"If I don't do well at one thing, it means I'll never be successful."	Black-and-white thinking
"Everybody thinks I'm a loser."	Mind-Reading
"My boss just criticized me—she thinks I'm incompetent."	

After identifying the type of errors you make in evaluating yourself, challenge and test the accuracy of your thoughts: What is the evidence? What are alternative explanations? What are the implications? Are there ways of testing the accuracy of this thought? In addition, examine the type of language you use in evaluating yourself by completing the Self-Concept Inventory.

Assignments

1. Complete Purchasing Record.
2. Complete Self-Concept Inventory.
3. Read next session.

Purchasing Record

Date	Time	Items[a]	Cost	Thoughts/Feelings	+/−

How much time did you spend shopping/buying today? ____ min.

How much time did you spend planning or thinking about shopping/buying today? ____ min.

[a] Indicate if by television (TV) or Internet (IN)

Self-Concept and Self-Esteem

1. Using the self-concept inventory (attached), please write descriptive comments about yourself for each of the categories. Include both positive and negative comments.
2. Now go back through the inventory and separate comments pertaining to your strengths and weaknesses. Rewrite.
    a. strengths: using synonyms, adjectives, and adverbs to elaborate
    b. weaknesses:
        1. Use nonpejorative language
        2. Use accurate language
        3. Use specific rather than general language
        4. Find exceptions or corresponding strengths
3. Write a new self-description, including your revised strengths and weaknesses
4. Remembering your strengths:
    a. Daily affirmations: Write your strengths down on a 3 × 5 index card and read them several times a day.
    b. Reminder signs placed in your home or at work to cue you to mentally repeat your affirmations.
    c. Active integration: Each day select three strengths from your list and remember situations from the past that exemplify those strengths. Consider as many examples as you can for each strength.

Self-Concept Inventory

Name:

Physical Appearance

How I Relate to Others

Personality

How Others See Me

Self-Concept Inventory

Name:

Performance at School/Work

Performance of Daily Tasks of Life

Mental Functioning

Friends/Romance/Sexuality

Revision

Weaknesses

    1.

    2.

    3.

    4.

    5.

    6.

    7.

Strengths (elaborate using detailed language)

    1.

    2.

    3.

    4.

    5.

    6.

    7.

Unit 9: Exposure

In learning to control urges to compulsively buy it is important that individuals who have had problems in this area learn to expose themselves to potential buying situations, and learn to master these situations by not buying things. This is particularly important, because for the rest of your life you will periodically be in situations where the potential for compulsive buying behavior is around you.

Maladaptive behaviors can be effectively changed "by doing, not talking ... by practicing new behaviors, as well as exposure to critical cues."

Exposure involves "planned, sustained, and repetitive exposures" to shopping situations that usually trigger buying behavior. It is important to stay in the situation until discomfort or the urge to buy decreases.

For this reason we would like you to do an exercise involving "exposure," wherein you will expose yourself to a situation that usually would have resulted in compulsive buying and learn to master the situation by not buying. There are several steps to this process:

Step 1. Choose someone with whom to go shopping. This could be a spouse or other family member, if they are aware of your problem and are interested in helping you. It could also be a friend.

Step 2. Decide in advance what difficult shopping situation (what store or other venue, time of day, day of the week) would be a high-risk situation for you.

Step 3. You need to arrange to meet with your "shopping partner" in advance and talk through your plans for visiting this high-risk situation with him/her. In particular you should discuss when and where you will go, and set up an appropriate time to visit the store.

Step 4. It's time for your visit. With your shopping partner, go to the high-risk situation and engage in the behaviors you would have engaged in previously that would have resulted in compulsive buying. This would involve visiting the department or departments that are high-risk for you: handling objects, trying on clothes, or engaging in other behaviors that would be prerequisites to compulsive buying. The idea is to basically recreate the ritual that would have resulted in compulsive buying previously. Don't forget to wait until the urge to buy decreases! Describe the experience.

_____

_____

_____

Step 5.   The next step is to repeat the process. Go to the chosen place with your "shopping partner," but have that individual wait outside for you. If it is a mall he/she can wait outside of the store, and if it is a store away from the mall he/she can wait for you in the car. You should go in and repeat all these high-risk behaviors. You should engage in these behaviors by yourself and refrain from buying anything. Describe the experience:

_____

_____

_____

Step 6.   The last step in this process is for you to engage in all of these behaviors by yourself. This involves going to the compulsive buying situation, engaging in the usual behaviors, and leaving without buying. Describe the experience:

_____

_____

_____

It is hoped that learning to master this situation, and other similar situations in the future, will allow you to feel a better sense of control in situations where you might be tempted to compulsively buy. People can learn to control their behavior, and this type of stepwise exposure can help in that process.

Assignments
1. Complete Purchasing Record.
2. Go Shopping! (Exposure)
3. Read session material for next session.

Purchasing Record

Date	Time	Items[a]	Cost	Thoughts/Feelings	+/−

How much time did you spend shopping/buying today? ____ min.

How much time did you spend planning or thinking about shopping/buying today? ____ min.

[a] Indicate if by television (TV) or Internet (IN)

Unit 10: Stress Management and Problem Solving

Introduction

In the popular press we are hearing more about the effects of stress on our physical and mental health. It is easy to assume that stress is something to be avoided because it is the "enemy." In reality stress is a natural phenomenon and essential to life. It is how we respond to stressful events and in particular what we tell ourselves about stressful events that determine whether we experience stress in a healthy or unhealthy way.

The following information on stress will help you begin to evaluate your attitudes about stress, how you perceive stressful events (stressors), how you choose to respond to (or cope with) these stressors, and how the consequences of stress affect you.

A. Stress and Its Components

    1. **STRESSOR**: The demand

        a. Could be of major proportions:
- moving
- loss of significant other
- marriage

        b. Could be of minor proportions:
- finding a parking place
- completing an assignment
- blind date

        c. Most people recognize and accept the major stressors, but minimize the significance of the minor ones. Repetitive minor stressors can accumulate and take on major proportions.

        d. **IMPORTANT**: Recognize **YOUR** stressors.

    2. **STRESS RESPONSE**: Involves thoughts, feelings, behaviors, and physical states that are triggered by the stressor.

	Positive Responses	**Negative Responses**
Thoughts	I like a challenge.	I am incompetent.
	I can get it done.	I must do this perfectly.
	Relax; I'm doing what I can.	I can't handle this.
Feelings	Exhilaration	Anxious
	In control	Angry
	Competent	Frustrated
		Sad
Behaviors	Assertive	Withdrawal
	Productive	Avoiding situations
	Task-Oriented	Overreacting

continued

	Positive Responses	Negative Responses
Physical States	Increased pulse rate	Knots in stomach
	More strength	Headache
	Increased speech	Trembling

B. How to Manage Stress Effective coping means that you are managing the **STRESSOR** and your **STRESS RESPONSE** (thoughts, feelings, behaviors, physical states) in such a way that the results (**CONSEQUENCES**) are positive—balanced and healthy.

1. Managing stress involves at least two tasks:

   Task #1: *Problem solving.* Dealing directly with the problem or the stressor that is triggering the stress response.

   Task #2: *Stress management.* Minimizing stressors in your life and managing the stress response.

   Sometimes you will need to deal with the problem first and then manage your stress response to that problem.

   At other times, you will need to handle the stress response first and the problem later.

   Most often, you will be doing both tasks interchangeably. That is, first dealing with the problem until the stress response gets you out of balance (negative consequences), then managing the stress response until you are back in balance (positive consequences). You will then be in the position to return to the problem.

2. **PROBLEM SOLVING** (Task #1)
   a. Identify feelings and behaviors.
   b. Define the problem.
      What has happened?
      What is upsetting about the situation?
   c. Decide what you want and establish goals.
      What do I want?
      What would I prefer to happen?
   d. Generate several possible solutions.
   e. Evaluate each alternative; choose the "best" alternative.
      How useful will this outcome be in solving my problem?
      How difficult will it be to do it?
      Do the benefits of this solution outweigh the possible costs?
   f. **IMPLEMENT.**
   g. Verify afterwards.
      What were the consequences of my action?
      Am I satisfied with the results?
      If not return to step E.

3. **STRESS MANAGEMENT** (Task #2)
   a. General well being—develop regular habits
      1. Eat three adequate, nutritionally balanced meals a day.
      2. Exercise regularly (but don't overdo it).
      3. Sleep adequately and regularly.
      4. Listen to your body and relax when needed.
      5. Provide time for pleasant and rewarding activities in your day.
      6. Provide time for peaceful solitude—for quiet time alone.
      7. Avoid excessive use of alcohol and caffeinated beverages.
   b. Organize yourself
      1. Set priorities. (No one can do everything at once. Protect yourself from overload—mental, emotional, physical, and behavioral.)
      2. Structure your time. (Plan your day so that you use your time and energy efficiently. Learn to pace your work and activities.)
      3. Set realistic and practical goals. (Monitor your progress toward these goals.)
      4. Make decisions. (Learn to identify alternatives, evaluate their pros and cons, and choose the alternative that is appropriate for you at that time. Note: Leaving a decision unresolved is a stressor in itself.)
   c. Establish friendships so that you:
      1. are emotionally involved with others;
      2. are exposed to different perspectives or ways of thinking;
      3. can validate your feelings and check out your perceptions with people whose feedback you trust and respect;
      4. have access to information and other resources;
      5. have opportunity to practice specific skills and receive support and encouragement.
   d. Control your environment
      1. Avoid too many changes in your life at any one time.
      2. Shield yourself when necessary. (Control the amount of stimulation in your environment. Avoid too little or too many stressors at one time.)
      3. Create a personal stability zone so that there is someone or something that you can fall back on.
      4. Remove yourself permanently from the stressor. (Change your environment or the situation—eliminate or avoid the stressful cue.)

    e. Manage your THOUGHTS and FEELINGS (emotions)

       1. Unwind. (Do a short relaxation exercise, meditate, go for a walk, stretch, take a deep breath, etc.)

       2. Work off the stress. (Exercise, garden, play tennis, get involved in another activity, etc.)

       3. Drain off the stress by using heat and/or massage. (Take a hot bath or sauna, etc.)

       4. Take time out. Take short breaks or do something else for a short period of time.

       5. Talk out the stress with another person.

Assignments

1. Complete Purchasing Record.
2. Stress Reduction Experiment.
3. Read next session.

Purchasing Record

Date	Time	Items[a]	Cost	Thoughts/Feelings	+/−

How much time did you spend shopping/buying today? _____ min.
How much time did you spend planning or thinking about shopping/buying today? _____ min.

[a] Indicate if by television (TV) or Internet (IN)

Stress Reduction Experiment

Identify a stressor in your life _____

_____

_____

Choose one technique to cope with or reduce this stressor _____

_____

_____

Describe the results of your experiment_____

_____

_____

List below some techniques you can use to try to manage stress this week:

1.

2.

3.

4.

5.

Unit 11: Relapse Prevention—Lapse and Relapse Plans

Lapse

A lapse is a single slip. Don't see it as an indication of failure because this way you are more likely to escalate into a full-blown relapse. See it as a temporary setback. Lapses can be viewed as valuable learning opportunities ("learning from mistakes"). Try to understand what led up to it and view it as a chance to renew commitment.

Relapse

A relapse is a series of lapses that continue. People give up.

1. Why do people relapse? People relapse for a variety of reasons. What sorts of problems/thoughts might contribute to your relapse? What are your **HIGH-RISK SITUATIONS**?

   _____

   _____

   _____

   _____

   _____

2. The following is a scenario of a relapse.
   Imagine that you have successfully completed the compulsive buying treatment program. You've been free from excessive buying for five months and have been following your purchasing plans. You start encountering some problems in your life. You are in a new job, are making more money and are meeting new people. You are finding it increasingly difficult to plan your finances because of your new schedule. You very much want to appear attractive and financially secure to the people around you. You start to shop for clothes at lunch. You acquire extra credit cards and soon you are shopping every day after work. During the period of one week you have gone from healthy habits to excessive spending again. You are early in the process of relapse. What are you going to do?

Lapse Plan (Write a step-by-step plan that you will carry out if a lapse occurs. Focus on not only what you would do, but also how you would change your thoughts.)

1. _____

_____

2. _____

_____

3. _____

_____

4. _____

_____

5. _____

_____

6. _____

_____

Relapse Plan (Write a step-by-step plan that you will carry out if relapse occurs. Focus on not only what you would do, but also how you would change your thoughts.)

1. _____

_____

2. _____

_____

3. _____

_____

4. _____

_____

5. _____

_____

6. _____

_____

1. To avoid a relapse, you need to be able to confront stressors, expected or unexpected, with increasing confidence and self-esteem. It is important to continue to practice the skills that have been suggested in treatment in previous sessions. If there is a stressor that you can predict, such as returning to school in the fall, a friend's wedding, moving, etc., it will be important to anticipate areas of concern, plan ahead, and talk it out with a friend.

   Listed are some of the skills to continue to practice:

   a. Problem-solving techniques and priority setting in times of crises.
   b. Stress management skills: relaxation, avoid too many changes at once, make decisions, adequate sleep.
   c. Alternative behaviors.
   d. Challenging dichotomous and catastrophizing thoughts.
   e. Improve self-esteem.
   f. Reward self for accomplishing goals.
2. It is also very important to have a support network established now that the group is coming to a close. This may include:
   a. Family and friends
   b. Support systems and groups such as self-help groups, assertiveness training groups, volunteer work, etc.
   c. Continue in an aftercare group or obtain ongoing individual therapy, couples therapy, etc.
3. Develop a healthy, positive, and balanced lifestyle.

Assignments

1. Complete Purchasing Record.
2. Lapse and Relapse Plan.
3. Read session material for the last session.

Purchasing Record

Date	Time	Items[a]	Cost	Thoughts/Feelings	+/−

How much time did you spend shopping/buying today? _____ min.

How much time did you spend planning or thinking about shopping/buying today? _____ min.

[a] Indicate if by television (TV) or Internet (IN)

Unit 12: Summary and Outlook

Positive changes in my thoughts and behaviors since I started treatment.

1.

2.

3.

4.

5.

6.

7.

8.

9.

10.

Positive change in my thoughts and behaviors that people have noticed in me (ask one to two people close to you who know of your treatment involvement; this can include group members).

1.

2.

3.

4.

5.

6.

7.

8.

9.

10.

Goal Setting

During the next three months, I need to continue to work on the following: (examples: take time out for relaxation three times a week, learn to be more assertive—read an assertiveness book, etc.).

1. _____

_____

2. _____

_____

3. _____

_____

4. _____

_____

5. _____

_____

6. _____

_____

7. _____

_____

Evaluate in three months to identify whether or not you reached your goals. Take some time to make a new list of goals. Make sure you don't set your goals too high. Keep them simple and achievable.

Index

A

Addiction, 5
  alcohol, 145
  behavioral, 69, 133
  CB classified as, 7, 65
  drug, 31, 33, 67
  gambling, 78
  Internet, 52, 60
  substance, 97, 134, 145
  treatment, 133
Addictive Buying Indicator, 33, 34
Adolescents, predictive modeling of
      CB among, 20
Advertising, influence of, 66
Affective spectrum disorders, 9
Alternative behaviors
  group treatment, 197–198
  planning of, 152
American Psychiatric Association
      (APA), 65
AMPA/kainate glutamate-receptor
      subtypes, antagonism of, 142
Anorexia nervosa, 52
APA, *see* American Psychiatric
      Association
Assessment, 27–49
  Addictive Buying Indicator, 33, 34
  anxiety disorders, 31
  bankruptcy, 37

Clinical Global Impression severity
      score, 37
Compulsive Buying Measurement
      Scale, 33
compulsive buying scale, 41–42
construct validity, 33
diagnostic criteria, 29
drug addiction, 33
dysfunctional home, 31
Edwards Compulsive Buying Scale, 43
excuse to medicalize behavioral
      problems, 28
experimental drug trial, 37
family history, 31
goal of evaluation, 29
identification and assessment, 28–29
Impulse Buying Tendency Scale, 35
media portrayals, 28
mental status examination, 32
Minnesota Impulsive Disorder
      Interview, 34
National Institute of Mental Health
      Obsessive-Compulsive Scale, 36
other assessments, 32–36
patient example, 37–38
postpurchase guilt, 35
prevalence estimation, 34
psychiatric history, 30–32
questionnaire about buying behavior,
      45

screening, 29–30
self-help program, 36
shopping diaries, 36–37
social history, 31
spending rush, 37
spousal relationship, 32
Yale-Brown Obsessive-Compulsive
      Scale-Shopping Version, 47–49
   degree of control over compulsive
      shopping, 49
   degree of control over thoughts
      about shopping, 48
   distress associated with compulsive
      shopping behavior, 49
   distress associated with thoughts
      about shopping, 47
   interference due to shopping
      behavior, 48
   interference due to thoughts
      about shopping, 47
   resistance against compulsive
      shopping, 49
   resistance against thoughts about
      shopping, 47
   time occupied by thoughts about
      shopping, 47
   time spent shopping, 48
Avoidance coping style, 92
Avoidant personality disorder, 98
Axis I disorder, 91, 141
Axis II disorder, 105, 162

B

Bankruptcy, 6, 37
Bariatric surgery candidates, 106
Beck Depression Inventory, 130
Behavioral addictions, 133
Big Five Model, 92
Big Five personality traits, 92
Binge eating disorder, 52, 87
Biopsychosocial model, 23–25
Bipolar disorder, 90
Blood oxygen level dependency (BOLD)
      time course, 74
BOLD time course, see Blood oxygen
      level dependency time course
Brain imaging studies, 133
Bricks-and-mortar buyers, 59
Brief Patient Health Questionnaire, 91

Bulimia nervosa, depression and, 96
Bupropion SR, 144

C

Carbamazepine, 144
Case examples, 149–159
   alternative behaviors, planning of, 152
   Amanda, 157–158
   CB, group therapist definition of, 156
   chat rooms, 153–154
   cognitive-behavioral treatment, 150,
      154
   Deborah, 151–152
   disciplined self-denial, 158
   eBay, 157
   glamorizing behavior, 154
   group participation, 151
   Internet shopping, 157
   intervention, 154
   narcissistic reaction, 154
   Nora, 155–157
   oniomania, 149
   relationship breakup, 156
   Ron, 153–155
   Sarah, 150–151
   self-confidence, lack of, 152
   settlement money, 153
   socialization, 151
   social support, 153
Cash
   declining use of, 80
   management, 164, 209–213
      assignments, 212
      cash management suggestions,
         209–210
      credit cards, 209
      definition of healthy buying,
         210–211
      hoarding, 211–212
      purchasing record, 213
Catastrophizing, 217
CB, see Compulsive buying
CBS, see Compulsive Buying Scale
CBT, see Cognitive behavioral therapy
CGI severity score, see Clinical Global
      Impression severity score
CIR, see Clutter Image Rating
Clinical Global Impression (CGI)
      severity score, 37
Clutter Image Rating (CIR), 117

Cognitive behavioral therapy (CBT), 120
  advantages, 130
  case example, 150
  cues, 131
  group participation, 155
  hoarding, 120
  randomized trial, 154
  trials comparing medication to, 145
Cognitive errors, 247
Compulsive buying (CB), 3, 27
  age at onset, 11, 31
  arousal of, 9
  assessment of in young people, 12
  characteristics, 149
  chronic nature of, 5
  consequences of impulse buying and, 4
  consumer focus on, 63
  criteria, 6
  definition of, 6, 52
  disorder evaluation, 28
  gender imbalance, 13
  group therapist definition of, 156
  incidence, 51
  misunderstanding of, 3
  preferred buying medium for
      individuals with, 60
  prevalence studies, 10
  recognition, 29
  secrecy, 28
  severity of symptoms, 119
  Web sites addressing, 52
  worldwide existence, 11
Compulsive Buying Measurement Scale,
    33
Compulsive Buying Scale (CBS), 8
  development of, 34
  scoring algorithm, 10
Compulsive exercise, MIDI assessment
    of, 34
Compulsive hoarding, definition of, 115,
    see also Hoarding
Compulsive sexual behavior, 93
  MIDI assessment of, 34
  pharmacotherapy, 132
  prevalence, 93
"Confessions of a Shopaholic," 64
Consumer(s)
  ability to buy unobserved, 59
  feeling of achievement, 20
  preoccupied thoughts, 52

Consumerism, social transmission of
    attitudes about, 20
Consuming-network notion, 79
Credit cards
  access to, 21
  debt, 37
  decision to give up, 209
  getting rid of, 164
  influence of on CB behavior, 21
Cronbach's alpha, 33, 57
Cue(s)
  chains and, 165–166
  cognitive behavioral therapy, 131
  consequences and, 164, 195–207
    alternative behaviors, 197–198
    alternatives to problem buying
      behaviors, 207
    assignments, 200
    maximizing healthy behaviors
      and minimizing buying
      behaviors, 205
    possible consequences that
      result from problem buying
      behaviors, 196
    purchasing record, 201
    rearranging consequences
      (goal setting and self-rewards),
      199–200
    strategies for change (focusing on
      consequences), 199
    strategies for change (focusing on
      cue), 196–197
  rearranging, 196
  ways of reacting, 215

D

DAPP, *see* Dimensional Assessment of
    Personality Pathology
Debt
  amounts incurred, 12
  attitudes toward money, 21
  counseling, 143
  credit card, 37
  current level, 32
  excessive, 149, 187
  extreme levels of, 64
  forgotten, 122
  gradual, 69
  nonmortgage-related, 6

payment on, 210
senseless amount of, 5
Demographics, 13, 57
Depression, 96
  history of, 31
  improvement of, 96
  measurement of extent, 75
Diagnosis and epidemiology, 3–17
  acceptance of problem, 14
  affective spectrum disorders, 9
  algorithm for scoring, 9
  arousing experience, 9
  bankruptcy, 6
  chronic nature of CB, 5
  classification of compulsive buying as
    disorder, 7–9
  Compulsive Buying Scale, 8
  consequences of impulse buying, 4
  debt, 12
  definition of CB, 6
  demographics, 13
  diagnosis, –7
  DSM-V, 9
  epidemiology, 9–11
  escape theory, 14
  excessive versus compulsive buying, 7
  German Addictive Buying Scale, 10, 11
  health-related studies, 10
  impulse buying, definition of, 3
  impulsive-compulsive disorders, 9
  income levels, 12
  intrusive thoughts, 9
  kleptomania, 9
  legal problems, 12
  materialism, envy dimension of, 4
  Maudsley Obsessive Compulsive
    Inventory, 8
  negative consequences, 7
  nonmortgage-related debt, 6
  oniomania, definition of, 5
  onset, 11–12
  Padua Inventory, 8
  pathological gambling, 9
  pyromania, 5
  random digit dialing sample, 10
  self-help groups, 5
  self-identification, 9
  spending goals, 4
  trial-and-error learning, 14
  trichotillomania, 9
  who is at risk, 12–14
  worldwide existence, 11
Diagnostic and Statistical Manual of
    Mental Disorders (DSM), 65
  Axis II personality II disorders, 106
  criteria, OCD behavior, 8
Dimensional Assessment of Personality
    Pathology (DAPP), 91
Dissocial behavior, 91
DSM, see Diagnostic and Statistical
    Manual of Mental Disorders
DSM-IV
  hoarding, 117
  ICDs, 93
  impulse control disorder not
    otherwise specified, 132
DSM-V, 9
  category of obsessive-compulsive
    spectrum disorders, 65
  inclusion of compulsive buying, 9
  Work Group on OCSDs, 97

E

Eating disorders, 31, 98
eBay, 157
Echo planar imaging (EPI), 74
Edwards Compulsive Buying Scale, 43
Emotions
  identifying feelings, 216
  negative, 21
Envy, materialism and, 4
EPI, see Echo planar imaging
Epidemiology, see Diagnosis and
    epidemiology
ERP, see Exposure and response
    prevention
Escape
  CB linked to, 92
  eBay, 157
  internal trigger, 110
  theory, 14
Escitalopram, 140
Etiology, 19–26
  behavioral factors, 22–23
  biological factors, 23
  cognitive and emotional factors, 21–22
  consumers, feeling of achievement, 20
  macrosystem, 20
  materialism, definition of, 21
  materialistic beliefs, 21

microsystem, 20
narcissism, materialism and, 22
negative emotions, 21
neuroeconomics, 23
predictive modeling of CB among
    adolescents, 20
psychodynamic factors, 23
retail therapy, 24
risk-taking behaviors, 22
self object equilibrium, 23
social factors, 20–21
socioeconomic strata, buying
    behaviors, 20
toward biopsychosocial model, 23–25
Exercise dependence, 99
Exposure and response prevention (ERP),
    121
Express checkout, 55, 57, 60

F

FFPI, *see* Five-Factor Personality
    Inventory
Five-Factor Model, 107
Five-Factor Personality Inventory (FFPI),
    107
fMRI, *see* Functional Magnetic Resonance
    Imaging
Functional Magnetic Resonance Imaging
    (fMRI), 68

G

GABA-A receptor subtypes, 142
Gambling, pathological, 52, 93, 98
    lifetime history, 9
    MIDI assessment of, 34
    pharmacotherapy, 132
    prevalence, 93
GCBS, *see* German Compulsive Buying
    Scale
Gender, controversy over women's CB
    problem, 13
German Addictive Buying Scale, 10, 11
German Compulsive Buying Scale
    (GCBS), 72
Go-around technique, 163
Group treatment manual, 169–278,
        see also Therapist's guide to
        treatment manual; Treatment
    alternative behaviors, 197

anxiety, 193
behavior change, strategies for, 235
cash management, hoarding, 209–213
    assignments, 212
    cash management suggestions,
        209–210
    credit cards, 209
    definition of healthy buying,
        210–211
    hoarding, 211–212
    purchasing record, 213
chain of behavior, 235
changes to expect, 193
cleaning house, 212
cognitive errors, 247
confidentiality, 171
consequences, categories of, 196
cues and chains, 235–245
    assignments, 237
    behavioral chain, 236
    identifying behavioral chains
        worksheet, 241, 243, 245
    purchasing record, 239
cues and consequences, 195–207
    alternative behaviors, 197–198
    alternatives to problem buying
        behaviors, 207
    assignments, 200
    maximizing healthy behaviors
        and minimizing buying
        behaviors, 205
    possible consequences that
        result from problem buying
        behaviors, 196
    purchasing record, 201
    rearranging consequences
        (goal setting and self-rewards),
        199–200
    strategies for change (focusing on
        consequences), 199
    strategies for change (focusing on
        cue), 196–197
difficulty in asking for help, 171
dysfunctional thoughts, examples, 247
exposure, 259–261
    assignments, 260
    purchasing record, 261
feelings, 216
goal behavior, 200
goal setting, 278
goals of treatment, 171

group expectations, 171
group reminders, 171
healthy buying, 210
identifying problem buying
    behaviors and their
    consequences, 183–193
    assignments, 189
    purchasing record, 191
    reasons for and against changing
        unhealthy buying habits, 187
    shopping rules, 185
    what to expect as you change your
        buying behavior, 193
involvement of family and friends,
    171–172
maladaptive styles of thinking, 217, 218
    catastrophizing, 217
    challenging of, 226
    dichotomous, 217
    overgeneralization, 217
    questioning of, 225
material rewards, 199
mental rewards, 199
numbing of unpleasant thoughts, 193
planning for high-risk times, 197
problem identification, 225
regaining control over behavior, 173
relapse prevention (lapse and relapse
    plans), 271–275
    assignments, 273
    lapse, 271
    lapse plan, 272
    purchasing record, 275
    relapse, 271
    relapse plan, 272
responses (thoughts, feelings, and
    behaviors), 215–223
    assignments, 218
    becoming aware of your
        responses, 223
    introduction, 215
    maladaptive styles of thinking,
        217–218
    overreliance on opinions of others,
        218
    purchasing record, 219
    restructuring thoughts worksheet,
        221
    self-fulfilling prophecy, 218
    thoughts, feelings, and behaviors,
        215–217

restructuring your thoughts, 225–233
    assignments, 227
    challenging maladaptive thoughts
        by questioning them, 225–226
    challenging maladaptive thoughts
        by testing them, 226–227
    introduction, 225
    purchasing record, 229
    restructuring your thoughts, 231
rewards, 199
self-esteem, 247–257
    assignments, 247
    definition of, 247
    purchasing record, 249
    revision, 257
    self-concept inventory, 253, 255
    self-concept and self-esteem, 251
self-fulfilling prophecy, 218
shopping partner, 259
stress management and problem
        solving, 263–269
    assignments, 266
    how to manage stress, 264–266
    introduction, 263
    purchasing record, 267
    stress and its components, 263
    stress reduction experiment, 269
summary and outlook, 277–278
treatment goal, 196
treatment program overview, 173–181
    assignments, 175–176
    contract for compulsive buying
        disorder treatment, 181
    definition of compulsive
        shopping, 174
    making commitment to change,
        181
    myths about compulsive buying,
        179
    purchasing record, 177

H

HAM-D, see Hamilton Depression
        Rating Scale
Hamilton Depression Rating Scale
        (HAM-D), 135
Health department survey, 116
Healthy buying, definition of, 210
Hemodynamic response function (HRF),
        74

Hoarding, 97–98, 115–126
assessment strategies, 120
background mood state, 121
clinical implications, 120–121
Clutter Image Rating, 117
compulsive hoarding, definition of, 115
disorder-specific group therapy, 119
dissociative state, 122
emotional attachment, 115
exposure and response prevention,
121, 122
health department survey, 116
hoarding, 116–118
hoarding and compulsive buying,
118–119
homelessness, 116
Hopkins Epidemiology of Personality
Disorder Study, 118
list of items, 211
maladaptive attachment patterns, 119
moment-to-moment events, analysis
of, 121
pharmacotherapy, 120
prepurchase questions, 122
prevalence, 118
Receiver Operating Characteristic
curves, 117
Saving Inventory-Revised, 116
self-criticism, 122
Socratic questioning, 123
treating excessive acquisition, 121–123
treatment difficulty, 123
value of objects collected, 118
work impairment, 116
Homelessness, 116
Hopkins Epidemiology of Personality
Disorder Study, 118
HRF, see Hemodynamic response
function
Hypomania, 29

I

ICD, see Impulse control disorder
ICD NOS, see Impulse control disorder
not otherwise specified
IED, see Intermittent explosive disorder
Impulse buying
consequences of, 4
definition of, 3, 107
Impulse Buying Tendency Scale, 35

Impulse control disorder (ICD), 8, 9, 65, 93
de novo onset of, 100
distinction between OCD and, 8
gender difference, 13
intrusive thoughts, 9
narcissism and, 92
prevalence, 93
underlying risk factors, 14
Impulse control disorder not otherwise
specified (ICD NOS), 132
Intermittent explosive disorder (IED), 93
MIDI assessment of, 34
prevalence, 93
Internet addiction (impulsive), 52
Internet shopping, see Measurement
and its application to Internet
buyers

K

Kleptomania, 5, 52, 93
depression and, 96
lifetime history, 9
MIDI assessment of, 34
naltrexone treatment, 141
pharmacotherapy, 132
prevalence, 93
treatment trial, 141
women engaging in, 13

L

Latent profile analysis (LPA), 90
Lithium carbonate, 144
LPA, see Latent profile analysis

M

MADRS, see Montgomery-Asberg
Depression Rating Scale
Major depressive disorder (MDD), 135
Mania, 29
MAO activity, see Monoamine oxidase
activity
Materialism
definition of, 21
envy dimension of, 4
narcissism and, 22, 92
social transmission of attitudes about,
20

Maudsley Obsessive Compulsive
  Inventory, 8
MDD, *see* Major depressive disorder
Measurement and its application to
  Internet buyers, 51–62
  ability to buy unobserved on
    Internet, 56
  bricks-and-mortar buyers, 59
  compulsive buying and Internet, 55
  compulsive Internet research, 53
  definition and positioning of
    compulsive buying disorder,
    52–55
  demographics, 57
  e-tailers, 55, 58
  express checkout, 55, 57, 60
  findings, 58–59
  hedonic motives, 57
  immediate positive feelings, 57
  implications of Internet buying, 59–60
  motivations to shop and buy
    on Internet versus from
    bricks-and-mortar stores, 55–56
  preferred buying medium for
    individuals with, 60
  product and information variety, 56
  public policy implications, 60–61
  public policy officials, Internet retail
    research and, 60
  self-report measures, 53
  survey, 57–58
Media portrayals, 28
Mental status examination (MSE), 32
MIDI, *see* Minnesota Impulsive Disorder
  Interview
Minnesota Impulsive Disorder Interview
  (MIDI), 34
Model
  Big Five, 92
  biopsychosocial, 23–25
  blood oxygen level dependency time
    course, 74
  cognitive, 21
  family dynamic models of causality, 66
  Five-Factor, 107
  relapse prevention, 167
Money
  adolescents, 96
  amount spent, 30
  anticipated loss of, 79
  attitudes toward, 21, 131

frustration, 150
  healthy buying, 210
  meanings of, 210
  mismanagement, 12, 66, 123
  power and, 179
  right amount of, 210
  settlement, 153
  students, 109
  windfall, 5
Monoamine oxidase (MAO) activity, 134
Montgomery-Asberg Depression Rating
  Scale (MADRS), 140
Motivation(s)
  hedonic, 57
  online shopping, 58
  primary, 5
  retail shopping, 55
  trigger as, 110
MSE, *see* Mental status examination

N

Nalmefene, 141
Naltrexone, 141
Narcissism
  CB and, 22
  materialism and, 22, 92
  measurement, 109
Narcissistic Personality Inventory (NPI),
  109
National Institute of Mental Health
  Obsessive-Compulsive Scale
  (NIMHOCS), 36
Nefazodone, 144
Neural basis, 63–86
  advertising, 66
  anticipated gain versus anticipated
    loss, 67
  cash, declining use of, 80
  CB, definition of, 64, 65
  compulsive buying, 64–66
  consuming-network notion, 79
  definition of CB, 64, 65
  discussion, 77–80
  echo planar imaging, 74
  Functional Magnetic Resonance
    Imaging, 68
  impulse-control disorder, 65
  knowledge gap, 64
  learning theory, punishment in, 67
  method, 71–75

fMRI analysis, 72–74
  participants, 71–72
  postscan analysis, 74–75
neural basis of compulsive buying,
  66–71
  insular cortex, 70–71
  striatum (nucleus accumbens),
    67–69
  ventromedial and ventrolateral
    prefrontal cortex, 69
neuroeconomics, 78
neuroimaging studies, 67
obsessive-compulsive disorder, 65
prevalence rates, 65
price condition, 79
product selection, 73
results, 75–77
  fMRI decision phase results, 75–76
  fMRI price phase results, 75
  fMRI product phase results, 75
  postscan results, 76–77
risk-averse decisions, 70
risk-averse strategies, 67
simulated purchasing decision, 68
tolerance, development of, 69
tradeoff of purchase decisions, 67
unambiguous classification, 80
Neuroeconomics, 23, 78
Neuroimaging studies, 67
Neuroticism, 107, 111
NIMHOCS, *see* National Institute
  of Mental Health
  Obsessive-Compulsive Scale
Nonmortgage-related debt, 6
NPI, *see* Narcissistic Personality Inventory

O

Obsessive-compulsive disorder (OCD),
  8, 65, 90, 96–97
characteristics, 53, 65
distinction between ICD and, 8
drugs useful for, 145
DSM criteria, 8
exposure and response prevention, 121
hoarding disorder and, 118
intrusive thoughts, 9
prevalence, 90
SSRI treatment, 145
symptoms, 97
underlying risk factors, 14

Obsessive-compulsive personality
  disorder (OCPD), 94, 117
Obsessive-compulsive spectrum
  disorders (OCSD), 97
conditions, 52
features, 97
OCD, *see* Obsessive-compulsive disorder
OCPD, *see* Obsessive-compulsive
  personality disorder
OCSD, *see* Obsessive-compulsive
  spectrum disorders
Olanzapine, 144
Oniomania, 5, 149, *see also* Compulsive
  buying
Online shopping, *see* Measurement
  and its application to Internet
  buyers
Opioid antagonist, 141
Overgeneralization, 217

P

Padua Inventory, 8
Parkinson's disease (PD), 99–101
PD, *see* Parkinson's disease
Personality, 105–113
  Axis II disorders, 105, 106
  bariatric surgery candidates, 106
  clinical samples, 106–107
  disorders, 92
  extraversion, 107
  Five-Factor Personality Inventory, 107
  impulsive buying, definition of, 107
  internal trigger, 110
  lack of premeditation, 108
  narcissism, measurement, 109
  neuroticism, 107, 111
  nonclinical samples, 107–109
  personality prototypes, 110
  personality typologies, 109–110
  self-regulatory resources, depletion of,
    109
  Structured Interview for DSM-III-R
    Personality Disorders, 106
Pharmacotherapy
  bupropion SR, 144
  carbamazepine, 144
  escitalopram, 140
  hoarding, 120
  literature, 132
  lithium carbonate, 144

n-acetyl cysteine, 145
nalmefene, 141
naltrexone, 141
nefazodone, 144
obsessive-compulsive disorder, 145
olanzapine, 144
opioid antagonist, 141
SSRI, 30
    literature, 143
    OCD treatment with, 144
    research, 132
    studies, 136
    treatment results, 135
    trial, 144
topiramate, 142
valproate, 144
venlafaxine, 142
Price condition, 79
Product selection, 73
Psychiatric comorbidity, 87–104
    avoidance coping style, 92
    avoidant personality disorder, 98
    Axis I disorders, 91
    Big Five personality traits, 92
    bipolar disorder, 90
    Brief Patient Health Questionnaire, 91
    cluster analysis, 92
    compulsive buying in psychiatric
        samples, 94–101
    compulsive hoarding, 97–98
    depression, 96
    Dimensional Assessment of
        Personality Pathology, 91
    dissocial behavior, 91
    eating disorders, 98
    exercise dependence, 99
    impulse control disorders, 93
    intermittent explosive disorder, 93
    kleptomania, 93
    latent profile analysis, 90
    lifetime criteria for mood disorders, 87
    obsessive-compulsive disorder, 96–97
    obsessive-compulsive personality
        disorder, 94
    obsessive-compulsive spectrum
        disorders, 97
    Parkinson's disease, 99–101
    pathological gambling, 93, 98
    personality disorders, 92
    personality prototypes, 92

prebariatric surgery patients, 91
prevalence rates, 88
psychiatric disorders, 95
psychiatric inpatients, 94–96
putative sampling bias, 94
Questionnaire for
    Impulsive-Compulsive
    Disorders in Parkinson's
    Disease, 99
restless legs syndrome, 99–101
social isolation, 92
Psychiatric disorders, 95
Pyromania, 5
    pharmacotherapy, 132
    prevalence, 93

Q

Questionnaire for Impulsive-Compulsive
    Disorders in Parkinson's
    Disease (QUIP), 99
QUIP, *see* Questionnaire for
    Impulsive-Compulsive
    Disorders in Parkinson's
    Disease

R

Receiver Operating Characteristic (ROC)
    curves, 117
Restless legs syndrome, 99–101
Retail therapy, 24
Risk-averse decisions, 70
Risk-taking behaviors, 22
ROC curves, *see* Receiver Operating
    Characteristic curves

S

Saving Inventory-Revised (SI-R), 116
SCS, *see* Self-Control Scale
Selective serotonin reuptake inhibitors
    (SSRIs), 135–140
    anxiety treatment with, 30
    literature, 143
    OCD treatment, 144
    research, 132
    studies, 136
    treatment results, 135
    trial, 144

Self-concept inventory, 251, 253, 255
Self-Control Scale (SCS), 75
Self-esteem
    definition of, 247
    group treatment, 247–257
        assignments, 247
        purchasing record, 249
        revision, 257
        self-concept inventory, 253, 255
        self-concept and self-esteem, 251
    session, 166
Self-fulfilling prophecy, 218
Self-help groups, 5
Self object equilibrium, 23
Self-regulation, 4
Shopping diaries, 36
SIDP, see Structured Interview for
        DSM-III-R Personality
        Disorders
SI-R, see Saving Inventory-Revised
Social isolation, 92
Socratic questioning, 123
SSRIs, see Selective serotonin reuptake
        inhibitors
Stress management, 167
Structured Interview for DSM-III-R
        Personality Disorders (SIDP),
        106
Substance dependence disorders,
        depression and, 96

T

Telescoping phenomenon, 133
Therapist's guide to treatment manual,
        161–168, see also Group
        treatment manual; Treatment
    Axis II personality disorders, 162
    cash management, hoarding, 164
    content, 161–163
    credit cards, 164
    cues and chains, 165–166
    cues and consequences, 164
    exposure, 166–167
    go-around technique, 163
    homework, 162, 163
    identifying problem buying behaviors
        and their consequences, 163
    relapse prevention, 167

responses "thought, feeling, and
        behavior," 165
    restructuring your thoughts, 165
    self-esteem, 166
    session format, 162
    stress management and problem
        solving, 167
    stylistic issues, 162
    summary and outlook, 167–168
Thoughtful buying, 210
Tolerance, development of, 69
Topiramate, 142
Treatment, 129–148, see also Group
        treatment manual; Therapist's
        guide to treatment manual
    addiction, 133
    AMPA/kainate glutamate-receptor
        subtypes, antagonism of, 142
    Axis I diagnosis, 141
    Beck Depression Inventory, 130
    behavioral addictions, 133
    brain imaging studies, 133
    bupropion SR, 144
    carbamazepine, 144
    challenges in pharmacotherapy
        research, 142–143
    escitalopram, 140
    future research, 143–145
    GABA-A receptor subtypes, 142
    Hamilton Depression Rating Scale, 135
    impulse control disorder not
        otherwise specified, 132
    kleptomania treatment trial, 141
    lithium carbonate, 144
    major depressive disorder, 135
    monoamine oxidase activity, 134
    Montgomery-Asberg Depression
        Rating Scale, 140
    n-acetyl cysteine, 145
    nalmefene, 141
    naltrexone, 141
    nefazodone, 144
    negative consequences, 131
    olanzapine, 144
    opioid antagonist, 141
    pharmacotherapy, 132–142
        genetics and neurobiology, 132–134
        miscellaneous agents, 142

opioid antagonists, 140–142
selective serotonin reuptake
    inhibitors, 135–140
prolactin response, 134
psychotherapy, 129–132
relapse rate, 135
serotonin dysregulation, 134
SSRI studies, 136
telescoping phenomenon, 133
topiramate, 142
24-hour rule, 131
valproate, 144
venlafaxine, 142
voltage-dependent sodium channels,
    blockage of, 142
Trichotillomania, 52
lifetime history, 9
MIDI assessment of, 34
prevalence, 93
Triggers, *see also* Cues
categories, 195
examples, 121
as motivation, 110
responses, 215
24-hour rule, 131, 189

V

Valproate, 144
Venlafaxine, 142
Voltage-dependent sodium channels,
    blockage of, 142

W

Web sites, 52
WHO, *see* World Health Organization
World Health Organization (WHO), 65

Y

Yale-Brown Obsessive-Compulsive
    Scale-Shopping Version
    (YBOCS-SV), 47–49, 130
degree of control over compulsive
    shopping, 49
degree of control over thoughts about
    shopping, 48
distress associated with compulsive
    shopping behavior, 49
distress associated with thoughts
    about shopping, 47
interference due to shopping
    behavior, 48
interference due to thoughts about
    shopping, 47
resistance against compulsive
    shopping, 49
resistance against thoughts about
    shopping, 47
time occupied by thoughts about
    shopping, 47
time spent shopping, 48
YBOCS-SV, *see* Yale-Brown
    Obsessive-Compulsive
    Scale-Shopping Version